English Grammar Instruction

That Works!

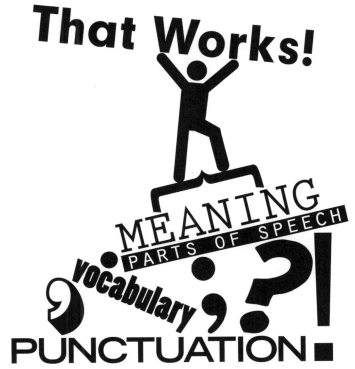

To my wife Myrna, my son Tyler—from Andy

To my children and grandchildren from Mom/Grandma

To my mentor and linguistic inspiration—Robert L. Allen—from your

grateful student—Evelyn

And thanks Wilma for your editing help.

English Grammar Instruction

That Works!

MEANING

PARTS OF SPEECH

vocabulary

PUNCTUATION

Developing Language Skills for All Learners

Evelyn Rothstein • Andrew S. Rothstein

CORWIN PRESS

A SAGE Company

For information:

Corwin Press
A SAGE Company
2455 Teller Road
Thousand Oaks, California 91320
www.corwinpress.com

SAGE Pvt. Ltd.
B 1/I 1 Mohan Cooperative Industrial Area
Mathura Road, New Delhi 110 044
India

SAGE Ltd.
1 Oliver's Yard
55 City Road
London EC1Y 1SP
United Kingdom

SAGE Asia-Pacific Pte. Ltd.
33 Pekin Street #02-01
Far East Square
Singapore 048763

Printed in the United States of America

Library of Congress Cataloging-in-Publication Data

Rothstein, Evelyn.
English grammar instruction that works! developing language skills for all learners/Evelyn Rothstein, Andrew S. Rothstein.
    p. cm.
Includes bibliographical references and index.
ISBN 978-1-4129-5948-3 (cloth)
ISBN 978-1-4129-5949-0 (pbk.)
    1. English language—Grammar—Study and teaching I. Rothstein, Andrew. II. Title.

LB1576.R7547 2009
428.2—dc22   2008021944

This book is printed on acid-free paper.

08   09   10   11   12   10   9   8   7   6   5   4   3   2   1

Acquisitions Editor:	Cathy Hernandez
Editorial Assistant:	Ena Rosen
Production Editor:	Veronica Stapleton
Copy Editor:	Tina Hardy
Typesetter:	C&M Digitals (P) Ltd.
Proofreader:	Dennis W. Webb
Indexer:	Sheila Bodell
Cover Designer:	Scott Van Atta
Graphic Designer:	Karine Hovsepian

Contents

Preface   **vii**
    Our Point of View   viii
    Objectives and Key Points   x
    Publisher's Acknowledgments   xiv

About the Authors   **xv**

1. **Introduction**   **1**
    The Premise of This Book   1
    What Do We Mean by Grammar?   1
    The History of Teaching Grammar in the United States of America   3
    Current Standards Related to Teaching Grammar   5

2. **Language and Metalanguage**   **7**
    Overview of the Terms *Language* and *Metalanguage*   7
    A Brief History of the English Language   16
    Internet Sites   18

3. **Builders of Linguistic Intelligence**   **19**
    Phonology   20
    Morphology   22
    Syntax   33
    Semantics   33
    Etymology   34
    Internet Sites   36

4. **Parts of Speech and the English Language**   **37**
    Teaching English Through the Structure of the English Language   38
    Morphological and Non-Morphological Words   39
    Expanding Definitions of Parts of Speech   46
    Organizing and Naming the Verb Conjugation Forms   51
    Verbs by Categories   54
    The Adjective in the English Language   57
    The Adverb in the English Language   63
    Internet Sites   65

5. **Syntax and Semantics**   **66**
    Getting Meaning   66
    Sentences and Semantics   70
    Internet Sites   83

6.	The Polyglot of English	84
	The Latin "DNA"	86
	Terms for Understanding the Structures of Words and Parts of Words	87
	Getting Meaning by Sorting and Clarifying	88
	Internet Sites	107
7.	The Polyglot: Beyond Latin and Greek	108
	Ich Spreche Deutsch—The Germanic Connection	109
	The French Connection—The Year 1066	111
	Hablo Español—I Speak Spanish	118
	Yiddish or Yinglish	119
	Worldwide Contributions—African Americans, American Indians, East Indians	121
	Contributions From China and Japan	125
	Internet Sites	126
8.	Return to Parts of Speech	127
	The Small Words	127
	Internet Sites	140
9.	Sentences, Paragraphs, and Other Structures of the Written Language	141
	Converting Spoken Sentences to Written Sentences	142
	Working With Sentence Units	142
	Finding Sentence Boundaries in Written Sentences	144
	"Deconstructing" Sentences to Find Their Deep Structure Meaning	144
	Subjects and Predicates	146
	Tenses and Agreement	147
	Verb Agreement	150
	The Paragraph	151
	The Grammatical Voice	152
	Internet Sites	153
10.	Grammar for Word Play	154
	Making Grammar Really Fun	154
	Internet Sites	165
11.	Reading, Writing, and Grammar	166
	Combining Reading With Grammar	166
	ABC Books for Building Language and Grammar Literacy	177
	Internet Sites	180
12.	Punctuation, Spelling, Text Messaging, and Other Consequences of Grammar	181
	Learning About Punctuation	183
	Spelling and Grammar	194
	Internet Sites	197
13.	Additional Learning Activities	198
	Building Sentence Power	198
	Paragraphs and Transitions	202
	Having Fun With Grammar and Words	211
References		213
Index		217

Preface

When you see a mother and son writing a book about teaching grammar, you might assume that there is a story behind their effort. The story behind this book dates back to Andy's ninth-grade English class. His teacher was Mr. T., who diligently taught us the *traditional* rules for English grammar.

One day, Mr. T. opened the class with the following statement: "You young people have much to learn about the English language. Of utmost importance is learning how to conjugate verbs. I am passing out several sheets of paper with all of the conjugations used in English. You are to study them tonight, for there will be a test on them tomorrow."

Upon returning home and raiding the refrigerator as fortification for the task ahead, the dutiful Andy sat at the kitchen table to pour over Mr. T's worksheets. When his mother (Evelyn), a newly minted college professor of linguistics, came into the kitchen, she observed Andy's perplexed expression. She asked him what he was studying.

"I have an English test tomorrow," said Andy.

"I love English," said Mom.

"I know you do," replied Andy.

"What are you learning about?" pressed Mom.

"How to conjugate verbs," answered Andy.

"Don't you already conjugate verbs?" quizzed Mom.

"Apparently not, according to Mr. T.," mumbled Andy.

"What do those sheets say?" asked Mom, as Andy pondered the wisdom of doing his homework in the kitchen under the watchful eye of his mother.

Andy sighed, "They contain all of the tenses and forms used to conjugate English verbs."

Mom peered over Andy's shoulder. Mom asked, "How many tenses and forms are on these sheets?"

"Eight," groaned Andy.

She clucked. She huffed. She puffed. Then, with conviction, she announced, "English only has two tenses. Any *linguist* will tell you that. These sheets are neither correct nor accurate!"

"They are tonight," deadpanned Andy. "And they better be tomorrow when I take the test. You can tell me the truth tomorrow."

Luckily, Andy got a good grade on the test and put the weekend to good use by forgetting everything he had studied for the test by shooting baskets.

This household event was one of many in which Evelyn challenged the merits of traditional ways of teaching grammar. Not that Evelyn didn't love grammar and everything related to this sometimes arcane subject. But she was now working with great teachers of language and linguistics at Teachers College at Columbia University and had a new and broader perspective, which often found its voice at our kitchen table. This book, which we have titled *English Grammar Instruction That Works! Developing Language Skills for All Learners,* is the culmination of our discussions and deliberations, combined with classroom practice, teacher workshops, and the research and wisdom of wonderful writers who have expanded our knowledge and understanding of the English language.

OUR POINT OF VIEW

The major purpose of this book is to guide teachers in teaching the grammar of English as it is, *not as we wish it to be.* These italicized words—*as we wish it to be*—may seem odd for a subject that, until recently, has been a mainstay of the English curriculum. However, if we examine the history of grammar teaching in schools, we discover that for generations, "school grammarians" have wanted English to be modeled on Latin—a *noble* language perhaps, but one that is no longer active and, furthermore, is extremely different in its structure from modern English.

Bill Bryson in *The Mother Tongue* (1990) exemplifies the point of view in this book, humorously stating that the teaching of grammar (in school) is confusing for one very simple reason: " . . . its rules and terminology are based on Latin—a language with which it has precious little in common. . . . Making English grammar conform to Latin rules is like asking people to play baseball using the rules of football. It is a patent absurdity" (p. 137).

Yet for generations, and until this very day, our school grammar books (unfortunately called *English* books) continue to perpetuate this misguided belief that English grammar should be based on Latin grammar, either stated or inferred. Some of us (including Evelyn) managed to learn what we were taught. We accepted and memorized the statements of teachers who told us that "English has eight parts of speech," or "English has nine [or was it eight?] tenses such as the preterit, the imperfect, the conditional, the progressive, the future, and so forth." We accepted that a "noun is a person, place, or thing" and that words such as *dog, joy, mathematics, discussion,* and *determination* are all *things* since they are not persons or places.

Some of us (but neither of the authors) enjoyed sentence diagramming. A sentence one of us had to diagram referred to Shakespeare's *Romeo and Juliet*: "A pair of star-crossed lovers take their lives." First, we had to remove the article from the noun so that the phrase could be Latinized since Latin has (or had) no articles. Then the adjective, which in English generally precedes the noun, had to be removed and shifted to come after the noun as in Latin. Finally the word such as *their* as in "their lives" would have to be removed because Latin did not have this type of construction. The sentence "A pair of star-crossed lovers take their lives" was reduced to "Lovers take lives!"

Some of us too might have enjoyed underlining the subject once and the predicate twice or finding the direct and indirect objects. We might have been gleeful over locating sentences that were declarative, interrogative, or imperative because this task seemed like a "no-brainer." And some of us might have liked the challenge of locating predicate nouns and predicate adjectives in sentences made up by the publisher of the grammar book. Some of us probably worked hard at grammar because we wanted to get a good grade and some us hoped (both authors) that knowing Latinized English grammar would make us good writers.

Then there were some of us who despairingly went along with what we had to do, but never quite caught on. We split infinitives, confused transitive verbs with intransitive verbs, never quite got the meaning of terms like "perfect" and "imperfect" as they applied to tenses (rather than people), and worried why in a sentence such as "It is raining," the subject was "It" when deep in our hearts we knew that "raining" was what the sentence was about.

So if the Latinized grammar of English is NOT useful, except as a game or "exercise of the brain," what grammar should we teach if, indeed, we teach grammar at all? A statement by VanTassel-Baska, Johnson, and Boyce (1996) illustrates what grammar is and supports why we believe it does have a place in teaching and learning, provided that we follow the premise of this statement: "Grammar serves meaning. . . . The rules of grammar . . . bend themselves to the needs of meaning . . . and these determine the success of the communication" (p. 156). Two statements from Crystal (2006a) also add to the importance of this topic, one of which is "No sentence can begin without grammar" (p. 96), and the other is Crystal's definition that "grammar is the study of all the contrasts of meaning that it is possible to make within sentences" (p. 97). Let's look at three examples of meaning and the *grammar* used to convey that meaning. One is from Eric Carle, one is from Dr. Seuss, and one is from A. A. Milne, three very respectable writers:

"Neigh! Neigh!" said the horse. "Want to go for a ride?"

"Moo! Moo!" said the cow. "Want to eat some grass?

"Cock-a-doodle do!" crowed the rooster. "Want to catch a pesty fly?"

And the spider caught the fly in her web . . . just like that! (*The Very Busy Spider,* Eric Carle, 1984)

Back feet

Front feet

How many different feet you meet (*The Foot Book,* Dr. Seuss, 1996)

"You see, what I meant to do," he explained, as he turned head-over heels, and crashed on to another branch thirty feet below, "what I meant to do———"

"Of course, it was rather———" he admitted, as he slithered very quickly through the next six branches.

"It all comes, I suppose," he decided, as he said good-bye to the last branch, spun around three times, and flew gracefully into a gorse-bush, "it all comes of liking honey so much. Oh help!" (*The World of Pooh,* 1957, A. A. Milne, p. 13)

Perhaps you're thinking, or you can hear your colleagues thinking, the following: "This is fine and good for an established author who probably already knows the *correct* way to write and doesn't have to write the *correct* way. But my students . . . ," and so forth. We understand the dilemma. When young students are learning to communicate, either in speech or writing, we feel that they must be grounded in the correct or standard ways and that by having these ways, they can then innovate or deviate because deep in their psyches they will know what is right. Perhaps there is truth to this idea because both of us, as parents, have tried to infuse in our own children this idea or ideal of "good and proper *standard*" English.

So what is the answer? That is, what is there about grammar that we should teach, and how should we go about teaching it? This is the question we hope to answer in this book, because if grammar indeed serves meaning, then the inclusion of well-defined grammar can be a powerful partner in the building of literacy. In this book, we hope to provide a fresh and accurate perspective, with practical application, that gives teachers the necessary background about the English language, combined with specific, lively, student-centered activities.

We have drawn from the research and writing of exemplary linguists and educators who offer teachers and students the knowledge and joy that comes from knowing how to write and speak and *is supported by understanding the grammatical structure of English.* Throughout this book, we cite the current and substantiated works of Chomsky, Pinker, McWhorter, Bryson, McArthur, Crystal, McCrum, Cran, and MacNeil, among others (in the References), who address the relationship between the structure of the English language and the educational needs of diverse speakers.

OBJECTIVES AND KEY POINTS

We have set out the following objectives to give teachers the linguistic background and structure of the English language so that their students will learn the following:

- How to apply knowledge of English grammar to improve their communication skills in a variety of situations and for a multitude of purposes.
- How English got to be English.
- The differences between spoken English and written English.
- Why different speakers of English speak different English.
- Different aspects of language—dialect, slang, standard, and more.
- Specific language terminology or metalanguage—sentences, parts of speech, vocabulary, written conventions, and more.
- Ways that language can be fun—riddles, oxymora, idioms, and more.
- How English grammatical structures relate to other languages.

By having in-depth knowledge of the English grammatical structure, your students will attain a high level language background that supports all aspects of literacy. We, therefore, address these questions:

- What should students know about language generally?
- What should students know about English grammar, specifically?
- What is the role of vocabulary in relationship to grammar?
- How do we help students enlarge their sentence-making repertories?
- What strategies relate grammar to speaking, reading, and writing?
- How do we integrate grammar with language arts and other subject areas?
- How can knowledge of English grammar help students who speak a language other than English?
- How do we make grammar fun to learn, really, really fun, and memorable and meaningful?

As in our previous books, *Writing as Learning* (2007) and *Write for Mathematics* (2007), we provide specific strategies, tables and figures, and accurate resources that can guide you in making the teaching of grammar lively, interesting, and above all, beneficial to your students' language needs. We've tried to keep this book user-friendly with activities for all ages and abilities which you can use directly with your students or modify them as necessary.

The 13 chapters of this book, summarized as follows, are organized to fulfill our objectives and are written in the order of what we believe will give you both an historic and application perspective of English grammar and its components. We hope you read it through and then go back to the chapters and sections that apply best to your students' needs and interests.

Chapter 1. The **Introduction** discusses

- what grammar is.
- the history of teaching grammar in America.
- current standards on the teaching of grammar.

Chapter 2. **Language and Metalanguage** provides

- an overview of the aspects of language and metalanguage and the terms we use to describe language.
- the origins and historic changes of the English language.

Chapter 3. **Builders of Linguistic Intelligence** gives an overview of five aspects of language that are essential to developing high level language and literacy skills, which are

- Phonology—The "sounds" or vocal aspects.
- Morphology—The structure of words.
- Syntax (or grammar)—The speaker's internalized rules for constructing sentences.
- Semantics—The deep structure meanings that sentences provide for both speaker and listener.
- Etymology—The history or story of words.

Chapter 4. **Parts of Speech and the English Language** focuses on English as primarily a morphological language where

- the majority of its words or lexicon has multiple forms (e.g., play, players, playful, playfulness).
- a limited number of non-morphological words (e.g., the, in, but, or) provide the "glue" for constructing sentences.

Chapter 5. **Syntax and Semantics** note the relationship of grammar to meaning and explain how

- the meaning of words is derived from sentences.
- the deep meaning or semantics is the basis of comprehension.
- students benefit from studying both aspects—syntax and semantics—in unity.

Chapter 6. **The Polyglot of English** explains how and why the lexicon of English is composed of vast numbers of Latin and Greek words and offers students the plethora of

- Latin stems, roots, and words or the Latin DNA that make up a large part of "high level" spoken and written English.
- Greek stems, roots, and words infused in science, literature, social studies, religion, and other subjects.

Chapter 7. **The Polyglot: Beyond Latin and Greek** adds the lexical contributions of the languages of peoples worldwide who have contributed to the diversity of the English-speaking world and includes the following:

- Germanic, French, Spanish, and Italian words.
- Words from African Americans and Yiddish speakers, as well as words from China, Japan, and India.
- Writing activities that provide students with expanded knowledge of the English polyglot.

Chapter 8. **Return to Parts of Speech** is mainly about the non-morphological English words that bind words into sentences, provide multiple meanings, and often defy classification as parts of speech, such as

- prepositions.
- two-part verbs.
- conjunctions.
- transitions.

Chapter 9. **Sentences, Paragraphs, and Other Structures of the Written Language** is mainly about written structures that guide students in

- converting spoken sentences into written sentences.
- working with sentence units known as phrases and clauses.
- finding sentence boundaries in written sentences.
- finding deep structure meaning in written sentences.
- working with subjects and predicates.
- learning about tenses and agreement.
- learning whether "to split or not to split."
- working with paragraphs.
- learning about writing formats such as *formal to friendly* and *friendly to formal.*

Chapter 10. **Grammar for Word Play** is to make "grammar" really fun by writing joyfully, using

- oxymora.
- eponyms.
- colorful words.
- affixes awry.
- comedic characters.

Chapter 11. **Reading, Writing, and Grammar** combines these aspects of literacy with student activities from

- fairy tales and other children's literature.
- the autobiography *Narrative of the Life of Frederick Douglass, an American Slave* (1845/2003).
- author Lewis Carroll.
- the novel *The Phantom Tollbooth* (Juster, 1989).

Chapter 12. **Punctuation, Spelling, Text Messaging, and Other Consequences of Grammar** offers students lively activities that have them

- do a personal punctuation assessment.
- clarify their writing by gaining a deep understanding of how punctuation attempts to "imitate" speech.
- explore why we use apostrophes, colons, semicolons, dashes, and parentheses.
- relate spelling to grammar.
- contribute to the new grammar of text messaging.

Chapter 13. **Additional Learning Activities** build sentence power and include the following:

- Plan to Expand.
- People in Apposition.
- Verbs of Locomotion for Getting Places.
- To + Verb = One Great Sentence.
- Past Tense Openers.
- Transitions for Unity.
- Powerful Paragraph Starters.
- Numerous Combinations.
- World-Wide Words.
- African American Proverbs.
- Double Meanings.
- Acrostic Varieties.

We have had the privilege of having our manuscript submitted to a variety of teachers and university faculty and have received many insightful comments and valuable suggestions for making this book "useful" in the classroom. We have incorporated what they have told us in as many ways as possible and know that this book has benefited from their careful reading and deep reflections. Hopefully, we have done justice to their suggestions.

Last, we want to thank the many teachers who have taken our courses in Linguistics and the Structure of the English Language and who have shared their own knowledge and provided us with invaluable feedback on what has worked (or not worked) for their own students. This book is our special tribute to these "students" of the English language.

We look forward to hearing from you. Your questions, comments, and successes will all be welcomed.

PUBLISHER'S ACKNOWLEDGMENTS

Corwin Press gratefully acknowledges the contributions of the following reviewers:

Mary Nell Anthony
English Teacher/Dean of Arts
   and Science
T.L. Hanna High School,
   Anderson, SC

Amy Benjamin
Educational Consultant
Fishkill, NY

Michelle Drechsler
Middle School Language Arts Teacher
Phoenix, AZ

Karen L. Fernandez
Literacy Instructor
Humanities Facilitator
Denver Center for International Studies,
   Denver, CO

Linda Irvin
Fourth Grade Teacher
Sunflower Elementary School
Paola, KS

Christine Landwehrle
Reading/Language Arts Teacher
Bedminster Township Public School,
   Bedminster, NJ

Tabia Lee
Gifted ELL English/Social
   Studies Teacher
Belvedere Middle School, CA

Arlene Sandberg
ESL Resource Teacher
Mountain View Elementary School,
   Anchorage, AK

Amy Shoultz
Assistant Clinical Professor of Teaching
   and Learning
University of Iowa, Iowa City

Barbara Stanford
Emeritus Associate Professor
University of Arkansas at Little Rock,
   Little Rock, AR

About the Authors

Evelyn Rothstein has been an educational consultant specializing in teaching writing across the curriculum for the past 20 years. With a background in classroom teaching and a specialization in linguistics and language development, she has trained teachers and implemented her strategy-based Writing as Learning and Write for Mathematics programs in hundreds of schools and school districts throughout the United States. In addition, she is a consultant for the National Urban Alliance, focusing on writing, language, and cognition. Dr. Rothstein is a graduate of the City University of New York and Teachers College, Columbia University with degrees in education, speech, reading, and psycholinguistics. She is the author of numerous books and articles, including *Teaching Writing* (Rothstein & Gess, 1992), *Staying at the Top* (Rothstein, Berliner, & Berliner, 1986), *Writing As Learning* (Rothstein, Rothstein, & Lauber, 2007a), and *Write for Mathematics* (Rothstein et al., 2007b). She is also the author of four children's books: *My Great Grandma Clara* (2005), *My Great Grandpa Dave* (2006), *Dave the Boxer* (2008a), and *Clara Becomes a Citizen* (2008b).

Andrew S. Rothstein has had a distinguished career as teacher, administrator, and researcher. His diverse and enriching experiences in international schools, U.S. public schools, special education, and consulting have given him a broad perspective on the contexts in which children learn. As an author and presenter, he has achieved wide acclaim for his work in improving school performance by focusing on improving instruction and its supervision. His work in integrating many subject areas through writing has been highly effective in improving test scores in districts across the country. Dr. Rothstein earned a master's degree in special education from the University of North Carolina at Chapel Hill and a doctorate in educational administration from New York University. As a school principal, Dr. Rothstein led site-based improvements that resulted in strong increases in student academic performance. While superintendent of a regional school serving children with severe physical disabilities and health impairments, Dr. Rothstein reorganized staff development, created new curricula, and integrated technology into the instructional program for children from prekindergarten through high school. He has taught and lectured at several major universities and has been a senior consultant with the National Urban Alliance. Currently he is Senior Director, Curriculum & Academics, for the National Academy Foundation. Dr. Rothstein is a coauthor of *Writing As Learning* (Rothstein et al., 2007a) and *Write for Mathematics* (Rothstein et al., 2007b), published by Corwin Press.

Introduction

*Language and
Metalanguage*

*Builders of
Linguistic
Intelligence*

*Parts of
Speech and the
English Language*

*Syntax and
Semantics*

*The Polyglot
of English*

*The Polyglot:
Beyond Latin
and Greek*

*Return to Parts
of Speech*

*Sentences,
Paragraphs, and
Other Structures
of the Written
Language*

*Grammar for
Word Play*

*Reading, Writing,
and Grammar*

*Punctuation,
Spelling, Text
Messaging, and
Other
Consequences of
Grammar*

*Additional
Learning
Activities*

CHAPTER ONE

*On the writing of grammars there is no end. . . . There have been
short grammars and complete grammars, practical grammars and
philosophical grammars, new grammars and improved grammars,
descriptive grammars and structural grammars, grammars without
tears and grammars for heretics, logical grammars and grammars on
historical principles, and even Grammar on English Grammars.*

Robert L. Allen (1972, p. xiii)

THE PREMISE OF THIS BOOK

The premise of *English Grammar Instruction That Works! Developing Language
Skills for all Learners* is that there is an important place for grammar (defined
later) in students' lives and learning. Grammar is integral to language and
provides us with the ability to speak, read, write, appreciate humor, express
emotions, and have a shared backdrop with others that provides closeness and
understanding. Students with a strong knowledge of language, including
grammar, enjoy expanded learning opportunities in all disciplines, including
a better understanding of themselves. They develop insights about thinking
and bringing thought to vocal and written expression. They are better
equipped to say what they mean and understand what others mean. Since
there is virtually no end to the amount of language that we can learn, students
of language develop a passion for all learning and never get a signal that says
"Hard drive full!"

WHAT DO WE MEAN BY GRAMMAR?

School grammar books have traditionally taught that grammar is to learn the
"correct rules" of a language, mostly for writing. They include topics such as
usage, sentence structure, punctuation, parts of speech, and possibly other features that are related to school purposes such as improved reading comprehension and development of presentation skills (Crystal, 2006a).

1

Many teachers, however, have had more questions about this subject than answers. They appropriately ask, "Does this concept of grammar as *correct usage* help my students improve their writing, reading, or speaking?" "Does it relate in any way to other subjects—social studies, mathematics, science?" Many teachers ask or ponder, "Why can't so many of my students remember to use a capital letter at the beginning of a sentence?" "Why can't they remember what a *complete* sentence is?" "They know what adjectives are, but why do I constantly have to remind them to use them?"

Then come the more challenging questions: "How do I get my students to make their verbs *agree?*" "How can I get my ELL students to understand plurals or prepositions or verb conjugations?" "How can I get *them* to stop using double negatives?" So before we can proceed to make sense of this subject and what we need to teach, we start with some definitions and concepts, because we need to have a common understanding of key terms. To get us started, we provide two definitions: One is adapted from *Random House Webster's Unabridged Dictionary* (2000), and the other is from *The Oxford Companion to the English Language* (McArthur, 1992).

The definition of *grammar* from *Random House Webster's Unabridged Dictionary* (2000) is

1. the study of the way the sentences of a language are constructed, including morphology and syntax.

2. a set of rules accounting for these constructions.

3. a body of rules, whose output is all of the sentences that are permissible in a given language, while excluding all those that are not permissible

The definition of *grammar* from *The Oxford Companion to the English Language* (McArthur, 1992) is

The systematic study and description of a language . . . in terms of either syntax and morphology . . . with aspects of phonology, orthography, semantics, pragmatics, and word-formation . . . . (p. 446)

Probably neither of these definitions will help classroom teachers. Does the five-year-old fluent speaker of English need to study sentence rules? What do native speakers need to *study* about sentence construction if they already construct standard English sentences fluently without direct instruction? On the other hand, you might ask: "What about children who speak a 'nonstandard dialect,' of English fluently. Which sentence constructions should they study? Their own? The teachers? Both?"

We also have students who speak a language other than English, with varying degrees of fluency and ability. Which sentence constructions should these students start with? Should they study their own and compare them to English or just begin with English? If we add the second definition from *The Oxford Companion to the English Language* (McArthur, 1992), we are broadening the base of what grammar is, but now we need to know what we should teach and with what purposes or objectives?

At one time the answer to teaching grammar was not this complicated. Every student had a grammar book, and the word *grammar* meant parts of speech, verb tenses, subject and predicate, transitive and intransitive, subjunctive and "nonsubjunctive," and *lots* of underlining such things as direct object, indirect object, predicate adjective, predicate noun, and so forth. In fact, some students (including these authors) did so much underlining that there was no time for writing.

We begin with the view that grammar is the glue that holds language together. Without grammar we have just words—phonology or meaningful sounds—which are what many first year foreign language students have and very little else. All of you reading this book are likely to know words in a foreign language (Spanish, French, Italian, Chinese, or whatever language you have had some contact with). But try to say something fluently in another language, and many of you will find yourselves inarticulate because you lack the grammar. Even more difficult is to understand the other speaker's reply, known as pragmatics, and reply back. Then try to carry on a conversation for 10 minutes.

Grammar glues our language together in a way that makes sense to the speaker and listener when words are placed in the "right order" of a specific language. This is where nature works its magic because that assemblage of order begins very early in a child's life. And the longer the delay, for whatever reason, the greater the difficulty in "fluent assemblage." Every English-speaking child with uninterrupted development knows to say "the red hat," while in France, the same-age child says with perfect confidence, "le chapeau rouge." And bit by bit, then with great rapidity, the assemblage continues and the native speaker knows his or her own native language fluently by age five or six and sometimes younger. Yet no young child can recite or explain the rules. According to Chomsky (1957, 1965), Pinker (1994, 1999), and others, learning a language is innate and is universally learned when the child is very young.

THE HISTORY OF TEACHING GRAMMAR IN THE UNITED STATES OF AMERICA

If language is innate and developmental, what is the grammar that schools want to teach and toward what end? The answer to this question lies in history, especially in the history of education, and for the purposes of this book, in the education of students in the United States. Among the earliest grammar books in the United States were those written shortly after the American Revolution by Lindley Murray (an American Loyalist), followed by Noah Webster. Their aims, like others who would follow, were to introduce foreigners to English and teach students their own language, as if a native speaker is not speaking his or her own language! Most important was preparing students to read Latin and apply its rules to English. All of these early grammarians viewed Greek and Latin as languages to be emulated and "saw [in English] a barbarous mass of material that seemed to lack all grammatical order" (McArthur, 1992, p. 448). This point of view was to influence subsequent grammarians well into the 20th (or 21st) century who continued to describe English as if it were Latin with terms such as declensions, case, subjunctive, participle, and so forth. From this heritage, English would remain in the shadow of Greek and Latin, even as English progressed to be a global language, while Greek (ancient and classical) and Latin became, in essence, a backdrop to English (Crystal, 2006a).

In addition to the aim of "Latinizing English," the writers of what would become "school grammar" began to see the study of grammar as "uplifting." Children of the poor and the uneducated, whose language was "substandard," meaning not like the language of people of affluence and power, would "morally benefit from parsing sentences" (McArthur, 1992, p. 449). For African American children (Delpit, 1998), the relation to grammar took on racist overtones. "Black Language" has been characterized as a kind of "broken English reflecting the supposed simplicity and lack of education of its users" (Delpit, 1998, p. 58). So the school grammar books focused even more on "prescriptive grammar," meaning how we *should* speak rather than on the study of how language develops, changes, and *is spoken*. Instruction in "correct English" became the norm of the school grammar books with emphasis on "having students memorize and recite definitions and rules" (e.g., a noun is a person, place, or thing; the subject is what the sentence is about, etc.). Tests in grammar have asked students to choose the "correct" answer, with no recognition that students who have learned a different form in their own community can only judge "correct" against what they have heard and know. One of the authors, Evelyn, remembers a grammar test in about sixth grade which asked the following: "Which is correct? I daren't open the box or I dasn't open the box." How ridiculous, Evelyn thought: "Who on Earth would use the word 'dasn't,' especially in the Bronx. It certainly wasn't a word my Eastern European immigrant mother would have used. On the other hand, she wouldn't have used 'daren't' either, but at least I had heard it someplace in New York."

Perhaps you're thinking by now, "But aren't there standards of good English or correct English? Don't we use the term, even in America, the 'Queen's English'? Doesn't the form of the language one speaks 'keep them in their place,' as Henry Higgins says in *Pygmalion* or *My Fair Lady*? And won't teaching [prescriptive] grammar in school solve 'their' language problems or deficits? Aren't there advantages to knowing and applying the rules of *standard* English?"

As we already know, however, school or prescriptive grammar hasn't done the job of "fixing" students' language. According, again, to the prestigious *The Oxford Companion to the English Language* (McArthur, 1992), "the grammarian's attitude toward language, combined with the mechanical instruction required by the texts, made the subject feared and despised by teachers and students alike" (p. 449). This statement may not be totally accurate because many teachers and some students were "good" at this subject, and being good at something makes it much more palatable or possibly pleasant.

However, we can make *grammar work and serve high literary purposes* when we teach students the following:

- The history of the English language with suggestions for further study for those who are interested.
- Different ways to describe language, known as metalanguage—the linguistic or symbolic system used to discuss, describe, or analyze a language.
- How we learn our (first) language and how we can expand on that learning.
- The different ways we use language—in speaking, in writing, in humor, in thinking.
- When and how to say or write what to whom, known as the conventions of language, both spoken and written.
- To explore second language learning, cyber language, other languages, and whatever is interesting about language.

CURRENT STANDARDS RELATED TO TEACHING GRAMMAR

The Assembly for the Teaching of English Grammar, as part of the National Council of Teachers of English (NCTE), has made the following statement related to the teaching of English grammar:

> Grammar is important because it is the language that makes it possible for us to talk about language. Grammar names the types of words and word groups that make up sentences not only in English, but in any language. . . . People associate grammar with errors and correctness. But knowing about grammar also helps us understand what makes sentences and paragraphs clear and interesting and precise . . . And knowing about grammar means finding out that all languages and dialects follow grammatical patterns. (NCTE, n.d.)

Included in the NCTE/IRA (International Reading Association) Standards for the English Language Arts, 4 of the 12 standards refer to students' understanding of language and sentence structure:

- Standard 3 refers to sentence structure as an important aspect of comprehending and appreciating texts.
- Standard 4 maintains that students need to know how to adjust their spoken and written language for different purposes, which requires an understanding of the conventions and style of language.
- Standard 6 states that students should "apply knowledge of language structure and language conventions" to create and critique both print and nonprint texts. (NCTE/IRA, 1998)
- Standard 9 calls for students to "develop an understanding of and respect for diversity in language, patterns, and dialects across cultures, ethnic groups, geographic regions, and social roles." (NCTE/IRA, 1998)

Every state education department has standards on language generally divided into reading and writing. Most states include expectations of using appropriate grammar. As stated, this book emphasizes the importance of knowing language and knowing *about* language, not only to meet the standards, but to raise the standards. State tests often assess student use of grammar, and students who achieve high scores on the SAT are likely to know a great deal about language.

The chapters that follow cover what we believe are the major areas that teachers need to know to make the teaching of grammar effective, exciting, and capable of providing students with deep, meaningful knowledge about language, literacy, and culture.

We believe that teachers need to know the history of the English language. First, the history itself is fascinating and informative. Today, English is a global language spoken all over the world by both people for whom it is their first language and by millions of people who have made it their second language. The history of the English language tells us why our nouns and verbs have their present forms, from what languages our words come, why we have so many variations in our spelling and sound-symbol systems, and why English is so widely spoken.

Teachers also need to be familiar with the terminology related to language such as grammar, dialects, sentence structure, word formation (morphology), among other terms. This information helps us understand the diversity of language and within language. While we may all speak English, we immediately recognize differences in accent, idioms, fluency, and more. Knowledge of metalanguage terms allows for accuracy of teaching and opportunities for sharing this information with students at the deepest possible levels.

Teachers also need to know how children learn language from birth through the school years. This knowledge is essential to guide students in reading, writing, and speaking beyond the "basics" so that by the end of high school, students know how to adjust their language for different purposes. Knowing how children learn language is particularly important in helping the multitudes of students who enter school with a language other than English and must quickly make the transition to a "second" language while simultaneously learning academic material.

In addition, there is the area of curriculum and methodology. How can we best teach what students need to know? What should students learn and how should they learn it? We have included ideas and strategies for learning more about the lexicon or the words—vocabulary, phonology, morphology, and spelling—and how the lexicon is inseparable from "grammar." Words make up sentences, so students need to enlarge their sentence repertoire to say more and possibly "say it better" or with greater variety and preciseness of meaning. Working with sentences will include terms such as syntax and semantics, among others. Students need to have and use a range of "linguistic registers." Linguistic registers include the language we use in conversations with family and friends, interviews, presentations both informal and formal, and writing to diverse audiences. Associated with linguistic registers is the important concept of sociolinguistics, the study of the social uses and social implications of language.

Teachers and students who become familiar with these terms have the benefit and joy of understanding the *culture* of language and the role that language plays in every human's life. Language is one of the great distinguishing characteristics of humans. The purpose of this book is to have your students communicate in ways that are practical, precise, delightful, creative, brilliant, humorous, and deep. The emphasis of this book is that learning about language is about becoming wise about language.

Introduction

Language and Metalanguage

Builders of Linguistic Intelligence

Parts of Speech and the English Language

Syntax and Semantics

The Polyglot of English

The Polyglot: Beyond Latin and Greek

Return to Parts of Speech

Sentences, Paragraphs, and Other Structures of the Written Language

Grammar for Word Play

Reading, Writing, and Grammar

Punctuation, Spelling, Text Messaging, and Other Consequences of Grammar

Additional Learning Activities

CHAPTER TWO

Language and Metalanguage

. . . all language is equal, even if some language is more equal than others.

(Howard, 1985, p. 1)

. . . languages would do very well . . . if they could only live up to the standards illustrated by Latin.

(Aelfric's Colloquy, Garmonsway, 1939, p. 23)

Key Concepts and Terms

Language, Metalanguage, Dialect, Grammar, Slang, Creole, Pidgin, Register, History of the English Language

---

OVERVIEW OF THE TERMS *LANGUAGE* AND *METALANGUAGE*

Everyone readily understands the word *language* as in "They speak a different language." We know when we don't understand someone else's *language*—perhaps Italian or Chinese or Hungarian. But when we encounter words which are related to language, or metalanguage (the language used to discuss, describe, or analyze another language), our understanding becomes less clear. What do we mean when someone speaks a *dialect* or speaks the English language with a different *accent,* or speaks it *incorrectly* or *impeccably?* What we do mean by *good grammar* or *bad grammar* and why are there these distinctions? Why do some accents carry *prestige* like the "Queen's English," while other accents are given short shrift or, worse yet, are considered *lowly* or get mocked? Almost all of

Taxonomy

A taxonomy is a strategy used to create a list of words related to a specific topic or subject area. Taxonomies can be developed for waterways, geometry, capital cities, animals, or any other category. By listing the words alphabetically, students have a retrieval system as well as a stimulus to think of related terms. For example, "I need a word for the category of language that begins with "s." The student might now think of *syllable* or at a more advance level *sibilant* or *sociolinguistics.* Taxonomies used for word categories help students build a personal thesaurus for expanding their vocabulary and having a ready source for using this vocabulary in their writing.

Figure 2.1   Taxonomy of Metalanguage*

• TAXONOMY •

A	accent, affixes
B	"borrowed" words, base forms
C	colloquial, Creole, conversational
D	dialect, discourse, descriptive grammar
E	etymology, Ebonics
F	formal, fluent
G	grammar, grammatical
H	
I	idioms, idiomatic, idiolect, informal, inflection
J	jargon
K	
L	linguistics, lexicon, language
M	morphology, morphemes
N	nonstandard, nongrammatical
O	
P	pidgin, patois, phonology, pragmatics, pronunciation, psycholinguistics, prescriptive grammar, punctuation, parts of speech, phonemes
Q	
R	register, regionalisms, roots
S	standard, slang, syntax, semantics, sociolinguistics, stress, syllable
T	
U	usage
V	vernacular, vocabulary
W	words
X	
Y	
Z	

*There are other metalanguage terms which can be found in texts on linguistics and language which you and your students can research (see Internet References).

these terms and questions are part of sociolinguistics, the social aspects of language, which include "attitudes" of language related to accent, dialect, region, and class (McArthur, 1992). Do teachers need to know this information, and if yes, what significance does this information have for teaching your students?

A good place to begin conceptualizing metalanguage is by understanding the terminology we use to describe aspects of language. In Figure 2.1, Taxonomy of Metalanguage, is a list of many of the terms that describe language. The list is set up as a taxonomy—a procedure of *classification,* presented in *Writing as Learning* (Rothstein, Rothstein, & Lauber, 2007a) and *Write for Mathematics* (Rothstein 2007b).

The sidebar provides a definition of taxonomy as used for classifying vocabulary.

Most of these metalanguage terms relate to classroom instruction. Some may appear to be value neutral, while others may influence how we view our students. By knowing and using their accurate meanings, we gain a deeper insight as to how language is constructed and the additional perspective about cultural and linguistic diversity. Furthermore, these terms set the stage for a study of language that will engage student interest because it deals with our most valuable human asset, the ability to communicate. Seven metalanguage terms are defined in this chapter: language, dialect, grammar, slang, Creole, pidgin, and register (Figures 2.1 to 2.7).

Language, Dialect, and Grammar

Throughout this book, you will encounter most of the terms listed earlier, but to get started we have set out the definitions of three metalanguage terms—language, dialect, grammar—that form the basis for the strategies and activities we propose (Figures 2.2, 2.3, and 2.4). We have used a template called Defining Format for these (and subsequent) definitions as described more fully in *Writing as Learning* (Rothstein et al., 2007a). Notice that the template begins with a question, followed by a category, and then with the essential characteristics of the term being defined. We suggest that you use this template with students beginning in intermediate grades to help them define terms they will need to know or understand.

By starting with the definition of language shown in Figure 2.2, we can now define the subcategories of two essential words related to language: *dialect* and *grammar*, shown in Figures 2.3 and 2.4. While the words dialect and grammar are in common usage, they have come to mean different ideas to different people. By accurately defining the meanings of these words, we can offer our students descriptive terminology that generates insight to language usage.

Sometimes, the word *dialect* has been linked to jargon or slang without a clear explanation of the distinctions. There are also occasions when people refer to dialects in a pejorative or judgmental way, assuming that their own speech patterns are not dialects at all. By stating the characteristics, we recognize that all languages are composed of dialects.

Similarly, all language forms have grammatical structures. The definition of grammar in Figure 2.4 provides the key characteristics for examining any language in any dialect.

Figure 2.2

What Is Language?

• DEFINING FORMAT •

Question	Category	Characteristics
What is language?		
Language is a	system that	1. humans use to communicate. 2. consists of arbitrary sounds, called phonemes, which give meanings, called words. 3. has precise patterns internalized by the speaker known as grammar. 4. can generate an infinite number of statements from a finite set of "rules." 5. has a structure of word order known as sentences. 6. is understood only by those who have learned those sounds and structure either in early childhood or through circumstances of later acquisition. 7. has different "registers" such as intimate, conversational, formal, literary. 8. can have "subcategories" such as dialect, Creole, pidgin, slang, and sign. 9. can be symbolized through alphabets and icons. Other characteristics can be added.

Figure 2.3

What Is Dialect?

• DEFINING FORMAT •		
Question	Category	Characteristics
What is dialect?		
Dialect is an	aspect of language that	1. refers to variations in pronunciations, words, and grammar of a *specific* language. 2. is part of every language, resulting from geographic, occupational, and social differences. 3. makes up part of everyone's speech. 4. is generally intelligible to speakers of other dialects within the same specific language, but with some exceptions related to pronunciation, accent, grammatical variation, or words. 5. is often "judged" by speakers of that specific language as socially distinct (standard vs. nonstandard, prestigious vs. nonprestigious).

Figure 2.4

What Is Grammar?

• DEFINING FORMAT •		
Question	Category	Characteristics
What is grammar?		
Grammar is an	aspect of language that	1. refers to the way the sentences of a specific language are constructed. 2. includes phonology, morphology (forms of the words), and syntax. 3. consists of a body of rules that allows for the generation of an infinite number of sentences.

By seeing language as composed of dialect and grammar, we get a clearer view of how language works. With this starting point, we can create knowledge-based language instruction that infuses the total curriculum, since every subject area requires a high level use of language. In the remaining portion of this chapter, we have added other metalanguage definitions that provide an expanded background of what language means and how it operates (see Figures 2.5, 2.6, 2.7, and 2.8). Share this information with your students as much as possible during language arts, social studies, reading, writing, mathematics, and so forth.

Figure 2.5

	DEFINING FORMAT	
Question	Category	Characteristics
What is slang?		
Slang is an	aspect of language that	1. occurs within a distinct group such as adolescents, students, sports figures, the military, and others, and results in group identity. 2. is generational or arises within a specific time period and eventually fades out (e.g., Shakepeare's slang vs. Dickens's slang vs. "today's" slang [e.g., cool, awesome, nerd, etc.]). 3. may be regional (e.g., bloke, guy). 4. is part of spoken language or when written is often within dialogue representing a specific character or personage.

slang (slang), n. (from *Random House Webster's Unabridged Dictionary*, 2000)

1. very informal usage in vocabulary and idiom that is characteristically more metaphorical, playful, elliptical, vivid, and ephemeral than ordinary language, as *Hit the road.*
2. (in English and some other languages) speech and writing characterized by the use of vulgar and socially taboo vocabulary and idiomatic expressions.
3. the jargon of a particular class, profession, etc.
4. the special vocabulary of thieves, vagabonds, etc.; argot.
5. to assail with abusive language.
6. nonstandard.

Slang

One of the most commonly used terms is the word *slang,* which often connotes "bad" or "low" language or refers to the speech of undereducated speakers. It is also a common feature of pop culture language. By defining a word judgmentally rather than linguistically, we do not get to the origin or "story" of the word or why we even have "slang," which occurs in all languages (Perry & Delpit, 1998). The metalinguistic word slang is an essential term for teachers (and students) to know, and we have defined it in Figure 2.5, adapted from *The Oxford Companion to the English Language* (McArthur, 1992, pp. 940–941). We have also compared this definition with that of the *Random House Webster's Unabridged Dictionary* (2000), which includes the judgmental slant often stated in dictionaries (see Figure 2.5).

Using judgmental definitions (rather than descriptive ones) often causes students to feel embarrassed about their own language rather than become inspired to understand language in all its varieties. The focus of language education is to equip the learner with a deep understanding of different forms of language that can be applied to a wide range of circumstances. The tone needs to be *additive* rather than *corrective.* For example, students in middle and high school are often very interested in slang as part of their "culture" and can become deeply engaged in discussing its meaning. There are many examples of leveraging slang in music and poetry to communicate very serious ideas. McArthur (1992) points out that "slang is used to establish or reinforce social identity and cohesiveness, especially within a group or with a trend of fashion in society at large" (p. 940). Slang is generally transient or it can often migrate to acceptance as standard English as in the formerly slang words of *jeopardy* (from gambling) and *crestfallen* (from cockfighting).

Creole and Pidgin

In Figures 2.6 and 2.7, we define two terms that are important parts of linguistic lexicon—*Creole* and *pidgin*. The word *Creole,* as a language, is often associated with Haitian Creole. However, the term has a broader meaning and encompasses many languages. It derives from the Latin *creare,* meaning "to beget" or "create." After the New World's discovery, Portuguese colonists used the word *crioulo* to denote a New World slave of African descent. Eventually, the word was applied to colonists of "mixed" ethnic origin, living along the Gulf Coast, especially in Louisiana. There the Spanish introduced the word as *criollo,* and during Louisiana's colonial period (1699–1803) the evolving word *Creole* generally referred to persons of mixed African and European heritage born in the New World. By the 19th century, black, white, and mixed-race Louisianians used the term to distinguish themselves from foreign-born and Anglo-American settlers. We define the term *Creole* in Figure 2.6, followed by the definition of the term *pidgin* in Figure 2.7. The term pidgin is often closely allied with Creole languages, with both terms likely to carry negative connotations (MacArthur, 2002).Your students can do exciting research projects related to these two terms and gain an important perspective on the historical impact of cultures merging through human migration or colonization.

We encourage you to teach your students how to research, analyze, and clarify the meanings of language and vocabulary using these terms. Here are several ways

Figure 2.6

What Is Creole?		
• DEFINING FORMAT •		
Question	**Category**	**Characteristics**
What is Creole?		
Creole is an	aspect of language that	1. develops through colonization or domination from a more powerful group or nation. 2. maintains some of the structure and vocabulary of the language which was spoken by the dominant or conquering group (e.g., French, Spanish, Portuguese, English). 3. maintains words and grammatical structures from the languages from which it sprung (e.g., Niger Congo or other African languages with English or French; Yiddish with Hebrew and German; Ladino with Spanish, Turkish, Greek, and Hebrew). 4. is grammatically and lexically complex like other languages (e.g., Haitian Creole, Papiamento, Ebonics).

Figure 2.7

DEFINING FORMAT		
Question	Category	Characteristics
What is pidgin?		
Pidgin is an	aspect of language that	1. comes into existence when people of two different languages attempt to speak to each other over a period of time (e.g., English with Chinese). 2. has resulted from trade and interactions of diverse language speakers. 3. results in the grammatical and lexical simplification of one of the languages (e.g., English). 4. may form the basis of a new language (see Creole) and eventually becomes grammatically and lexically complex.

What Is Pidgin?

to engage and encourage your students to find out the history of these terms and their accurate meanings. Students can do the following:

- Check Internet sources of these terms that specify Creole as a language.
- Discuss the difference between using the word *Creole* as a reference to people in contrast to using the word as a language.
- Research world languages that have the characteristics of the definition of Creole in Figure 2.6. (see also Figure 2.7).
- Collect Creole words from different Creole languages (Haitian, Jamaican, Cajun, West African Creoles, African American Creoles, Yiddish, and others).
- Check Internet sources on different pidgins and their origins.

When students make these terms part of their knowledge, they can look at their own language metacognitively and with a conscious awareness as to why they speak the way they do, whether it be due to family background or heritage, belonging to a particular group, or living within a particular community. From this awareness, students expand their linguistic repertoire and cultural understandings of language. Imagine being able to speak comfortably and fluently with your family and friends as *they* speak, then speak just as fluently and comfortably with teachers and other "school" people, and finally "code switch" to the "formal language" of occupations, professions, and *writing*.

Registers

The word *register* refers to the various formalities or informalities of language. For example, we are likely to speak one way to a prospective employer using "formal" English, another way to a peer using "conversational" English, and quite differently to a baby using "baby" talk. Teenagers speak in a different register to fellow teenagers in contrast to how they are likely to speak to their parents, known often as "intimate" or peer group register (Joos, 1957).

Another example of register is when an English speaker "switches" from using walking to walkin' or Mr. to Hey Man or keeps or avoids the use of ain't. This type of change in register is often called code switching. This aspect of language has been widely written about by educators and linguists, especially in relationship to the reading, writing, and social challenges faced by children with diverse language backgrounds (Berg, 2003; Delpit, 1995; Delpit & Dowdy, 2001; Gomez & Madda, 2005; Joos, 1957; Labov, 2003; Trudgill, 1974). The term *register,* defined in Figure 2.8, has often been the reason, explicit or underlying, for teaching prescriptive grammar, or often colloquially stated as "correct" grammar, the grammar that has also been termed *proper* or *polite* (Delpit, 2001).

Everyone has a range of registers, and education can be used to expand one's register and increase student awareness of its social uses. For example, look at these sentences and think about where you would assign them (formal, informal, colloquial, etc.) and under what circumstances you would speak in these different registers:

I expect you to be punctual.

I want you to be on time.

Management is expending a considerable time on this task.

The bosses are taking a lot of time getting this job done.

Mother is always fatigued after a long journey.

Mom is just plain worn-out after one of those long trips.

If you were to speak these sentences, you most likely would say them differently, perhaps speaking more carefully or slowly and placing different emphasis on the words so that the rhythm of the utterances changes. Then *who* we are talking to makes all the difference in our choice of register—our children, someone else's children, family, friends, colleagues, employers, medical and legal professionals, and so forth.

Registers are both developmental and learned (Joos, 1957; Piaget, 1954, 1972). Parents in all cultures instruct their children to "speak politely," by which they are likely to mean "formal." For example, parents may insist that a child uses the honorific (Aunt or Uncle) rather than just using a first name (i.e., Mary or Carlos) when addressing these family members. In parts of the United States, the word *Miz* is often required when a child addresses a female friend of the family, as in "Miz" Evelyn. Words like *sir* and *ma'am* are absolute register requirements in some communities, but shunned or ignored in other communities. What is a *respectful* or formal register

Figure 2.8

What Is Register?		
• DEFINING FORMAT •		
Question	**Category**	**Characteristics**
What is register?		
Register is an	aspect of language that	1. refers to the social or situational context of speech (or writing). 2. can be labeled as child [language], adult, colloquial, conversational, formal, or informal. 3. may be referred to as occupational, academic, journalistic, scientific, or legal. 4. develops in family, cultural, and educational settings.

in one geographic area may be insulting elsewhere. (See Forms of Address in *The Oxford Companion to the English Language,* McArthur, 1992.)

Delpit and Dowdy (2001) make an emphatic statement about how children are taught and learn the social aspects of language or registers in her reference to African American children. They state the following:

> From rhyming games to rap songs, from talking their way out of trouble to instigating trouble, many African-American children use language to display their intelligence and their competence to negotiating the world. In their communities, they are applauded for their quick verbal responses, their creative plays on words and sounds, their imaginative improvisations of familiar stories and themes, and their ability to best an "opponent" through superior verbal reasoning. (p. 61)

Each of these forms of language (i.e., rap, play on words, improvisation, verbal reasoning) represents a subset of register. Raps and word play are generally used with peers and formed with peer language forms; verbal reasoning requires different linguistic structures and often code switching.

Register as Power

An important aspect of register has to do with societal relationships (Delpit, 1995; Trudgill, 1974). Delpit (1995) uses and analyzes the terms *culture of power* and *codes of power,* which relate to ways of talking (linguistic forms), ways of writing (communicative strategies), ways of dressing, and ways of interacting (presentation of self). Success socially, in school and in the workplace or career, is heavily dependent on having a range of registers, which means knowing the "grammar" of different registers. Knowing multiple language registers widens one's social range and brings to the individual what Trudgill (1974) calls *linguistic power,* a term that can have positive connotations, but has often been used to exclude speakers with a limited range of registers. The negative effect of linguistic power is when the dominant group of a society or social setting expects and demands that *they, members of the dominant group,* be spoken to in a way that they consider acceptable. This scenario plays out frequently when students interact with teachers.

The dialogue that follows illustrates an example of exercising linguistic power in a conversation between a student and a teacher. In this instance, the teacher chooses to address the language used by the student—prescriptive language—before addressing the need of the student.

Student: Teacher, I got to go to the bathroom.

Teacher: You mean, "I have to go to the bathroom."

Student: Yes, ma'am.

Teacher: O.K., you may go.

Another example of linguistic power is in the use of "boy" or "girl," as in this conversation between an African American doctor in an encounter with a police officer:

Officer: What do you think you are doing here, boy?

Doctor: I'm Doctor Smith and I'm calling on my patient.

Officer: I said, "Boy, you have no right to be here."

Less confrontational register power, but still common, is the reference to an employee in the following manner: "I hired a new girl to answer the phone and do my letters," which ignores the adulthood of the employee and the occupational term of receptionist or office assistant.

Register as Solidarity

Register is often a form of linguistic solidarity where the group speaks the "same" language, using words, expressions, and sentence structures that bond the speakers and often exclude those who don't know that language. Here is an example about the use of the word *cool,* which has nothing to do with climate or temperature and may define the ages of the persons with whom you have or do not have linguistic solidarity:

> . . . by all the laws of language, *cool* should have died a natural death around 1963 along with most of the hipster lingo. . . . Who would have figured that cool would survive the decade, much less the century?. . . Hey, *cool* is eternal. The hippies picked up on it in the 70s and spun off a new antonym *uncool.* . . . And finally there's the cool of the digital age—"Click here for cool stuff" or "Today's cool Web site." (Nurnberg, 2001, p. 75)

On a personal note, picture this exchange that took place between one of the authors, Evelyn, and her grandson. Evelyn knew she and her grandson Tyler had linguistic solidarity, when in a conversational register, Tyler said, "Grandma, your matzoh ball soup is cool." In case Grandma thought he meant the temperature, Tyler then added, "I mean Grandma, it's awesome."

With this beginning background of metalanguage terms—*language, dialect, grammar, slang, Creole, pidgin,* and *register*—you can listen carefully to your students' speech or read their journals and get to know the variations in your classroom. Every student has an *idiolect* (personal speech profile), which reflects one's family and community. In addition, every student already has a variety of registers, intimate with their peers, conversational with family members and others, formal with teachers and certain adults that are markers of their culture. Every student (except perhaps those with serious language impairment) speaks a first language with the fluency that all second language learners seek to achieve. What you want to listen for is what they are communicating and what grammatical structures they use. When your head is filled with your students' voices, you can guide them on the exciting voyage of learning the different ways to speak and write in many dialects and unique idiolects.

A BRIEF HISTORY OF THE ENGLISH LANGUAGE

With this background in metalanguage, we present a brief history of the English language with its antecedents on the Asian, European, and African continents and its continuous changes as it "migrated" across northern Europe and eventually across the globe. As the number of people speaking English around the world rapidly increases, dialects are now ubiquitous, spoken with different accents and with local lexicons. Yet English speakers generally understand each other because it is held together by rules and words that English speakers recognize and can respond to.

An understanding of the history of English is helpful for putting the instructional approaches offered in the book into context. Most of us have received instruction in the English language that emphasizes certain aspects of English history and downplays others. This phenomenon has contributed to confusion among students and, in many cases, misleading information. Another unfortunate consequence of not understanding English history is that many students are given rules to follow in the absence of purpose or underlying logic.

Origins of English

A good place to start is to begin with the question, "Why is English called English?"

The answer is related to a term well known to many of us: *Anglo-Saxon*. English is a morphed form of "Anglish." Not much is known about the early settlers of the island known as England, but we can use our current language to figure out some of the events. What is known is that the people we now call Anglo-Saxons came to England as invaders from northern Europe. They were composed of Angles, Saxons, Jutes, Frisians, and Franks. They arrived sometime during the 5th or 6th century, conquering the Celts who were already there. Since the invaders came from different places at different times, the Anglo-Saxon language that emerged was probably a combination of many languages spoken in northern Europe at that time. We retain many words from the Anglo-Saxons, including the days of the week: Tuesday, Wednesday, Thursday, and Friday, and a huge number of words that refer to family, home, farm life, and animals and plants indigenous to the English countryside. In addition, almost all our non-morphological words that connect sentences are of Anglo-Saxon origin.

Starting in the 7th century, written English appears, initiating the period now known as Old English. In the 9th century, the Norsemen began invading England. They continued to drive into England into the 11th century until it was fully conquered by the Danish King, Canute. Since the Norse language was also Germanic, Old English grammar continued to develop along those lines. Among the words of Norse origin in modern English are *anger, bag, birth, call, husband, mistake, skin,* and *take*.

Key Point to Remember

English grammar, at its core, is Germanic.

The Norman Invasion and the Middle English Period

In 1066, William the Conqueror led the Norman invasion of England, marking the beginning of the Middle English period. This invasion brought a major influence to English from Latin and French. As is often the case with invasions, the conquerors dominated the major political and economic life in England. While this invasion had some influence on English grammar, the most powerful impact was on vocabulary.

Because of the power of the Norman conquerors, the trend was for their vocabulary to become associated with high society, centers of power, and commerce. Nevertheless, some of the original vocabulary remained, and the basic grammatical structure of Anglo-Saxon survived. The pattern of development was very fragmented due to a lack of communication throughout the country, but English continued to spread. Gradually, the power of the press started to create a form of standardization on English. This was also the period of the "great vowel shift" that differentiated the vowel sounds of English speakers from the people on the European continent.

Key Points to Remember

- The influence of Latin was greater on the vocabulary of English rather than its grammar.
- English began its continuing tradition of acquiring vocabulary from many languages.
- Many of today's confusing English grammatical and vocabulary idiosyncrasies resulted from the merging of major language groups.

Modern English

In 1755, Samuel Johnson published the first widely accepted English dictionary, part of a general movement to formalize the rules of English usage. Noah Webster followed with an American version in 1828. Robert Lowth (1762) was among the first people to publish a book that sought to standardize English grammar. The early grammarians were enamored of Greek and Latin and believed they represented the best model for English. This mindset resulted in a number of rules that force fit English into rules associated with Latin and Greek. Hence, "rules" were established, such as the banning of double negatives, split infinitives, and the use of prepositions at the end of a sentence.

Simplistically stated, the effort to regulate English has led to two major camps with different opinions about what to teach students about grammar and how to use English. The Rule-Based camp accents the importance of mastery of standardized rules that are approved by organizations that are deemed authoritative. The Constructivist camp, which has created various models, emphasizes that grammar is best understood as a system of families of constructions (structures).

This book does not attempt to resolve the debates surrounding these points of view, but the authors seek to enlighten educators about the various constructions, how they work, and what are the considerations for making informed grammatical decisions.

Key Point to Remember

The goal of this book is grammatical empowerment, not judgment.

INTERNET SITES

- http://www.krysstal.com/borrow_norse.html
  Words Borrowed from Norse—An excellent Taxonomy of Terms for all students.

- http://www.ielanguages.com/enghist.htm
  History of English—A very good overview that can be introduced to older and intermediate students.

- http://www.askoxford.com/worldofwords/history/?view=uk
  A superb source for students interested in finding the history of words.

- http://www.askoxford.com/worldofwords/worddetectives/dictionaryeditors
  Cites the work of Philip Durkin, principal etymologist at the *Oxford English Dictionary*, (2008) who chose five events that shaped the English Language: the Anglo-Saxon settlement, the Scandinavian settlements, the events of 1066 and what followed, standardization, and colonization and globalization. An excellent Web site for combining interest in history with language.

Introduction

Language and Metalanguage

Builders of Linguistic Intelligence

Parts of Speech and the English Language

Syntax and Semantics

The Polyglot of English

The Polyglot: Beyond Latin and Greek

Return to Parts of Speech

Sentences, Paragraphs, and Other Structures of the Written Language

Grammar for Word Play

Reading, Writing, and Grammar

Punctuation, Spelling, Text Messaging, and Other Consequences of Grammar

Additional Learning Activities

CHAPTER THREE

Builders of Linguistic Intelligence

Language is like a flowing stream sweeping onward with few discernible breaks in the flow.

(Lederer, 1991, p. 11)

A mastery of syntax . . . is a . . . sine qua non of poetry.

(Gardner, 1993, p. 76)

The goal of this chapter is to show the interrelationship of five major aspects of language that are necessary to provide an effective instructional model for improving student literacy. These five aspects make up the greater part of what we call language, which by definition is the sum of its parts (Crystal, 2003) and includes the following:

- Phonology—its sounds or *phonemes*
- Morphology—its words and their formations
- Syntax—its "rules" for composing statements
- Semantics—its meanings
- Etymology—its historic changes in phonology, morphology, and grammar that occur in every language over time.

Figure 3.1 illustrates the interrelationship of these language aspects with grammar in the center in line with Crystal's (2006a) statement that grammar is "absolutely central to the study of language" and that "no sentence can begin without grammar" (p. 96).

Figure 3.1   Interrelationships of Five Aspects of Language

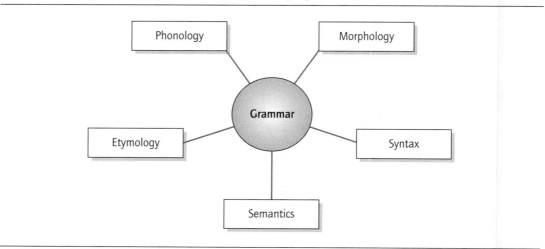

Every native speaker of every language makes use of phonology, morphology, syntax, and semantics *with ease,* the term *with ease* being used in contrast to how a speaker composes in a second language (Peregoy & Boyle, 2004). Most people who have studied a second language have experienced the fatigue that sets in when speaking the second language for any length of time and the relief that comes when switching back to one's first or native tongue. The native speakers generally know what they want or have to say and how to say it. In addition, native speakers assume that they will understand the responses. Along with these aspects are the etymological aspects of language—its historic changes—which underlie native speakers' idioms. This means that no English speaker today speaks like Shakespeare or George Washington or Charles Dickens. We all "speak modern" without ever giving a thought to the history of English.

Understanding this principle of "ease" is essential in the teaching of language or "language arts" in the classroom. Students who have acquired this *ease* will generally have little difficulty in learning to read or write. Even more significant is their specific awareness and expanded use of language, which Gardner (1993) refers to as "linguistic intelligence." While socialization plays a significant role in language development in individuals, educational forces are powerful assistants to the acquisition of words, creative sentence structure, and a conscious awareness of one's speech and its power or potential (Gardner, 1993; Jensen, 1998). By engaging students in exploring the five cited aspects of language, they can develop a deepened understanding of these "central aspects of language" and the knowledge that accrues. Fortunately, with the superb knowledge that has been given to us by linguists and educators, teachers can provide all of their students with the language tools they need to succeed by showing them how *their* language works.

In defining the five aspects of language, we have to keep in mind that they represent the unity of language, so that in explaining one term, we often have to use the other terms as part of the explanation.

PHONOLOGY

We begin with phonology: the study of the distribution and patterning of speech sounds in a language and of the rules governing pronunciation. Phonology comes from the Greek forms of *phono-* for sound and *-logy* meaning study. However, to understand phonology we need a broader definition, because phonology relates to sounds that convey meaning. Meaning is conveyed only to those who have acquired it in early childhood (as first language) or through study or explicit instruction (generally as in second language). Some children are exposed to two first languages. Even then, one of the languages tends to be "primary" depending on which the child hears and uses more. Furthermore, phonology relates the sounds (of speech) to the "grammar of the language" (McArthur, 1992, p. 772), and without grammar we have sounds or words without context, which convey limited or even no meaning. Figure 3.2, Taxonomy of Terms Related to Phonology, shows the many words related to phonology and its importance within the framework of language.

We suggest that by intermediate grades, students are introduced to these (and subsequent) language terms using the taxonomy template. Students should have a simple composition notebook for keeping taxonomies (Rothstein, Rothstein, & Lauber, 2007a). During lessons related to language, which should normally be part of all literacy related lessons, many of these words will arise during instruction or discussion. Have your students keep track of them, and discuss their meanings and importance for speaking, reading, and writing. You may wish to set up student "committees" to research the history or background of these terms and form discussion groups for sharing this important and interesting knowledge.

Figure 3.2 Taxonomy of Terms Related to Phonology

• TAXONOMY •	
A	accent, articulation, alphabet
B	
C	consonant
D	dialect
E	etymology, emphasis
F	
G	glossary
H	
I	idiolect
J	
K	
L	language, lexicon
M	morphology, minimal pair
N	
O	orthography
P	phonemes, phonics, phonetics, phonemics, pronunciation, prosody, phonology, pragmatics
Q	
R	
S	sound, sound-symbol, syllable, stress, speech
T	
U	unvoiced
V	voice, voiced, vocalization, vocabulary, vowel
W	word
X	
Y	
Z	

Following is an explanation of several of the terms shown in Figure 3.2 for use with your students to expand their understanding of phonology and its application to "high literate performance."

The "Sounds" or Phonology of Language: The sounds of language are described by various words such as *accent, articulation,* and *pronunciation.* However, teachers are less likely to refer to these terms except when students have specific problems with the intelligibility of their speech. More likely, teachers will focus on "sounds" when they teach beginning reading and have to refer to the *alphabet* and its "sounds," a process known as *phonics.* Terms less used by classroom teachers are terms such as *phonetics* and *phonemes,* although *phonemic awareness* is currently in use in relationship to teaching reading (Armbruster & Osborne, 2001).

The Basic "Sight Words" and the Study of Phonology: In *Putting Reading First* (Armbruster & Osborne, 2001), the authors refer to five areas of reading instruction:

phonemic awareness, phonics, fluency, vocabulary, and text comprehension. The authors explain terms such as *phoneme isolation, phoneme identity, phoneme categorization, phoneme blending,* and *phoneme segmentation,* among others (pp. 5–6).

The term *phoneme* refers to a sound or sounds that are *meaningful* to a native speaker. For example, English speakers rarely hear "vl" as in Vladimir, which is common in Russian. Many English speakers can't correctly pronounce the word "challah," a Hebrew word for Sabbath bread, or the Arabic word "Aleikim," because the guttural phoneme in these languages is unfamiliar. They are likely to substitute the phoneme [k] because they cannot pronounce the low throat or guttural sound that Hebrew and Arabic speakers learn in childhood.

But learning phonics or developing phonemic awareness is often not enough for successfully learning to read. Because of the complexity of English spelling, which has resulted from historic changes in pronunciation (Bryson, 1990), beginning readers must also learn what reading methodology books call "sight words" to build fluency. These are the words that in many cases defy "phonemic identity" and "phonemic categorization" and are exemplified by words such as *the, have, know, right, come.* Students are often told that they must memorize these words and pay only scant attention to the "phonemics." This complexity of English (phonology/phonics/phonemics/spelling) has led to the often vociferous polarization of how to teach reading with such slogans as "Phonics First" versus "Whole Language." But since our focus here is to relate grammar to reading, we suggest ways to provide students with the language knowledge that underpins effective and efficient language and results in good reading.

We have taken six representative verbs from "sight word" lists and preprimer and primer levels (www.createdbyteachers.com/dolchlist.html) to show how the *phonological* aspects of language can be combined to provide students with phonemic awareness, followed by *morphology* (the structure of words) and *etymology* (the origin and history of words), all of which are extensions of *grammar* (see Figure 3.3 on page 24) and will continue to be discussed throughout this book. You can use Figure 3.3 with all levels of students to make them aware of the spelling history of English words of Anglo-Saxon or Germanic origin and introduce them to the fascinating world of morphology and etymology. Encourage your students to become curious about these spellings and to see the "logic" of the spelling as their pronunciation changed over time. A wall of questions, along with a word wall, referred to frequently, can raise the bar of interest and high level knowledge. See the boxed text for start-up questions. Then ask students to create their own questions.

> Are you curious about English spelling? Find the answers to these questions. Then add your own questions about spelling. You're on your way to becoming a great etymologist.
>
> Why is there a *w* in the word *two?*
>
> Why is the numeral *8* spelled *eight?*
>
> Why is there a *k* in the word *knee?* Or *know?* Or *knight?*
>
> Why do we have the letters *gh* in *right, enough, daughter,* and so many other English words?
>
> Why do we use *sh* for *share,* *ch* for *chair,* and *th* for *there?* And why are there three different spellings for the rhyming parts of these words?

MORPHOLOGY

The term *morphology*—the study of the changes in structure or forms of words—comes from the Greek god Morpheus, the god of dreams and sleep. In this role, Morpheus had the ability to change his shape and also change the shapes of images in a mortal's sleep. In linguistics, morphology refers to the patterns of word formation in a particular language that includes changes in words which result from affixing (prefixes, suffixes, inflections) or from shifts in pronunciation. Morphology is closely tied to etymology, the study of word origins and their changes over time and is also an extension of phonology.

In the following pages and throughout the subsequent chapters, we present learning strategies and activities that you can introduce to your students to expand their knowledge of the five aspects of language. In each chapter, we label the first of these direct student activities as "APPLICATION TO LEARNING."

Figure 3.3 (see page 24) shows the patterns of morphology, phonology, and etymology of six representative words that have traditionally been called "sight" words. You can introduce this material to students at different grade or learning levels as appropriate to their needs. For example, all beginning readers should see and learn to read the full morphology of morphological words as illustrated in this figure. Along with the introduction of these words, you can point out the sound and symbol consistency that is in the *past tense* form. As you guide your students to become curious about the spellings, add the information on etymology. Post these charts visibly and refer to them frequently for reading, spelling, and high level learning. Following Figure 3.3 is an activity that can engage students in expanding their language knowledge beyond the "sight word."

APPLICATION TO LEARNING

Figure 3.4 (see page 25) shows representative *verbs* from the "sight word" list with their full verb morphology. The benefit of morphology is to provide students with the complete patterns or conjugations of the verbs rather than an isolated word. You will notice that when the past form of the verb has a different vowel or a different consonant, that form is listed separately as another way for developing phonemic awareness. Notice too, that we use linguistic terminology—*vowel changing* and *consonant changing*—rather than "irregular," since we are focusing on phonology (sound) and on the accepted and used patterns of the English language (*run/ran; find/found*). Further explanations of these terms continue throughout the book.

We strongly recommend or even urge that you structure the teaching of "beginning reading" words morphologically so that students can see the spoken and written patterns of English as suggested here:

- Provide students with these templates so they can enter the morphology, or post the template on a wall and complete the morphology with the students.
- Teach the concept of a verb as a word that has four or sometimes five forms and that there are some verbs, always of Anglo-Saxon origin, that have several ways to change their past form. For example, a specific feature of English verbs is that all verbs must have four forms, with some verbs having five forms (e.g., take, takes, taking, took, taken). This description of a verb is fully expanded on in Chapter 4, which you may want to read before your students do this activity.

By showing all the morphs or forms of the verb, the student gets a bonus in fluency because English verbs are not limited to only one form. By learning the full pattern of "sight word" verbs, beginning readers can read (and write) a wide range of natural language text and make use of phonics or phonemic awareness. Figure 3.4 provides you with a visual overview of the morphologies of representative "sight" words that are generally taught in the early reading stages.

Figure 3.3   Morphology, Phonology, and Etymology of Six Sight Words

Directions: Your teacher will guide you in completing this activity following the patterns. The etymology or the history of these words has been done for you. At the end of this activity are the explanations of the etymology abbreviations.

When you and your classmates have completed the chart, write your observations in the paragraph frame that follows.

"Sight Word"	Morphology	Phonemic Awareness (Sound/Symbol Consistency)	Etymology (Origin or Basis of Word)
come	come comes coming came	came (follows rule of "silent e")	[bef. 900—ME *comen*, OE *cuman*; D *komen*, G *kommen*, Goth *qiman*, ON *koma*]
eat	eat eats eating ate eaten	ate (follows rule of "silent e")	[bef. 900—ME *eten*, OE *etan*; G *essen*, Goth *itan*, L *edere*]
give	give Add the other forms or morphs.	gave (follows rule of "silent e")	[bef. 900—ME < ON *gefa* (cf. D *give*); ME *yeven*, *yiven*, OE *gefan*, *giefan*; c. D *geven*, G *geben*, Goth *giban*]
drink	drink Add the other forms or morphs.	drank (follows rule of "short vowel")	[bef. 900—ME *drinken*, OE *drincan*; D *drinken*, G *trinken*, Goth *drinkan*]
fall	fall Add the other forms or morphs.	fell (follows rule of "short vowel")	[bef. 900—ME *fallen*, OE *feallan*; G *fallen*]
do	do Add the other forms or morphs.	did (follows rule of "short vowel")	[bef. 900—ME, OE *dᴈn*; c. D *doen*, G *tɹn*]

Etymology Key:

Bef—900 means spoken before the year 900 A.D. or Common Era

ON—Old Norse

OE—Old English

ME—Middle English

D—Danish

G—German

Goth—Gothic

L—Latin

Figure 3.4 Morphology of Representative "Sight Words"

Verb	Vowel Changing Past	Consonant Changing Past	Other Variations of the Past
come comes coming	came		
find finds finding	found		
make makes making		made	
run runs running	ran		
see sees seeing	saw		seen*
eat eats eating	ate		eaten
get gets getting	got		gotten
do does** doing	did		done**
ride rides riding	rode		ridden
give gives giving	gave		given
have has having		had	

(Continued)

Figure 3.4 (Continued)

Verb	Vowel Changing Past	Consonant Changing Past	Other Variations of the Past
know knows knowing	knew		known
take takes taking	took		taken
put puts putting			put (null change)
buy buys buying		bought	
go goes going			gone*** went
read reads reading	read****		
sing sings singing	sang sung*****		
sit sits sitting	sat		
sleep sleeps sleeping	slept		
write writes writing	wrote		written
bring brings bringing	brought		

Verb	Vowel Changing Past	Consonant Changing Past	Other Variations of the Past
draw draws drawing	drew		drawn
drink drinks drinking	drank		
grow grows growing	grew		grown
hurt hurts hurting			hurt
hold holds holding	held		
keep keeps keeping	kept		
light lights lighting	lit		

*The *en* form exists in a limited number of English verbs of Anglo-Saxon origin.

**This form has gone through a pronunciation change resulting from the earlier form of "dost" as in "dost thou."

***This is another *en* verb only with reversed spelling as in "gone."

****This verb maintains the same spelling in the base or present form and in the past even though the pronunciation of the vowel changes.

*****This is another variation of the past, and it is rare or nonstandard (drank, drunk).

To further help students see patterns in written words, we can organize many of the sight words phonemically where the rules of phonics show some stability. Students must be able to read these words to make (grammatical) sense of text. In Figure 3.5, the "sight" words are arranged by their short vowel phonemes so that once again students can work with patterns. Whether you are teaching reading to young students or working with older students who need reading help, have them put this chart in their notebook and post the chart on the wall. Then have students complete the activities, using accurate metalanguage.

By rearranging the "sight" words using *phonological* and *morphological* patterns, students do not have to depend on rote memory, but will have the benefit of phonemic support (sound and symbol relationships) combined with the grammar of the words, particularly the verbs.

Now follow the path of morphology where there is more for the students to explore and learn.

Figure 3.5   Patterns in Short Vowel Words

Directions: By learning about the spelling patterns of English, you can quickly become a fluent reader and learn more about the English language. Follow these steps:

- Copy this chart into your notebooks. Be sure to write the title.
- Be sure to put the "short" vowel symbol, which is called a *breve**, over each vowel letter.
- Pair up with a classmate and add at least five more words to each column which has the same phoneme as the sample word.
- Write your own story using as many of these words as you can.
- Illustrate your story.
- Share your story with your partner and other classmates.

Words Arranged by "Short" Vowel Phonemes*

ă as in cat	ĕ as in pet	ĭ as in bit	ŏ as in hot	ŭ as in bun
and	help	in	not	funny
am	every	is	on	run
after	let	it	stop	up
an	when	if	got	jump
as	best	little		us
ask	very	into		cut
fast	better	him		much
black	never	his		
	seven	think		
	ten	bring		
		six		
		sing		
		sit		
		pick		
		will		

*This list excludes "short" vowel sounds in words spelled with a final e as in *give, live,* and *have,* which have their own etymological history.

Morphology—An Extension of Phonology

Morphology refers to the structure of words and more specifically to the structure of a specific word and its forms (*Beyond Root Words,* 1997).

In English, for example, the word *help* offers the speaker an array of forms called morphs, with each morph providing a shade or variation of meaning. In addition, each form has a *phonological* variation (e.g., help, helps, helping, helped). These morphed forms of the word also take on different parts of speech, meaning they are used in different parts of the sentence to form the grammar of the word, as illustrated in Figure 3.6. At this stage of exploration of words, do not ask your students to define the parts of speech, but let them discover how the "parts" work by having them set up Morphology Templates to discover the organizational patterns. Have your students follow the steps outlined in Figure 3.6 as a strategy for expanding their phonological skills in combination with their morphological skills as part of building sentence (syntactic) fluency. Figure 3.7 shows a completed template.

To further expand your students' concept of morphology, Figure 3.8 (see page 31) provides a template that shows the conjugational forms of

The Importance of Morphology

The morphology of English is the basis for our understanding "parts of speech." To understand parts of speech, we need to analyze English as English, meaning that we cannot impose the parts of speech of say French or Spanish onto English (Bryson, 1990).

The authors remember that when we began to learn French, we had to compare the French imperfect *Je parlais* with the English "imperfect" (a strange word) and the teacher said that *Je parlais* meant *I was speaking*. Where, we asked, was the word *was* in French, and the teacher said it was in the form *-ais*. How odd this seemed. Later we learned the French future—*Je parlerai*. The teacher said this could be *I will speak* or *I will be speaking*. We thought, how could that be? Neither the English teacher nor the French teacher told us that every language has its own morphology (or no morphology), and every language does just fine in either case.

Figure 3.6   Building Morphology Templates

Follow these directions for your Morphology Templates, and you will have an amazing vocabulary for writing and reading:

- In your notebook, using a double-page spread (two blank pages facing each other), fold each page in half to get four columns.
- Label the columns VERB, NOUN, ADJECTIVE, and ADVERB, as shown in the table that follows. These words are called "Parts of Speech." Don't worry about their definitions. You will discover what they are after you have constructed many Morphology Templates.
- To get started in understanding morphology, begin with the word *help* from your Short Vowel Phoneme Chart. Your teacher will guide you, and soon you will know how to do these Morphology Templates by yourself.
- Write the word *help* in the VERB column.
- A verb must have four forms called "morphs," so write the other three forms, which are *helps* as in *She or he helps*, *helping* as in *I am helping*, *helped* as in *Yesterday I helped*.
- With your teacher's help, write the other forms or morphs of the verb *help*, such as *helper, helpers, helpful, helpless, helpfully, helplessly, helpfulness*.
- Your teacher will help you decide in which column you should put these words.
- Soon you will be able to construct Morphology Templates by yourself, because you will see the patterns.
- Just a point to remember: Not all words have all the parts of speech.
- Now see if you can do Morphology Templates for these words: *sit, sing, think, pick, stop, run, jump*. What patterns did you notice?

Verb	Noun	Adjective	Adverb

Figure 3.7   Completed Morphology Template of the Word *Help*

Verb	Noun	Adjective	Adverb
help (I) helps (she/he) helping (they are) helping helped (yesterday I)	helper helpers helpfulness helplessness	helpful	helpfully

The English speaker will easily recognize these forms and possibly the reasons for division into parts of speech, especialy if asked to create a "morphological" sentence as in the example that follows:

The teacher thanked the six *helpful helpers* who *helpfully helped* some *helpless* people and praised their *helpfulness* while others stood by *helplessly.*

the verb using linguistic terminology (Allen, 1972; Pinker, 1994). The verbs in this template are also part of the vocabulary of beginning readers (at any age) and can expand both reading and vocabulary knowledge and skills. As in the previous templates, have your students put the Morphology Templates in their notebooks and, if possible, on the wall. Have the students follow the directions to complete the template.

English words come mainly in two classes: morphological and non-morphological (which we explain in more detail in Chapter 4). The morphological words are our nouns, verbs, adjectives, and in a related way, the -ly adverbs and pronouns. When laid out, as in the template that follows, we can see the formation of parts of speech. There are two examples, *defend* and *progress,* both of which illustrate the many forms or "morphs" a word might have (see Figures 3.9, 3,10, and 3 11). To accelerate students' progress in reading and related aspects of literacy, have them create Morphology Templates following the patterns illustrated in these figures. Guide them through the process with several words that illustrate the morphological patterns, and then have the students work in groups or independently. Then have them write morphological sentences to build powerful syntactic skills as previously illustrated with the verb *help* and shown in the following paragraph as part of the morphology of the word *defend.*

The **defendant** in the trial was successfully **defended** by the lawyer for the **defense** who at no time was **defensive** about the client's innocence and refused to behave **defensively** at any time.

As students create more and more templates of morphological words, they both formulate and internalize how their language works. Furthermore, they begin to learn how the same word in a different form offers nuances of meaning (e.g., *As we progressed through the forest that was becoming progressively dense, we made progressive progress, assuring ourselves of the certainty of our progression in a dangerous setting*).

Figure 3.8   The Forms of the English Verb

Directions: The verb in the English language always has a minimum of four forms. However, there are some English verbs that have a fifth form. Verbs with five forms always come from the Anglo-Saxon heritage of the English language. Now you know something about the etymology (word history of these verbs). Now follow these steps to complete this template:

- Look at how the verbs' morphs are named: base, verb -s, -ing, past, -en past
- Complete each form. The four forms for the verb *run* have been done and the five forms for the verb *hide* have been done.
- When you have finished your template, work with a classmate. Complete the statement that follows to explain the patterns of these verbs.
- You are on your way to becoming a great explainer of the English language.

Base	Verb -s	-ing	Past	-en Past**
run	runs	running	ran	not applicable
hide	hides	hiding	hid	hidden
give				
take				
eat				
speak				
buy				
think				
teach				
hit				
quit				

Complete this statement of your observations. You can work with a partner.

- From this template of the forms of the English verbs, I have made the following observations:
- First, I observed that all of these verbs have at least _____ forms or morphs.
- But then I noticed that some of these verbs also have _____.
- I realized that the verb forms or morphs of the English language are 1 _____, 2 _____, 3 _____, 4 _____, with some verbs having _____.
- When I looked in the first column labeled *past,* I noticed that some verbs _____, while other verbs _____,
- From this template, I now know that all verbs _____.

Figure 3.9   More Practice With Verb Morphologies

Here are the directions: Check out the "rule of four" plus a "possible rule of five" with the verbs that follow.

1. Complete this Morphology Template.
2. What observations have you made about verbs that you can explain to friends or family who might not know what you now know about English verbs?

Base	Verb -s	-ing	Past	-en or n Past
add	adds	adding	added	not applicable
borrow				
calculate				
catch				
divide				
engage				
freeze				
gather				
justify				
know				
leave				
unite				
verify				
wake				

Figure 3.10   Morphology of the Word *Defend*

Verb	Noun	Adjective	Adverb
defend defends defended defending	defender defenders defendant defendants defense defenses	defensive	defensively

Figure 3.11   Morphology of the Word *Progress*

Verb	Noun	Adjective	Adverb
progress* progresses progressed progressing	progress* progression progressions	progressive	progressively

*This word indicates its "part of speech" by stress with pro´gress as the noun and progress´ as the verb. Other stress combinations of noun and verb are *subject/subject, project/project, record/record,* and *import/import,* among others.

SYNTAX

Syntax refers to the rules for forming phrases and sentences. The ability to form these phrases and sentences comes from a "storehouse" of memorized or learned words, which Pinker (1999) calls the "mental lexicon." Combined with this lexicon are the "rules" that combine words into bigger words or variations of the words, which are the morphology. These components of rules, phonology, and morphology make up the syntax and are generally regarded as the major constituents of grammar (McArthur, 1992, p. 1016). All children with uninterrupted development (e.g., hearing impairment, learning disabilities, serious psychological deprivation) learn these components of their first language early and effortlessly, or as stated by Noam Chomsky (1957), as a "genetic predisposition." We see how these interrelationships of rules, phonology, and morphology work when we hear children say "I buyed a toy," or "I goed home," indicating that they have internalized the "past" form of the English verb, even though they are (at this stage) overgeneralizing. Parents often smile at these constructions when the child is just learning to speak, but if the child, by school age, "fails" to master the "correct" or expected syntactic or morphological constructions, parents begin to worry.

To have a clear understanding of syntax, we must relate this aspect of language to semantics because of their powerful inter-relationship, as illustrated in the following section. An APPLICATION TO LEARNING activity follows the explanation of semantics.

SEMANTICS

Semantics is the study of meaning as part of the grammatical and lexical (word) structures of a language. This word, another contribution from the Greek, comes from *semantikos*, meaning the study of signs. Pinker calls semantics the "interface between language and mind (1999, p. 22). For teachers, semantics is likely to be related to understanding or comprehension, particularly in the area of reading. One of the higher levels of students' reading achievement is the ability to make inferences or "read between the lines," a semantic skill for understanding the deep meaning of a text. Yet, the term *semantics* has rarely been part of school grammar, although "you can't have grammar without semantics or vice versa. "The influential grammarian Robert L. Allen used to write the following sentence on the board during his linguistic class and then ask the students for its "meaning:"

They tossed the salad in the bathtub.

Did the speaker or writer mean that because there was such a big party no salad bowl was big enough and therefore the bathtub had to be used? Or was the salad so terrible that the guests just tossed it in the bathtub? Another example can be the inferential information a word can provide. If you are intrigued by these types of sentence meanings, try the activities found in Figures 3.12 and 3.13 with your students (about fourth grade and up). The syntax is simple, but the meaning may be "semantically challenging."

Figure 3.12   Semantic Challenges From Simple Syntax

Directions: What might these sentences mean? Write two meanings for each sentence. The first two are examples.

Sentence	Meaning 1	Meaning 2
She always ate the vegetables.	She never ate meat.	Even if there was meat, she ate the vegetables.
He's too tired to do his homework after dinner.	He always does his homework before dinner.	He never gets to do his homework.
I could never believe that story.		
I tried to call you yesterday.		
Six people were declared winners.		
He ran the New York Marathon.		

Figure 3.13   Semantic Inferences From Specific Words

Directions: Read each sentence, then tell what you know because of the bolded words in the sentence. The first one is done for you.

Sentence	What I Know
The **Queen** of England wears a pearl **necklace.**	England has a queen.
The **St. Patrick's Day** parade in **New York** was **almost** cancelled because of snow.	.
Whenever **avalanches** happen in **Colorado**, the **snow patrol** is ready.	
The **explorers** in the **15th century** only knew **something** about **latitude**.	
We traveled by the **bright light** of the **moon**.	

ETYMOLOGY

Etymology tells the history of our words, which we have already touched on because it is so essential to understanding phonology and its effect on English spelling. In fact we have coined the slogan "Every Word Has a Story" (Rothstein et al., 2007a), because this is indeed true. The story of English words in particular is a lesson in history, migration, immigration, colonialism, and now technology. As we indicated in Chapter 2 on the history of English, the language has traveled, changed, and borrowed and continues to grow. But basic to every English speaker's vocabulary (first in speaking, then in reading) are the words which came from the Anglo-Saxon linguistic heritage and are the older words of the language. And being old, the pronunciation of these words has changed since the time that they were first written (and therefore spelled.) So a brief lesson in etymology begins here with the words that students learn to read first, because these are the words for which they already have meanings.

Figure 3.14 is a template of words that have the spelling combination *gh*, with the etymology of these words. The taxonomy shows why we now have silent letters that

Figure 3.14   Taxonomy and Etymology of Words Spelled With *gh*

Word	Etymology
cough	[1275–1325; ME *coghen*, appar. < OE *cohhian* (cf. its deriv. *cohhettan* to cough); akin to D *kuchen* to cough, G *keuchen* to wheeze]
daughter	[bef. 950; ME *doughter*, OE *dohtor;* c. G *Tochter*]
eight	[bef. 1000; ME *eighte*, OE (e)ahta; c. D acht, , OHG *ahto* (G *acht*), Goth *ahtau*, L oct∃]
enough	[bef. 900; ME *enogh*, OE gen∃h; c. G *genug*, Goth *ganohs*, ON n∃gr; akin to OE *geneah* it suffices]
high	[bef. 900; ME *heigh*, var. of HEGH, HEY, HEH, OE h ah, h h; OHG *hoh* (G *hoch*)]
laugh	[bef. 900; ME laughen, OE hlæh(h)an (Anglian); G lachen, ON hlja, Goth hlahjan]
light	[bef. 900; (n. and adj.) ME; OE l oht; , OFris liacht, D, G licht, Goth liuhath (n.) (G leuchten), Goth liuhtjan]
right	[bef. 900; (n. and adj.) ME; OE reht, riht; c. D, G recht, ON r ttr, Goth raihts; akin to L rectus, OIr recht law, Gk orektós upright; (v.) ME righten, OE rihtan, c. OFris riuchta, G richten

Etymology-Language Derivations:
bef.—before
OE—Old English
ME—Middle English
D—Danish
G—German
OHG—Old High German
ON—Old Norse
OF—Old Frisian
OIr—Old Irish
G—Gothic
Gk—Greek
L—Latin

once "spoke." Share this taxonomy with your students when they ask you why we have "silent" letters. Point out that the current words we use in English have old histories and that these words come mainly (or are derived) from Germanic and Scandinavian languages where the pronunciations were different from what they are today. As a result, the spellings reflect much older ways of pronouncing these words. You might want to have Etymology Committees or Etymologists of the Week to make presentations. The Internet is a treasure trove of word histories.

If you are a good linguistic detective or are about to embark on a linguistic "career," you will easily notice that all of the words in Figure 3.14 once had a guttural or glottal sound (from the throat) that required letters to symbolize that sound. Since none of the Latin letters stood for the guttural symbol (Latin only had the phoneme [k]), a *ch* or *gh* were combined as the symbol. Gradually speakers on the English isle softened the sound until it became "silent" (recht became right). As your students ponder why English spelling is so "strange" or varied, ask them to check the etymology and "write the story." We return to etymology frequently throughout this book, with further study on the story of *gh* and other spelling information in Chapter 12.

INTERNET SITES

- http://www.ling.upenn.edu/~rnoyer/dm

  Detailed and interesting questions and answers about different aspects of etymology. Excellent for older students.

- http://www.utexas.edu/courses/linguistics/resources/morphology/index.html

  Here you can find information about the Linguistic Olympics. This site was developed as an educational Web site for secondary school students and teachers and includes puzzles dealing with real language data. Most of these puzzles are essentially morphology problems.

- http://www.etymonline.com

  This online etymological dictionary includes explanations of what our words meant and how they sounded 600 or 2,000 years ago.

- http://www.behindthename.com

  A wonderful history of names from many languages and cultures that will interest all students, especially if they find their own name.

- http://www.sil.org/linguistics/GlossaryOflinguisticTerms/WhatIsA Phoneme.htm

  An expansive response to the question, What is a phoneme?

- http://www.auburn.edu/~murraba/phon.html

  A delightful explanation of phonemes written for elementary level students.

- http://facweb.furman.edu/~wrogers/phonemes

  Designed to help students trace the development of the phonemes of English from the Old English period into present-day English. Interesting for middle and high school students.

CHAPTER FOUR

Parts of Speech and the English Language

Introduction

Language and
Metalanguage

Builders of
Linguistic
Intelligence

**Parts of
Speech and the
English Language**

Syntax and
Semantics

The Polyglot
of English

The Polyglot:
Beyond Latin
and Greek

Return to Parts
of Speech

Sentences,
Paragraphs, and
Other Structures
of the Written
Language

Grammar for
Word Play

Reading, Writing,
and Grammar

Punctuation,
Spelling, Text
Messaging, and
Other
Consequences of
Grammar

Additional
Learning
Activities

A noun's the name of any thing:
A school, a garden, hoop, or swing.
Verbs tell of something being done:
To read, count, sing, laugh, jump, or run.

(Pinker, 1994, p. 97)

They've a temper, some of them—particularly verbs: they're the
proudest—adjectives, you can do anything with, but not verbs—
Humpty Dumpty in Through the Looking Glass.

(Carroll, 1872/1995b, p. 94)

Defining a language by its "parts" is always risky, since language, by definition, is a system for getting meaning that is always more than the sum of its parts. We understand our native language not because we necessarily know much *about* it, but because we just *know it!* So with this warning, we begin on parts of speech, a topic deeply embedded in our school culture and curriculum.

The long-standing tradition has been to offer students definitions of the "parts of speech" as a series of one-sentence aphorisms (A noun is a _____; a verb is a _____; an adjective is a _____; and so forth). Pinker (1999, p. 153) states that "a part of speech . . . is not a kind of meaning; it is a kind of token that obeys certain formal rules . . ." He gives examples that English speakers recognize, but that will never make it to the school grammar books, because they don't "fit" the definitions. Why is a noun a *thing* in the following sentence: "I have three *reasons* for writing this story"? What is the verb "justifies" *doing* in the following sentence: "The end justifies the means"? Which word is the adjective in *"I have six beautiful hanging desk lamps"*? And what is the verb "have" in this same sentence *doing*? Let's discuss parts of speech and what they really are and how knowing or recognizing those parts of speech helps students expand their linguistic knowledge and intelligence.

The definitions presented here are based on the *structural components* of specific types of words in the English language. For example, in English, only a noun (or its subcategory pronoun) can have or convey the plural form as in *one girl—two girls* or *one mouse—two mice* or *one sheep—two sheep.* Another structure of a noun, in English, results from affixes such as *-ion* to form *attraction*, *-ment* to form *resentment*, *-ity* to form *creativity*, and so forth. Notice that we keep saying "in English," because these structures of a noun are different in other languages. Italians, for example, order *due pizze* while English speakers prefer *two pizzas*. And in many languages, such as Korean for example, the plural is formed by a plural word, which is why a Korean person who is just beginning to learn English might say, "I have *ten* nail."

Defining by structure will show your students the patterns of their language that they already know intuitively but can now also know metacognitively. While there appears to be a surface logic in telling students that the word "running" can be a *verb* (I am running), a *noun* (Running is good exercise), or an *adjective* (I need running water), *depending on how you use it*, we ignore the "deep structure." This distinction between surface structure and deep structure was cogently brought out by Noam Chomsky in his work on transformational grammar, which focuses on the linguistic structures and processes of the mind (see McArthur, 1992). If you were to ask your students to draw a picture for each of the aforementioned sentences that use the word *running*, you will find that the students will illustrate all three sentences with "running" as a verb. None of your students would be able to illustrate *running* as a noun or adjective. Try it!

TEACHING ENGLISH THROUGH THE STRUCTURE OF THE ENGLISH LANGUAGE

By using the strategies in this chapter to teach grammar through structure, you get your students to first explore the different organizational structures of the words and then categorize them by their patterns. From this categorization system, the students can generate the "rules." Finally, they can discover the deeper, rather than the surface, meanings of sentences or statements. Furthermore, they can create rules that have some stability or construct without constant referencing to "exceptions" and "irregulars." And above all, by exploring the "parts," they can begin to see the wholeness and richness of their language and its potential for creating meaning. Describing a language accurately and engagingly is not easy, so we need to be patient in presenting this information to our students. This patience, however, will pay off in giving all your students a deepening knowledge of their language and how it works for reading, writing, and formal, as well as informal, communication. As David Crystal's (2006a) witty and informative book *The Fight for English* emphasizes, by learning about language accurately your students will develop standards, appropriateness, perspicuity, clarity, and context in their use and understanding of their language—a worthy menu indeed.

MORPHOLOGICAL AND NON-MORPHOLOGICAL WORDS

English is predominantly a morphological language, and its grammar is dependent on and intertwined with this morphology, as we have stated in Chapter 3. The number of morphological words is vast, and when a new word enters the English language, it is most likely to have more than one form (e.g., *computer, computers, computerize, computerizes, computerizing, computerized*). The morphological words include nouns, verbs, adjectives, adverbs, and the subclass of nouns known as *pronouns*. When your students learn vocabulary within the expansive system of morphology, their word knowledge becomes exponential.

In addition, there is a much, much smaller English lexicon of single item or Non-morphological words such as *the, in, on, but, each, all,* and a few dozen others. These words are the syntax or sentence builders that "tie" or bind the morphological words together. Traditional school grammar books have tried to classify these words as articles, conjunctions, and prepositions, but often have to "make exceptions," such as trying to explain why or why not the word *up* is a preposition, as in *give up* or *loosen up* or *back up*, which are among the dozen *up* verbs in the English language. (See Chapter 8 on *up verbs*.)

Figures 4.1, 4.2., and 4.3 illustrate the organization of the parts of speech into two major categories: morphological and non-morphological, which form the basis of the English lexicon. The morphological words are categorized as noun, verb, adjective, and adverb (in Figure 4.1), plus there is the subcategory of pronouns (Figure 4.2). Nouns, verbs, adjectives, and adverbs are morphological because they have "affixed forms," commonly known as prefixes, suffixes, and inflections (see sidebar). Pronouns are morphological because they also "morph" as in *he, his, him, himself.* The non-morphological words, meaning those words that rarely have more than one form, are illustrated in Figure 4.3. We continue to elaborate on and clarify the concepts of parts of speech in subsequent chapters and in the APPLICATION TO LEARNING activities later in this chapter.

> ### Inflections
>
> A grammatical inflection is a phoneme or syllable that is added to the main stem or part of a word but does not change the part of speech.
>
> Example: *talk, talks, talking,* and *talked* all remain verbs even though they are *inflected*.
>
> However the form -er to create *talker* is a suffix because this word has changed from verb to noun.
>
> In the adjective *fine, finer,* and *finest,* all three forms have remained adjectives and -er and -est are inflections.

Figure 4.1   Morphological Parts of Speech

Nouns	Verbs	Adjectives	Adverbs
1. names many categories 2. may pluralize (e.g., hat, hats) 3. may take specific affixes (e.g., -ion) 4. may be preceded by an adjective (e.g., happy woman)	1. has four forms called a conjugation 2. may have a fifth form if of Anglo-Saxon origin (e.g., given) 3. has many categories (e.g., verbs of locomotion)	1. often compares (e.g., big, bigger, biggest or more/most beautiful) 2. may take various affixes (e.g., magical, attentive, useful) 3. may have the semantic feature of describing (sweet, pleasant)	1. is generally formed from an adjective (e.g., wise, wisely) 2. can take different positions in the sentence (e.g., finally she left; she left finally; she finally left)

Pronouns and Morphology

The pronouns of English also have a morphological system. The English pronoun, also called a pronominal, has four forms (morphs), which have been traditionally categorized as nominative, accusative, possessive, and reflexive. Native English speakers learn these (Anglo-Saxon) words in early childhood and by age five generally use them effortlessly. However, certain conventions of "correct" and "incorrect" are associated with pronoun usage, with "Me and him" or "Me and my friend" being most troublesome to teachers and also to parents. But before we move into the issues of "correct," let's look at how this part of speech lays out.

The pronouns take forms that have much greater variation than the other parts of speech. Historically, these forms have gone through great change throughout the history of English. Examples can be found from reading the King James Version of the Bible or Shakespeare, not to mention the more distant writings of Chaucer. As English speakers, we intuitively know these pronouns, but their relationships become clearer when we see them set out as in Figure 4.2. Following the template on pronouns is Figure 4.3 on non-morphological words.

Figure 4.2   Patterns of the Pronoun in English

Nominative	Accusative or Dative	Possessive (note two forms)	Reflexive
I	me	my, mine	myself
you	you	your, yours	yourself
we	us	our, ours	ourselves
she	her	her, hers	herself
he	him	his, his	himself
they	them	their, theirs	themselves
thou*	thee*	thy*, thine*	thyself*
it	it	its	—

*Relics of an earlier time, known as the "familiar" in contrast to the "polite," terms that are still part of French, Spanish, Italian, Portuguese, German, and other languages.

With structural information as background, you can give your students deep and meaningful knowledge about their language and apply this knowledge to speaking, reading, writing, and history. By defining accurately and using template organizers, they will be able to clarify not only linguistic concepts, but possibly transfer this skill of clarification to other subject areas. We begin with the noun.

Nouns and Morphology— A Word That Names

"A noun is a person, place, thing, or possibly an idea." For generations students have been taught this incomplete and somewhat misleading definition of a noun. The definition is in grammar books and posted on the walls of schools almost everywhere. When students question teachers about words such as *discussion, animation, mystery,* and *joyfulness,* they are demonstrating the shortcomings of the traditional definition. When students notice that words such as *difference, creativity, action,* and *fright* are called "things" or "ideas," they are told that these are "exceptions." Sometimes they are told that English is a confusing language and to leave it at that. So what is a better way to teach a noun?

We first focus on what we want our students to know or understand when we ask them to define any part of speech. The goal is for students to think about language by collecting, organizing, and categorizing examples. This process is designed to strive for clarity as well as communicate knowledge.

Begin this process with the etymology of the word *noun* as coming from the Latin word *nomen,* meaning name. A noun is a word that names, but that alone is not sufficient. We must ask, "What does a noun name?" "How do we recognize a noun?" "What are the characteristics of a noun in English (which is different from a noun in French, Spanish, Russian, or Chinese)?"

To guide your students into learning about the meaning of the word *noun,* we have set up what we call a "Noun Department Store," shown in Figure 4. 4. Figure 4.5 shows an example of the completed Noun Department Store. This is followed by a more advanced template for nouns with affixes, shown in

Figure 4.3 Taxonomy of Frequently Used Non-Morphological Words*

• TAXONOMY •	
A	all, about, as, a, an, after, also, above, almost, always, any, anywhere, anyone, and
B	but, by, below
C	
D	down, during
E	each, every, everyone, everybody, everything, either
F	for, from
G	
H	how, however, him, her, himself, herself
I	in, into, indeed, if, indeed
J	just
K	
L	
M	many, maybe
N	no, not, nothing, none, nobody, no one, never, nevertheless, neither, nor, nowhere
O	on, over, once, only, or
P	perhaps
Q	quite
R	rather
S	so, several, such
T	to, too, the, then, that, this, these, those, therefore
U	under, up, upon
V	very
W	with, without, who, whom, what, where, when, whenever, why, which, wherever, whoever
X	
Y	you, your
Z	

*Several of these words have been created through compounding, but none of them normally have affixes such as plurals, and they are not likely to shift as parts of speech. However, speakers will change these words in what is termed *colloquial* or *informal* speech as in "no ifs, ands, or buts" or the "ups and downs of life." So we must leave a little room for "occasional variations."

Figure 4.6. For this activity, students collect and sort nouns. Just have your students follow these directions. Students in third grade and up can do this activity and expand their vocabulary as well as their understanding of the metalanguage related to the word *noun.* Guide your students into setting up the template. This activity should be done over several lessons so that the students have the opportunity to see the organizational schema of the patterns of nouns (and other parts of speech as well).

Figure 4.4   Build a "Noun Department Store"

Directions: Set up a "Noun Department Store" with your teacher's help.

- Make the template below in your notebook by having two pages facing each other. This arrangement is called a double-page spread.
- Fold each of the pages into four columns so you now have eight columns.
- Place these nouns so that they are in the column that names their "category," as shown in the template: *friend, Mexico, cup, zebra, joy, Zeus, truth.*
- Now work with a classmate and add three or more other nouns to each column that fit the category. You can find nouns for these categories on the walls of your classroom or in your textbooks or reading books.
- If you are not sure of a category of a word, place it in the column called "other."
- Then sort the words into their appropriate columns.

Person	Place or Location	Object*	Animal	Emotion	Deity**	Principle***	Other****
friend	Mexico	cup	zebra	joy	Zeus	truth	

Notes for the Teacher

*Notice what happens when you substitute *object* for *thing.*

**Add this category because "person" is not exactly accurate.

***A word such as *truth* requires a deeper search for a category and may be categorized in other ways, for example as a quality or characteristic.

****There are nouns that are not easy to classify—*trial, worry, fame,* among hundreds. Therefore, always have a "category" called *Other* for placing these words. Students can also create their own categories, a skill that involves thinking and defining.

Figure 4.5   A Start-Up "Noun Department Store"

Person	Place or Location	Object*	Animal	Emotion	Deity**	Principle***	Other****
friend	Mexico	cup	zebra	joy	Mars	truth	discussion
Betty	home	desk	fox	sadness	Zeus	honesty	birthday
teacher	street	sink	insect	anger	Hera	commitment	mathematics
dad	sky	phones	puppy	delight	Apollo	virtue	song
babies	rooms	shelf	bird	love	Isis	sincerity	joke

Notes for the Teacher

*Notice what happens when you substitute *object* for *thing.*

**Add this category because "person" is not exactly accurate.

***A word such as *truth* requires a deeper search for a category and may be categorized in other ways, for example as a quality or characteristic.

****There are nouns that are not easy to classify—*trial, worry, fame,* among hundreds. Therefore, always have a "category" called *Other* for placing these words. Students can also create their own categories, a skill that involves thinking and defining.

In Figure 4.6, students from fourth grade and up can begin to do high level classification of nouns that will expand their vocabulary and deepen their understanding of the morphology of words from their academic subjects. Guide your students through this activity, and have them continue independently as much as possible to build a personal and class thesaurus of nouns.

The chart students create using the template in Figure 4.6 can be expanded as in Figure 4.7. By now, students are moving into higher level vocabulary and should start noticing that the noun covers a wide span of categories and organizational schemas. As students sort the nouns in different categories, they will realize how the system of affixing is part of the larger morphological system.

Figure 4.6   Build a Department Store of Nouns With Affixes

Directions: The English language has hundreds of nouns that have been created with special syllables called affixes, which you may also know as suffixes. Set up the template below in your notebook using a double-page spread and fold both the left-hand page and the right-hand page into three parts, so that you have six columns for sorting nouns with affixes.

- Copy the template with the affixes. If you look carefully, you will notice that all of these nouns have an "end affix," which is usually called a suffix and is written with a hyphen when it stands alone. Sort these nouns as illustrated in the template below: *ambition, preference, loveliness, creativity, friendship, humanism, devotion, difference, wildness, generosity, hardship, Hinduism.*

- Now add to each column five or more nouns that have the same affixes. You can work with a classmate, look on the walls of your room, or check your books for words with these affixes.

-ion	-ence (-ance)*	-ness	-ity	-ship	-ism
ambition	preference	loveliness	creativity	friendship	humanism
devotion	difference	wildness	generosity	hardship	Hinduism

*There is only a spelling difference between -ence words (difference) and -ance words (attendance).

Figure 4.7   An Expanded Affix Chart

-ion	-ence (-ance)*	-ness	-ity	-ship	-ism
ambition	preference	loveliness	creativity	friendship	humanism
devotion	difference	wildness	generosity	hardship	Hinduism
emotion	conference	seriousness	curiosity	worship	populism
generation	attendance	greatness	integrity	courtship	socialism
location	reliance	hardness	nobility	scholarship	Buddhism
preparation	tolerance	neediness	paternity	baptism	naturalism
vacation	endurance	quietness	scarcity	criticism	rationalism

*There is only a spelling difference between -ence words (difference) and -ance words (attendance).

For a follow-up morphology activity, see Figure 4.8 and follow these directions with your students. This activity shows the relationship of nouns that take affixes to other parts of speech. Here are the directions:

1. Ask the students to set up a Morphology Template as in Figure 4.8, with the parts of speech labels.
2. Have them enter the word *generation* in the noun column (-ion words are nouns).
3. Ask them to think of the verb that is related to the noun. Write the verb in the base form and add the other three forms.
4. Ask them if they can think of the adjective or just guide them.
5. Tell them to form the -ly adverb.
6. Continue with the other nouns.
7. Ask them to write morphological sentences. For example, "All students can work creatively by creating different artistic creations and be applauded for their great creativity."

By completing this activity, students will discover that not all the words have all the parts of speech, but that each word has several parts of speech. In addition to this discovery, students will have a good reason to "surf an unabridged dictionary" to

Figure 4.8   Building a Morphological Vocabulary From Nouns

Verb	Noun	Adjective	Adverb
generate generates generating generated	generation generations	generative	generatively
differ differs differing differed	difference differences	differential	differentially
create creates creating created	creativity creation creations	creative	creatively
populate populates populating populated	population populations popularity	popular	popularly

find the different forms. While "surfing," they will also discover interesting etymological bits of information, which they can report on and share.

Figures 4.9–4.14 define the morphological parts of speech using the Defining Format Template and other organizers.

After your students have explored the wide range of nouns and noun categories, have them set up a Defining Format Template (see Figure 4.9) and guide them through the steps of creating a full explanation of a noun. The students should set up this template in their notebook by again using a double-page spread. On the left-hand side, they fold the page in half. The right-hand page stays unfolded and serves for expanded note taking.

Figure 4.9

What Is a Noun in the English Language?

• DEFINING FORMAT •

Question	Category	Characteristics
What is a noun in the English language?		
A noun is a	word that	1. names many categories, including, but not limited to (a) persons or humans (e) deities (b) places or locations (f) emotions (c) objects (g) subjects (d) animals and whatever can be named 2. may have singular and plural forms or meanings:* (a) pencil–pencils (e) alumnus–alumni (b) watch–watches (f) addendum–addenda (c) man–men (g) index–indices (d) mouse–mice (h) cherub–cherubim 3. may be formed by adding specific affixes to other forms, such as (a) -ion (e.g., attraction) (b) -ness (e.g., gentleness) (c) -ment (e.g., disappointment) (d) -ence/-ance (e.g., conference) (e) -ity (e.g., creativity) (f) -ism (e.g., humanism) (g) -ship (e.g., relationship) *The deep structure of the English noun is that a large class of nouns can have one or more than one, including the null form as in *This farmer has one sheep; the other farmer has twelve sheep.* The speaker clearly knows by the number marker how many sheep (or deer) there are. Notice from the list that although adding the grapheme -s is the most common way of forming the plural, there are alternate ways, depending on the word's etymology (e.g., Anglo-Saxon, Latin, Greek, Hebrew).

The Concept of Proper Nouns

Traditional grammar books have included the terms *proper* and *improper* as part of the definition of nouns. These are not linguistic classifications, but rather spelling conventions that different languages use differently. For example, while English uses capital letters for months and days of the week, French, Spanish, and Italian do not. German capitalizes many nouns that English does not. Many languages do not capitalize the names of their language (French vs. francais). The concept of proper (and improper!) belong in the teaching of spelling, and we suggest you make this distinction with your students.

EXPANDING DEFINITIONS OF PARTS OF SPEECH

Follow up this definition of a noun by having the students continue to build their department store of additional noun categories as illustrated in Figure 4.10. The chart will further expand your students' vocabulary, especially if they search for other parts of speech that are extensions of these nouns, particularly verbs; for example, celebrate from celebration, capitalize from capitalization, and so forth.

Figure 4.10 Nouns by Categories

For this activity, you will continue to build your Department Store of Nouns. By now you know that there is a vast world of nouns you can use for speaking and writing. As you learn and categorize these nouns, you will notice that almost all nouns with affixes have other parts of speech forms. Your teacher will guide you in setting up your template with these directions:

- Set up a double-page spread with four columns as illustrated. The first column is labeled "Nouns for Events or Happenings" followed by a second column labeled "Related morphological Forms." The third column is labeled "Nouns for Actions" and is followed by a column labeled "Related morphological Forms."
- The template gives you examples for these labels. Then work with a partner and add your own examples of related morphological forms. You can add one or more forms.

Nouns for Events or Happenings	Related Morphological Forms	Nouns for Actions	Related Morphological Forms
accident	accidental	activation	activate
celebration	celebrate, celebrity	capitalization	capitalize
experience	experiential	beautification	beauty, beautify
graduation		destruction	
inauguration		evolution	
naturalization		fragmentation	
normalization		hospitalization	
presentation		magnification	
participation		memorization	
revolution		observation	
recognition		rotation	

Defining the Verb

Have your students set up the Defining Format Template shown in Figure 4.11 for *What Is a Verb in the English Language?* Have students follow the same procedures in their notebook.

The BE Verb

Often when we illustrate this definition of the verb, teachers have asked, "But what about the verb 'to be'? How does this verb fit into the definition of a verb that is provided in Figure 4.11? Explaining to your students the structure of the BE verb is essential to helping them understand its multiple uses in English sentence construction. In addition, the use of the BE verb has many variants in different English dialects, as in "We *be* friends for a longtime," or as in the conjugational form in "Bess you *is* my woman," from the opera *Porgy and Bess.* In addition, the BE verb of the English language has often puzzled students, especially when they have been told that *be* is a helping verb, a linking verb, or an auxiliary. Students who probe deeper or question the use of words such as *helper* or *auxiliary* may wonder why some verbs have to "help" other verbs.

Explain to your students that the verb BE separates itself from all the other English verbs in that it both carries the rule of the conjugation (four forms, plus a fifth form) and also has forms that bear no resemblance to the base, such as **am, are, is, was,** and **were.** This arrangement is Anglo-Saxon or Germanic and provides English with a structure that other languages may not have. An example is in comparing French with English and is one of the puzzling lessons Evelyn remembers in her first week of French in seventh grade. The teacher wrote the words *je parle* on the board. He then told the students that these two words meant the following (in English): I speak, I do speak, or I am speaking. Evelyn raised her hand and asked how would someone French say the last two forms (do, am speaking). The teacher said the French do not bother with those forms.

Students who know Spanish or know about Spanish will also notice that the BE verb in English is expressed by two Spanish verbs, ser and estar, with specialized uses, and is never used to form statements such as I am speaking or I do speak. Like the French, Spanish speakers simply use *hablo* and don't even need to say *Yo* or *I* because the o ending signals that it can only be *I* or *yo.*

Figure 4.11

What Is a Verb in the English Language?		
• DEFINING FORMAT •		
Question	Category	Characteristics
What is a verb in the English language?*		
A verb (in the English language) is a	word that	1. has four forms called a conjugation as in the following example: (a) I work (b) She/He works (c) We are working (d) Yesterday we worked 2. may have a fifth form limited to certain words of Anglo-Saxon origin as in the following: eat–eaten take–taken hide–hidden choose–chosen rise–risen give–given show–shown know–known 3. may have five forms as in these words: lie, lies, lying, lay, lain sing, sings, singing, sang, sung
*This definition serves for all English verbs, except for the verb *be*, which has a two-part system that is illustrated in the following section.		

In Figure 4.12, we have divided the BE verb into two sections. As you read the forms on the left, read them aloud, adding an appropriate pronoun or expanded form. You have probably heard constructions such as the following: (a) I *be* home late tonight. (b) She *bes* my best friend for years. (c) She *being* sick so long, she can't come. (d) We *beed* in the woods a long time or We *beer* in the woods a long time. The forms *bes* and *beed* are thought of by speakers of standard English as part of young children's emerging language or *nonstandard dialect*.

Figure 4.12   Double Morphology of the BE Verb

Directions: Copy this morphology chart into your notebook. Put Form 1 on the left-hand page and Form 2 on the right-hand page.

Form 1: The Conjugation of the BE Verb	Form 2: Other Forms of the BE Verb That Are Different From the Word BE
be (base)	am
bes (verb -s)	is
beed (past)	are
being (-ing)	was
+	were
been (-n form)	

Be a linguist—a person who studies about language.

- Look at the words that are related to the verb BE in Form 1. Put a check mark next to those BE words you have used. Write a sentence for each of the verb forms you have used.
- Now look at the verb BE that makes up Form 2. Write a sentence for each of these forms.

Have your students set up this template, and have them note the double morphology. By developing this double morphology, students will observe that while there is a consistent conjugational pattern in the English verb, there can also be variations that can be traced to the historic development of a language and the different word and grammatical usages that occur in different parts of the English-speaking world.

More on the BE Verb

The verbs of English follow fairly regular patterns, with the main variation in the formation of the past tense. By having the BE verb, we can expand our statements and give further meaning or nuance to the other verbs.

This verb, with its two-part system, has many functions, as in the examples that follow.

I *am* a teacher.

She *was* my best friend.

We *are* in the living room.

We *were* a happy family.

All *is* well.

Be a good girl and bring me my sweater.

Being a scholar means being a conscientious student.

Where have you *been?*

The BE verb also serves as an *expander,* which is a more descriptive word than *helper* or even auxiliary. Because the English verb (unlike the verbs of Romance languages) is limited to four or five forms, it uses a system of expanders to provide a sense of time. A sense of time does not necessarily mean tense, although it may coincide. This distinction between time and tense has often confused English-speaking students when teachers refer to present, past, and future tenses as if they are always time-bound. The problem gets worse when students are then given terms such as *present-progressive, past-progressive, future progressive, imperfect, conditional,* and so forth. Robert L. Allen of Columbia University stated the story simply:

> English has two tenses—present and past—and with these two tenses, English speakers can express a whole range of time from the distant past to the distant future. (1972, p. 48)

By adding the appropriate forms of the verbs *do* and *have,* English effectively operates with its two tenses. Here are some examples. You can also make up some of your own.

We *have been* going to school for several years (*have* is the base or present; *been* is the past).

Tomorrow we *are going* to have a picnic (*are* is the present; *going* is unmarked by tense).

I *do* not *have* to *be* in school until later today (*do* is present, *have* is present, *be* is present).

Last week we *were* told that we *did* not *have* to *be* at the award ceremony (explain this one yourself).

The BE Verb and Contractions

With the second forms of the BE verb, we get the contractions *isn't, aren't, wasn't,* and *weren't.* We no longer use *amn't,* which has been transformed into *ain't* and has its own story of being considered "low" level, but popular and ubiquitous. By checking the *Random House Webster's Unabridged Dictionary* (2000), we find that the word *ain't* has a long and interesting story, which you might want to share with your students. For further understanding of *ain't,* we have included the dictionary definition and its unusual relationship to the word *aren't.* You will notice that there are both prescriptive and descriptive explanations (see Figures 4.13 and 4.14). Students are likely to find the discussion of *ain't* very interesting and will have many questions, so be prepared to go to the Web sites we have cited at the end of this chapter. *Ain't* is more common in uneducated speech than in educated, but it occurs with some frequency in the informal speech of the educated. This is especially true of the interrogative use of *ain't I* as a substitute for the formal and—to some—stilted *am I not* or *aren't I,* considered by some to be ungrammatical.

Some speakers avoid any of the preceding forms by substituting *Isn't that so.*

Ain't occurs in humorous or set phrases: *Ain't it the truth! She ain't what she used to be. It ain't funny.* The word is also used for emphasis: *That just ain't so!*

It does not appear in formal writing except for deliberate effect in such phrases or to represent speech: *You ain't heard nothin' yet!*

The contraction *aren't* is simply a different outcome of the same historical development that yielded *ain't,* but the fact that it is spelled and pronounced like the contraction of *are not* (as in *You are staying, aren't you?*) apparently gives it, for some, an acceptability that *ain't* lacks. The use of *aren't I* is objected to by others because a declarative counterpart, *I aren't*, does not exist. Many speakers, however, prefer *aren't I* to the uncontracted, rather formal *am I not*.

Figure 4.13 The "Story of Ain't" (including a definition adapted From *Random House Webster's Unabridged Dictionary*, 2000)

---

ain't

1. Nonstandard except in some dialects from am not 1770–80; variation of *amn't* (contraction of *AM NOT*) by loss of *m*

Usage. As a substitute for *am not, is not,* and *are not* in declarative sentences.

Figure 4.14 The Relationship of *Aren't* to *Ain't* (*Random House Webster's Unabridged Dictionary*, 2000)

---

1. contraction of *are not.*

2. contraction of *am not* (used interrogatively as a doublet of AIN'T)

Usage. The social unacceptability of *ain't* has created a gap in the pattern of verbal contractions. *I'm not*, the alternative to *I ain't*, has no corresponding interrogative form except *ain't I*. In questions, *ain't I* is often avoided by the use of AREN'T I: *I'm right, aren't I? Aren't I on the list?*

ORGANIZING AND NAMING THE VERB CONJUGATION FORMS

By organizing the English verbs, based for the most part on etymology, students can figure out the patterns and "rules" that govern these words by doing the activities that follow. This first set (Figure 4.15) illustrates verbs that only have four forms known as a base, a verb -s, an -ing, and a past. All the past forms in this template add the grapheme (letters) -ed, but they may not have the same pronunciation (e.g., jumped [t] or pinned [d] or wasted [Ãd], known as the *schwa*). The -ed grapheme, you will notice, serves to mark three different phonemes as shown in the examples of the verbs *jumped, pinned,* and *wasted.*

Give your students a copy of this verb organizer and ask them to find another five to ten verbs that follow this pattern. Explain that the word *phoneme* refers to the pronunciation of the *grapheme* -ed and that the grapheme -ed is the most commonly used written symbol to signify the past form of thousands of English verbs. Have them also observe that the grapheme -ed represents three phonemes written as [t], [d], and with a schwa symbol [ə].

Figures 4.16 and 4.17 give examples of verbs that have traditionally been called "irregular." However, the verbs in Figure 4.16 have a pattern of changing the vowel

Figure 4.15 Examples of Verbs With Four Forms That Add -ed on the Past

Directions: The template shows all four forms of three verbs—ask, breathe, and expect:

1. **Base,** which means no "endings," known as inflection.
2. **Verb -s,** as in "she or he asks," which adds the inflection -s.
3. **-ing,** as in "we are asking."
4. **Past,** as in "yesterday we asked for help."

You will also notice that the letters -ed, also called the grapheme –ed, are written in the fifth column as a phoneme. A phoneme means the sound or pronunciation of the grapheme and is written between brackets [t] or [d] or with a special symbol called a schwa [ə].

Six more verbs have been added to this template. Write the remaining three forms for each of these verbs. Then write the phoneme that you hear. Put the phoneme in brackets [t] or [d] or [ə].

Base	Verb -s	-ing	Past	Past Phoneme
ask breathe expect perform repeat jump talk decide noticed	asks breathes expects	asking breathing expecting	asked breathed expected	[t] [d] [ə]

in the past and are called vowel changing verbs, known as a phonemic shift. Figure 4.17 lists Anglo-Saxon verbs that have both a vowel changing past and a fifth form of -n or -en. By using descriptive language, students can explain the differences. Figure 4.19 (Page 53) shows a very small group of verbs that do not change their form in the past (e.g., "Today I quit. Yesterday I quit.") and are called "null change" verbs.

Figure 4.16 Examples of Verbs With Four Forms That Have a Vowel Change in the Past

Directions: Some verbs in the English language change their vowel phoneme in the past. Verbs that have vowel-changing pasts come from the Anglo-Saxon heritage of our language. Here are three examples of the vowel-changing verbs. There are three more verbs for you to complete. Be sure to change the vowel in the past. Then add three more vowel changing verbs to this list.*

Base	Verb -s	-ing	Past
come feed run speak give ride	comes feeds runs	coming feeding running	came fed ran

*Notice that the past form is named by linguistics as *vowel-changing* form, rather than the empty word *irregular.* All English verbs that have this vowel-changing structure can be traced to Anglo-Saxon or Germanic verbs.

Figure 4.17   Verbs With Vowel-Changing Past Plus a Fifth Form With -en or -n.

Directions: Here is another Anglo-Saxon verb pattern. These verbs have the same four forms as other verbs, but they have a vowel-changing past and a fifth form that ends with the grapheme -en or -n. Five more verbs with this pattern have been added. Complete the missing forms.

Base	Verb -s	-ing	Vowel-Changing Past	Past -en or -n
drive	drives	driving	drove	driven
take	takes	taking	took	taken
speak	speaks	speaking	spoke	spoken
see	sees	seeing	saw	seen
hide				
know				
give				
eat				
bite				

Another feature of English verbs, derived from Anglo-Saxon, are vowel changes and dentalization [t] in the past form of the verb, as shown in Figure 4.18. Figure 4.19 illustrates a very small group of words that do not change their form in the past, known as "null" verbs.

Figure 4.18   Verbs With Four Form Forms That Have Both Vowel Changes and the Phoneme [t] Ending in the Past

Directions: These are a very small group of verbs, all Anglo-Saxon. Two of the verbs show their complete forms. Complete the forms that are missing from the other verbs.

Base	Verb -s	-ing	Vowel Changing Past
buy	buys	buying	bought
catch	catches	catching	caught
fight			
think			
teach			

Figure 4.19   A Very Small Group of Null Change Verbs

Directions: These verbs are part of a very small group that have no change (null) in the past. Two of the verbs show all the forms. Complete the forms for the other verbs.

Base	Verb -s	-ing	Past
hit	hits	hitting	hit
quit	quits	quitting	quit
hurt			
put			

The verbs in Figure 4.20 go back to Old English and show variations in pronunciation changes (e.g., do, does).

Figure 4.20   Other Anglo-Saxon Verbs That Show the History of Pronunciation Changes

Directions: These verbs go way back in the history of the English Language or the Anglo-Saxon times. Complete all the forms. Then complete the statements that follow.

Base	Verb -s	-ing	Miscellaneous Changes	Past -ne
have	has	having	had	
say	says	saying	said	
do	does	doing	did	done
go	goes	going	went*	gone

- When I completed the verb forms for these words, I noticed that all the verbs had _____ forms, but two of these verbs also had _____ .
- I also noticed that three of these verbs had a _____ past. These verbs are _____ , _____ , and _____ .
- I then noticed that HAVE does not change to HAVES, but is _____ .
- Then I noticed that the verb SAY has a different vowel sound when I add _____ . and a different vowel when the word ends in -d.
- The verb DO changes its vowel sound three times as in (1) _____ , (2) _____ , and (3) _____ .
- Finally, the verb past form for the word GO is _____ , which is different from every other verb pattern that I know.

*This is the only form in the English verb system that breaks from the pattern and might be called *irregular*. The form *went* is the past form of the archaic verb *wend*, as to *wend your way*, and became a substitute form for *go*, or as a young child might say, *goed*.

VERBS BY CATEGORIES

Verbs are complex words that permit speakers to request, command, state desires and wishes, gesture, express thoughts, and create clauses, sentences, paragraphs, and lengthy narratives and expositions. With verbs we can be the actor, the passive recipient, the mover and shaker, the thinker and ponderer, the predicate or the subject. With verbs we can tell the truth or lie; we can express love or hate, fear, or courage. Good speakers and good writers own thousands of verbs and use them well, surrounding them with glorious nouns, adjectives, adverbs, and other parts of language that provide their listeners and audience with rich meanings and images.

What are some of the categories of verbs in the English language? Figure 4.21 gives some examples of verbs that form in the *mind*, verbs that express *locomotion*, verbs that tell us we are making or hearing sounds of *vocalization*, verbs that provide us with ways to "express silence" through *gesture*, verbs that allow us to be *positive*, and verbs that accentuate the *negative*. And these are only some of the categories of verbs which your students might collect, as in the example in Figure 4.22 illustrating verbs that denote positive and negative meanings.

Figure 4.21   Verbs of the Mind, Locomotion, Vocalization, and Gesture (Add Others)

	The Mind	Locomotion	Vocalization	Gesture and Body Language
A	admire, appreciate	amble	announce	
B	believe	bound	bellow	blink, blow
C	care, comprehend	careen	chant, chuckle	clap
D	desire	drive	discuss	
E	envy, emulate		explain	
F	forgive			
G		gyrate	guffaw	grab
H	hope	hobble, hop	holler	hug, hold
I	imagine, infer			
J	judge	jump		juggle
K	know			kick
L	love	leap	laugh	lunge
M	miss	meander	mumble, mutter	
N	need		narrate	nod
O			opine	offer
P	ponder	prance	pronounce	point, puff, push
Q				quake
R	realize	rocket, run, race, ride	respond	
S	sympathize	stagger, skid, skate, slide, slip, scurry, saunter	speak, scream, shout, snicker	smile, stamp, squint, sign, shake, shiver
T	think	tiptoe	tell	tremble, throw
U	understand	undulate		
V	value			
W	wish, worry	waddle	whisper, whistle	wink, wave
X				
Y				
Z		zoom		

Figure 4.22   Verbs That Denote Positive and Negative Meanings

Many of the verbs can be classified as "verbs of the mind."

	Positive	Negative
A	admire, adore	abhor
B	beautify	berate
C	care, cherish	calumniate
D	dedicate	detest, demean, deplore
E	enjoy, ennoble	envy
F	forgive	frighten
G	glorify	
H	honor	hate
I	inspire	inflame
J		
K		
L	love	lament
M		malign, misappropriate
N		negate
O		
P	praise	penalize
Q		
R	respect	revile
S	sympathize	sneer, scold
T		terrorize
U	understand	upbraid
V	value	vilify
W		waste
X		
Y		
Z		

Will, Can, Shall, and May

You may be wondering what happened to the "future." Doesn't English have at least three tenses—past, present, and future? If we use tense and time interchangeably, we might say yes. But if tense refers to grammatical structure and time refers to one's sense of events, the terms are barely synonymous. What the English language has (unlike Spanish, Italian, or French) are expander words such as *will, would, can, could, shall, should, may, might,* words from our Anglo-Saxon heritage that once operated as full conjugational verbs, but are now reduced to two forms, present and past. These words have traditionally been called the "conditional" or "modals" and no longer operate within the "tense" structure of English that they once had.

When we ask teachers and students to give us the present and past of these "conditional" verbs, they easily sort them into present and past and they are now "reduced verbs," as in Figure 4.23.

Figure 4.23   Reduced Verbs From the Anglo-Saxon Past

Present	Past
will	would
can	could
shall	should
may	might

By checking out the meaning and usage of the word *could* in *Random House Webster's Unabridged Dictionary* (2000), we find a whole range of usage, beyond the conditional:

could

1. past of can
2. (used to express possibility): *I wonder who that could be at the door. That couldn't be true.*
3. (used to express conditional possibility or ability): *You could do it if you tried.*
4. (used in making polite requests): *Could you open the door for me, please?*
5. (used in asking for permission): *Could I borrow your pen?*
6. (used in offering suggestions or advice): *You could write and ask for more information. You could at least have called me.*

You can arouse your students' curiosity about these words by asking them to do a dictionary and Internet search and trace their history. Then for a "fun with words" activity, ask them to create a word wall of these reduced verbs, using them in as many different expressions as they can think of.

THE ADJECTIVE IN THE ENGLISH LANGUAGE

Students are traditionally taught that an adjective is a word that *describes* a noun or, in more traditional statements, students are told that an adjective *modifies* a noun. There is a certain truth to this, but we believe that students learn more when they explore the organization first and develop the rules after.

We begin by having the students use the template that follows to list words (adjectives) that have a base, the -er affix, and the -est affix, as illustrated in Figure 4.24.

Figure 4.24   Three-Part Adjectives in the English Language

The following template is set up to show English adjectives that have three forms: a base, an -er inflection, and an -est inflection. Three examples of these types of adjectives are listed. Add as many other adjectives as you can that follow this pattern. When you have finished, add the missing words to the sentences that follow.

Base	-er	-est
big	bigger	biggest
deep	deeper	deepest
easy	easier	easiest

Complete these sentences that can help you understand *one* definition of an adjective. Use the adjectives from your template.

1. An elephant is _____ than a squirrel, but _____ than a _____.

2. A truck is _____ than a car, but _____ than _____.

3. A bicycle is _____ than a wagon, but _____ than _____.

I noticed from these sentences that adjectives with three forms are used to _____

After the students have collected a sampling of these words, ask them what they notice about all of these adjectives. They are likely to say that these words all "compare." In fact, the affixes of -er and -est, also known as inflections, have been labeled "comparative" and "superlative," or in simple Anglo-Saxon as "more" and "most." However, there are other adjectives that came through the Latin lexicon that are bisyllabic (e.g., courageous) and, rather than adding the -er and -est affixes, the words "more" and "most" became the format. We can see the connection of these two words to -er and -est by thinking of "more" as the -er form and "most" as a contraction of "morest."

After the students have completed this initial work on these adjectives which, like verbs, have inflections in contrast to "suffixes," have them collect adjectives that are formed by affixes that are commonly known as suffixes. The collections that follow (see Figures 4.25, 4.26, and 4.27) are examples of patterns of adjectives. Figure 4.23 uses the Defining Format to define an adjective. The adjectives in these templates represent a high level of vocabulary and are generally appropriate for students in middle and high school grades. But you will notice that several are likely to appear earlier (e.g., *numerical, intelligent, magnificent,* and others). To build a high level vocabulary, you might want to set up these templates for fourth, fifth, and sixth grades too.

Another feature of adjectives is the ending -y or -ly as illustrated in Figure 4.27. Adjectives that end in -ly differ from -ly adverbs in that they are not added on to an already existing adjective. For example, *daily* derives from *day.*

Figure 4.25   Adjective Formed by the Affixes -al, -ic, -ive, -ent (Add Other Adjectives With These Affixes)

	-al	-ic	-ive	-ent
A	antithetical	alcoholic	appreciative, attractive	ambient, apparent
B	bilateral	balsamic		beneficent, benevolent
C	comical	comedic	cooperative	convergent
D	dialectical	despotic, demonic	divisive, distributive	divergent
E	ethereal	empathetic, energetic	elusive	emergent
F	funereal	frenetic	furtive, figurative	
G		genetic	generative	
H	hysterical	Homeric, horrific		
I	inimical, infinitesimal, intellectual		imperative, investigative	impertinent, intelligent
J	judicial			
K				
L	lackadaisical	laconic		latent
M	musical, magical, maniacal	metric	massive	magnificent, malevolent, maleficent
N	numerical			nascent
O	occasional, oppositional	opportunistic	oppressive	
P	peripheral, prepositional	philanthropic, peripatetic, pathetic	permissive, persuasive	persistent
Q	quizzical	quixotic	quantitative	quiescent
R	rhetorical, rhythmical	romantic	restive, reclusive, responsive, retentive	reticent
S	sensational, spherical	sympathetic, sybaritic	supportive, subjective	sentient
T	temperamental, tyrannical, transcendental	toxic	transformative, tentative, transfigurative	
U	universal			
V	visual		vituperative	
W				
X				
Y				
Z				

Figure 4.26 Adjectives Formed by the Affixes -ous, -ory, -ary, -able, or -ible (Add Other Adjectives With These Affixes)*

You can write creative sentences by using high level adjectives. Here are two different activities.

1. Select three adjectives with the same letter, but three different suffixes. Then write a sentence using all of these adjectives in the same sentence. Here's an example:

The *capable* explorer, *contrary* to the Queen's belief, was extremely *cautious* in his choice of a route to the west.

2. Select three adjectives, all with the same suffixes, and write a sentence using all of these adjectives in the same sentence. Here's an example:

The *hospitable* hostess set out a *formidable* display of delicious food for her *notable* guests.

You may wish to create additional sentences using other combinations of adjectives.

	-ous	-ory	-ary	-able/-ible
A	amphibious, ambiguous, abstemious	anticipatory	antiquary	able
B	bituminous		binary	
C	cautious, capacious		cautionary, contrary	capable, comprehensible
D	deleterious, delicious	defamatory, declamatory derogatory		desirable, dependable, destructible
E	envious, enormous. efficacious	expository, explanatory	exemplary	expendable
F	famous, fractious		funerary	formidable
G	generous, gracious, gratuitous			
H	humongous, horrendous, herbivorous			hospitable
I	infectious. infamous, industrious	inflammatory incriminatory	illusionary	impossible, inflammable, indestructible, invisible, insupportable
J	judicious			

	-ous	-ory	-ary	-able/-ible
K				
L	laborious loquacious luminous	laudatory		lamentable, lovable
M	monstrous, magnanimous	mandatory, migratory		malleable, manageable
N	noxious. numerous, notorious			notable
O	ostentatious	obligatory	obduracy	
P	poisonous, pernicious	participatory, preparatory	proprietary	possible, permissible
Q				
R	ravenous, rapacious			reprehensible, responsible, remarkable
S	supercilious, stupendous, serious, specious, serendipitous, synchronous	satisfactory, statutory	stationary	supportable
T	timorous, tenacious, tendentious		temporary	tenable
U	unctuous	unsatisfactory		understandable
V	vicious, vicarious, voluminous			visible
W				washable
X				
Y				
Z				

*Some of these affixes may also form nouns (e.g., laboratory, calligraphy, geography).

Figure 4.27   Adjectives That End in -y and -ly* (Add Others)

	-y	-ly
A	antsy	ably
B	busy, bony	bubbly
C	crazy, cozy	costly
D	dizzy, dusty	daily
E	easy	
F	funny	friendly
G	greedy	
H	hazy, happy	
I	itchy, icy	
J	juicy	
K		
L	lazy	lovely, lonely
M	merry	
N	needy	
O		only
P	pretty	pearly
Q		
R	rosy, rusty	
S	scary, sassy, sunny	
T	tiny	
U		ugly
V		
W		
X		
Y		
Z		

*Generally, adverbs have the -ly affix, but there are a few adjectives as illustrated. Now set up the Defining Format for the Adjective similar to the templates for the noun and verb as illustrated in Figure 4.28. Have the students put this definition on a double-page spread with two columns on the left-hand page and a complete page on the right-hand side.

Figure 4.28

What Is an Adjective in the English language?		
• DEFINING FORMAT •		
Question	Category	Characteristics
What is an adjective in the English language?		
An adjective is a	word that	1. compares by having a base to which -er and -est can be added (e.g., *big, bigger, biggest*). 2. compares by using *more* and *most* as in more beautiful, most beautiful. 3. compares by semantically related words such as *good, better, best,* or *bad, worse.* 3. can be qualified or intensified by words such as *very, rather, quite, less,* and *least.* 4. can precede the noun (e.g., quiet child) or follow a form of the BE verb (e.g., The child is quiet). 5. may be formed by specific suffixes (e.g., *heroic, delightful, adorable, foolish, attractive, tasty*). 6. may be formed from certain verbs (e.g., a *completed* document, an *expected* answer).

THE ADVERB IN THE ENGLISH LANGUAGE

This part of speech has been defined as virtually any word that "relates to the verb," hence its name ad-verb. However, when we lay out the morphological words of English, the adverb is clearly a word that is related to the adjective, also confirmed in *The Oxford Companion to the English Language* (McArthur, 1992). In fact, an adverb can be defined as a word that has been formed by adding the suffix -ly to an already existing adjective. The list in Figure 4.28 defines what an adjective is. Figure 4.29 gives examples of other adverbs that have variations because of etymological

Figure 4.29   Adverbs From Adjectives

Adjective	Adverb*
attractive	attractively
benevolent	benevolently
calm	calmly
delightful	delightfully
elegant	elegantly
fierce	fiercely
Etc. through the alphabet	

*We have to be careful to not say that a word that ends in -ly is an adverb (e.g., friendly), but that there must be a pairing of adjective with -ly adverb. A stable rule of the -ly adverb is that it is almost always formed from an already existing adjective.

Figure 4.30 Adverbs That Look Like Adjectives

A few words of Anglo-Saxon origin have the (seemingly) same forms as both adjectives and adverbs, as in the word *bad*, where we have "This is a bad day" and "I feel bad." Somehow, saying "I feel badly" has a different nuance than "bad" and remains one of the inexplicable aspects of semantics. Here are several of these words that you can discuss with your students as part of their etymological search. Ask the students to write a sentence for each pair in which they use the same word as an adjective and adverb.

Adjective	Adverb	Sentence
bad	bad, badly	There was a bad storm and
fast	fast	I felt bad because so many
quick		people were hurt.
slow		

Figure 4.31 Words of Time or When (Add Others)

• TAXONOMY •	
A	about the time, after, afterwards, a while, as soon as
B	by and by, before, by the time
C	
D	during
E	eventually
F	for the moment
G	
H	
I	immediately, in an instant
J	just then
K	
L	later, long ago, lately, a long time ago
M	minutes after, midnight
N	now, noon
O	over time, once upon a time
P	
Q	
R	
S	soon
T	today, tomorrow, tonight
U	
V	
W	while
X	
Y	yesterday
Z	

history or phonology. What has made defining the adverb confusing to so many students has been the attempt to incorporate other classes or categories of words that are not part of the morphological system such as *just, now, there, up, same,* and so forth. The moment we sort out the words as morphological and non-morphological, we separate the adverb from the unrelated forms. When we have students do morphology, we clearly see the amazing, but not unexpected, patterns of the English language. However, Figure 4.30 illustrates adverbs that look like adjectives.

Reclassifying Adverbs

Many grammar books include words that tell "when" as adverbs. We prefer to list these words separately because of their semantic meanings. For example, the word *today* is semantically very different from a word such as *happily*. In Figure 4.31, we have a Taxonomy of Words that expresses time, which your students will find useful when they write and will not have to think about their "parts of speech." These words resist parts of speech classification, many because they are non-morphological (e.g., *after*) and others because they are part of the phrase (e.g., *by and by*). Have students put this Taxonomy of Words of Time or When in their notebook as part of their ever-growing personal thesaurus.

Now have your students write the definition of an adverb, knowing what it is and what it is not (Figure 4.32).

Figure 4.32

What Is an Adverb in the English language?		
• DEFINING FORMAT •		
Question	Category	Characteristics
What is an adverb in the English language?		
An adverb in the English language is a	word that	1. adds -ly to an adjective as in *wise/wisely*, *happy/happily* 2. can sometimes have the same form as an adjective as in "I am a fast runner. I can run fast."

There is a great deal of information on parts of speech on the Internet, but we advise that you use it selectively, keeping to the major patterns and the morphology.

The "Other" Parts of Speech

In addition to the previously mentioned parts of speech, the traditional grammar books have added prepositions, conjunctions, and interjections. These predominantly non-morphological words are best taught within the context of where or how they are used in sentences because of the shifts in meaning (semantics) that can occur. Therefore, we continue with these other parts of speech in Chapter 5, "Syntax and Semantics: Getting Meaning."

INTERNET SITES

- http://www.ucl.ac.uk/internet-grammar/nouns/nouns.htm

  This Web site gives an accurate descriptive statement about nouns and includes a lively activity for students.

- http://www.scientificpsychic.com/verbs1.html

  An excellent resource for intermediate and secondary students that fully shows English verb conjugation and inflectional morphology of just about every verb.

- http://www.ucl.ac.uk/internet-grammar/adjectiv/adjectiv.htm

  Similar to the noun Web site listed earlier, the statement about adjectives is clear, and the site includes some good activities.

- http://web2.uvcs.uvic.ca/elc/studyzone/410/grammar/adverb.htm

  There is a good activity here for elementary and secondary students.

Introduction

*Language and
Metalanguage*

*Builders of
Linguistic
Intelligence*

*Parts of
Speech and the
English Language*

**Syntax and
Semantics**

*The Polyglot
of English*

*The Polyglot:
Beyond Latin
and Greek*

*Return to Parts
of Speech*

*Sentences,
Paragraphs, and
Other Structures of
the Written
Language*

*Grammar for
Word Play*

*Reading, Writing,
and Grammar*

*Punctuation,
Spelling, Text
Messaging, and
Other
Consequences of
Grammar*

*Additional
Learning Activities*

CHAPTER FIVE

Syntax and Semantics

*It does not follow that all word groups expressing complete thoughts
are sentences.*

(Allen, 1972, p. 3)

The sentence is notoriously difficult to define.

(McArthur, 1992, p. 918)

GETTING MEANING

No matter how little we remember of school grammar, we undoubtedly all remember the definition of a sentence—"a group of words that expresses a *complete thought.*" Many of us may have wondered how we would know when a thought is complete, but few have had the courage to ask. When we did ask, we were told that we would recognize a "complete thought" when there was a subject and predicate. Evelyn remembers writing a list of sentences when she was in seventh grade such as the following: *Yes, it is. No one knows. Nothing happens. Can't you see? It's fine.*

After underlining all the subjects once and the predicates twice as per instructions in the English class, she asked the teacher what was complete about each of these thoughts. All she remembers was being told to sit down and accept the rule that was in the grammar book. Many years later, Robert Allen, author of *English Grammar and English Grammars* (1972), gave a lecture on "the sentence." The views expressed by Allen remain accurate, current, meaningful, and important to know. Understanding the sentence is one of the most difficult aspects of grammar.

The word *sentence* comes through Old French by way of the Latin word *sententia*, which means a way of feeling and thinking (McArthur, 1992, p. 918; *Random House Webster's Unabridged Dictionary*, 2000). Linguists refer to a sentence as a structural unit in the metalanguage of grammar. It is the most complex unit to explain, as teachers know when "correcting" their students' writing. Coupled with the word sentence is the term *syntax,* from the Greek, meaning to put words together or connoting the "rules" of a specific language for conveying meaning.

You may be thinking that if children automatically learn the syntax and morphology of their language, what grammar do we have to teach in school? The answer is probably very little until we get to teaching reading and the more difficult literacy counterpart—writing. Learning to read requires the child to think metacognitively about language: "What sound do you hear?" "Read with expression." "When you add an *e* to a word, the first vowel says its name." The child now goes from the natural ease of speech to having to understand and apply the language of speech, a high level and no longer automatic language task.

Writing or composing is even more complex. Now children are told to "edit their speech." What is so easy to say is so difficult to write. New rules get imposed:

- Start with a capital letter.
- End with punctuation (previously a change in our voice told the listener we had finished or that we were asking a question).
- Don't begin with "Me and my friend."
- Don't use the word *nice* in your sentences.
- Never write a run-on sentence.
- Don't write fragments.
- Make sure your sentences make sense.

The shift from speaking to writing brings about the need for teaching grammar, with the further expectation that through grammar instruction, the students will not only write better, but will "speak better," meaning "correctly," according to the rules of what came to be called *standard* English (McWhorter, 1998). Yet English and language arts teachers often find that teaching their students "correct usage" and the rules of sentences does not result in improved writing and speech.

Students are often told to avoid *run-ons* and *incomplete sentences* or underline the subject once and the predicate twice, find direct objects, circle predicate adjectives, and find "errors" in sentences. Yet, even those students who do these tasks conscientiously and correctly still make "mistakes" in their own writing. Why does this happen generation after generation?

One answer to this question is that the "rules" that are stated in the grammar books rarely, if ever, refer to the thousands of sentences that English speakers use without following *those* rules (see Pinker, 1994, Chapter 4). According to traditional grammar rules, these sentences would be deemed incorrect. Can you tell why?

Traditional grammar rule: The subject is the doer of the action. The verb is the action.

Now read these sentences:

The three little pigs were afraid of the big bad wolf. (The pigs didn't do the frightening.)

I received a gift from my sister. (I didn't do any action. It was my sister.)

My mother recently underwent surgery. (My mother did not perform the surgery.)

Try this one. According to traditional grammar rules, *a sentence is a sentence when it has a subject and predicate.* What do you think?

The lion devoured.

The defendant alleged.

The student put.

Just one more. (Oops! Incomplete sentence.) Traditional grammar states that *the subject is what the sentence is about.*

What would your students say for these examples?

There are several ways to eat an avocado. (Subject is "there.")

It is essential that we take notes. (Subject is "it").

This is what I mean about the rules of grammar. (Subject is "this.")

Yet, tests are demanding knowledge and use of *standard* English, a challenging demand when classrooms across America are populated by students from different socioeconomic and ethnic backgrounds who speak varieties of English. The troublesome word is "standard" because, as we have already emphasized in Chapter 2, there are different forms of English for different purposes. Nevertheless, there is an *accepted standard*, determined ad hoc, by educated people. This standard focuses mainly on *formal* or written language which demands clearly defined hallmarks such as "complete" sentences, limited use of contractions, pronoun sequences such as "Sally and I," avoidance of double negatives, among others. However, even in written language, a wide variety of "syntax" is used. Compare, for example, the syntax in a "love and romance novel" versus a "scholarly paper."

As we **teach** students to write, we need to help them focus on these major principles of writing:

- "Who they are writing to," which will determine the register—friendly, formal, humorous, academic.
- The syntax or sentence structure that relates to the register (e.g., *So what's going on?* in contrast to *"What have been your most recent experiences in your travels to China?).*
- The vocabulary that they use in relation to the audience (e.g., *noisy/boisterous, happy/elated, hard-working/conscientious*).

Writers learn that syntax must be related to semantics or the study of meaning and can include a word, a sign, a sentence, or sentences. For example, the meaning of a word or words is derived from the meaning of sentences (McArthur, 1992, p. 915). An example is the sentence "There was a run on the market." These basic primary level words in this arrangement would be meaningless to any young child and possibly to an adult not familiar with the word *market,* meaning the stock market, and *run,* meaning a "panic to sell stocks." The semantics (or deep meaning) of a sentence will often determine whether one understands that sentence. It is this deep or inferential understanding that forms the basis of a child's reading comprehension. By studying semantics as part of grammar, students develop deep comprehension skills as well as high level writing skills.

APPLICATION TO LEARNING

The student activity Taxonomy of Semantic Terms (Figure 5.1) illustrates the topics and terms that can serve as a guide for developing strategies that can make students better readers, writers, and learners. Throughout this book, we refer to many of these terms with instructional strategies. This taxonomy can be presented to students in intermediate grades or higher with the following instructions.

Two Semantic Words Seldom Used in School

Prosody

- The stress and intonation patterns of an utterance
- A particular or distinctive system of metrics and versification

Pragmatics

- The analysis of language in terms of the situational context within which utterances are made, including the knowledge and beliefs of the speaker and the relation between the speaker and the listener

Figure 5.1   Taxonomy of Semantic Terms

Directions: Here are terms related to many aspects of language. Terms that describe language are called *metalanguage.*

- Enter these terms in your notebook.
- Underline all the words that are new to you.
- Team up with a partner and find the meanings of these unknown words using an Internet dictionary.
- With your partner, team up with two other partners, and write at least four sentences using the new words you now know (e.g., "People from England speak English with a different cadence or rhythm than people from the United States.").

• TAXONOMY •

A	antonym, ambiguity, accent
B	body language
C	connotation, clichés, cadence
D	definition, dialect
E	eponym
F	
G	gesture
H	homophone, homograph, humor
I	idiolect, inference, intonation, inflection
J	
K	
L	
M	metaphor, morphology
N	
O	oxymora
P	pragmatics, prosody
Q	
R	reference, rhythm
S	stress, symbolism, synonym, simile, satire
T	tone
U	
V	voice
W	word play
X	
Y	
Z	

SENTENCES AND SEMANTICS

Because semantics and syntax are a linked system, we need to teach our students the many different types of sentences, beyond what grammar has traditionally defined as declarative, interrogative, imperative, and exclamatory, and also make a distinction between spoken sentences and written sentences. By tapping into the vast fund of "different sentences," students can begin to expand both their spoken repertory and their writing voice. Certainly, we would not want all writing or speaking to be expository, and we would not want it to be all conversational or dialogue. It is the great variety of language and language usage that makes us literate and lively. For building sentence sense, we begin with our own working definition of a sentence, and amend it with the definition of a *written* sentence.

A sentence is a word or group of words that conveys meaning to the listener and can be responded to, or is part of a response.

A *written* sentence is a word or group of words that conveys meaning to the listener, can be responded to or is part of a response, ***and is punctuated.***

These definitions avoid the confusion of referring to an "incomplete sentence" or "an incomplete thought" and allows for the semantic elements of communication.

In this wide-open field called *syntax* and *semantics*, we also need to allow our students to *code-switch* among the *syntactic* and *semantic registers.* They can maintain their community and familial voices, yet be capable of writing (and speaking) using the *standard* forms that are associated with being educated (Delpit, 1995, 1998). This result is achievable when we provide students with a deep understanding of how language works and how each person's individual language (or idiolect) works. The activities that follow may be adapted to grade-level or achievement needs.

Sentences and Sentence Sense

The term *syntax* is almost synonymous with the term *sentence,* and most of us are likely to agree that a good writer makes "good sentence sense" or uses "good syntax." Just as in mathematics where students need to have number sense to move into more advanced study, so students need to develop a conscious sentence sense as they *write,* which is often very different from how they *speak.* This distinction between written and spoken sentences becomes crucial for writing. Look at the following example of a conversation you may have heard.

E: Good morning.

J: Morning.

E: What's going on?

J: Just heard from the boss. No raises this year. Not one.

E: Even for the boss?

J: The boss calls hers a bonus.

E: Bonus or raise. The same difference. Unfair. Just unfair.

J: Absolutely. Couldn't agree with you more.

Is this conversation spoken in "sentences"? Do you agree with how we punctuated this conversation? If these statements are not sentences, why bother to punctuate them? As a semantic activity (getting meaning), use Figure 5.2 to begin a discussion with your students on this topic. Ask your students which *statements* they think are "sentences" and why they think so?

Figure 5.2   Sentence? Not a Sentence? What Is Your Opinion?

A spoken sentence is *punctuated* by your voice. You pause between sentences or words. You often raise your voice to ask a question. You can sound excited or keep your voice at the same pitch. In writing your sentences, however, you have to use punctuation marks to clue the reader as to what you mean and where your sentences begin and end. This idea of punctuation and when a sentence is a sentence can be complicated.

Directions:

- Work with a partner. Read each statement and decide whether you think it is a *sentence* or *not a sentence according to the rules you have learned*. If you think the statement is not a sentence, rewrite it or restate it. If you can't change it, just write "don't know."
- Discuss with your partner what you think is the difference between *spoken sentences* and *written sentences*.

Statement	Is a Spoken Sentence	Would not be Called a Written Sentence	Change to a Written Sentence (if possible)
Good morning, students.			
So many smiling faces this morning.			
Jane. Jane. Jane!			
Thanks, Jane.			
Now. Who's ready?			
One, two, three.			
Good. Really good.			
Open your books.			
Quietly.			
Read to the end of the page.			

Elliptical Sentences

Probably only the last sentence in Figure 5.2 would fit a traditional grammar book definition. Yet if we converted the other statements to "sentences" we would not only sound unnatural, we would still remain uncertain as to whether we have stated "complete thoughts." One reason for this dilemma is that many sentences are *elliptical*, meaning that they are likely to be responses to prior statements or questions (e.g., *Later. As soon as possible. Definitely.*). If the question is "When will you be home?" the expected grammatical answer could be "Later." If the person answered, "I will be home later," the semantic implications are quite different, conveying possibly anger or displeasure.

Figure 5.3 provides several other statements (Allen, 1972, p. 3) for your students to consider and discuss as to whether they are sentences.

In Figure 5.4 there are *elliptical* sentences that are responses to possible questions or previous statements. For this activity, your students will write what they think prompted these responses.

Figure 5.3   Sentence? Not A Sentence?

How might you revise these statements to turn them into "written sentences"? Is there any reason they need revision? Discuss your ideas with a partner.

Statement	Sentence? Not a Sentence?	Revised Version
No taxation without representation.		
No parking from here to corner.		
This week only—two bottles of spring water for the price of one.		
Will arrive on the five o'clock train.		

Figure 5.4   The Elliptical Sentence

An elliptical sentence is a response to a statement or question.

Directions:

- Here are several elliptical sentences. Notice that they are punctuated.
- Write what statement you think might have prompted these responses. The first one is done as an example.
- Compare your responses with a partner.

Elliptical Sentences	Possible Statements or Questions That Might Have Preceded the Ellipsis
Tomorrow.	(example) When is the test?
Yes.	
No thanks.	
Maybe.	
Rarely.	
Never.	
Once in a while.	
If you say so.	
Serves you right.	
So what?	
How?	
Where?	
Why?	
Who?	
When?	
How many?	

In Figure 5.5 there are elliptical sentences organized by the number of words in each statement. Have your students write elliptical sentences that range from one word to eight words. Then discuss what statements might have prompted these *ellipses*.

Figure 5.5   More Elliptical Sentences

Directions:

- Here are elliptical sentences organized by the number of words in each "ellipsis." There is an example for each number.
- Write your own elliptical sentences, ranging from one word to seven words.

Number of Words in the Ellipsis	Example of Elliptical Sentences by Number of Words
One	Maybe.
One	
Two	Next week.
Two	
Three	Whenever we can.
Three	
Four	Minding my own business.
Four	
Five	In April almost every day.
Five	
Six	Lots of reading, writing, and math.
Six	
Seven	By reading books that teach us something.
Seven	

Advertising Sentences

Students are bombarded with elliptical sentences in the world of advertising and, not unexpectedly, are likely to use them in their own writing. For this reason, lessons and discussions of advertising sentences often engage student interest. These types of sentences are often *clipped* to get attention and to convince people to buy a product by using the fewest words possible. Figure 5.6 illustrates a piece of "advertising copy" and asks students to rewrite this copy in a longer, nonadvertising style. Figure 5.7 contains "nonadvertising" sentences for students to convert into "advertising sentences."

Figure 5.6   Converting Advertising Copy Into Nonadvertising Copy

Here is a paragraph written in the style of advertising copy.

Imagine that you have been asked to rewrite this copy in nonadvertising style. After you have read the copy, follow the instructions.

Advertising Copy

The Unmistakable X-Master (Revised example: We are selling the unmistakable revised X-Master.)

Incredible styling. Combined with unfailing performance.

Brilliant features. Computerized speed systems. Video monitors. Laser controls.

Easy to park. Easy to own.

X-Master to make you the master.

Instructions

- Copy the paragraph onto your computer.
- Copy and paste this paragraph so you have a second copy.
- Revise the second copy so that you change the "elliptical" sentences into "full" sentences. The first sentence of the advertising copy has been revised as an example.
- Read both paragraphs aloud to a classmate and discuss which you think is better for advertising and why.
- Example of revised sentence: "The X-Master has incredible styling combined with unfailing performance."

Figure 5.7   Convert Nonadvertising Sentences Into Advertising Sentences

Directions: Revise the nonadvertising sentences so that they are "clipped" for advertising. The first one is an example.

Nonadvertising Sentence	Advertising Sentence
This is a time to celebrate.	Time to Celebrate.
Make this dream come true.	
You will always remember this moment.	
This is the best music you will ever hear.	
Do you love to sing?	
You can have five hours of music at your command.	
There are hundreds of great features.	
With this new invention, you will have a whole world of rock, hip-hop, jazz, and reggae at your fingertips.	

Grammatically Complete Versus Semantically Complete

The grammatical statement that a "sentence contains a subject and predicate" can be baffling when the "sentence" has these two ingredients, yet doesn't make (semantic) sense. The sentences in Figure 5.8 are grammatically "complete" yet semantically incomplete. Have your students "complete" them and discuss the importance of this distinction. The sentences in Figure 5.9 need a prior statement to make them "complete."

Fragments, Run-ons, and Other "Faults"

For generations (and still continuing), students have been warned about sentence fragments or incomplete thoughts and its opposite *fault*—the "run-on," which runs two *sentences* together, often with what is called a "comma splice" (see Blue, 2000, http://www/grammartips.homestead.com/spliceok.html).

In fact, during Evelyn's time in the New York City schools, these faults were so grievous as to result in a failing grade on any piece of writing with fragments or run-ons. Not that we are advocating the neglect of these sentence deviations, but rather to point out the need to clearly help students understand the *conventional rules* of writing, which have become codified by the "educated" American English-speaking population. The words *codified, educated,* and *American English* are important to understand because the written codes of punctuation and sentence separators differ in different languages. For example, in French, "run-ons" (from the point of view of American teachers) are the accepted and praiseworthy French style of academic and literary writing.

What we propose here on this difficult or controversial issue is to give students extensive opportunities for writing and learning about the many varieties of sentence structure and the "rules" for punctuation (see Chapters 11 and 12).

Following are additional sentence development activities.

Figure 5.8   What's Missing? When Does a Sentence Make Sense?

Here is a set of sentences. Each one contains a word called a *pronoun* and a word called a *verb*. Each sentence is punctuated with a capital letter and a period. But what's missing?

Directions:

- Work with a partner and "complete" the sentences from the Grammatically Complete column into the Semantically Complete column. The first one gives an example.
- Discuss why you think there is a difference in "completeness."

Grammatically Complete	Semantically Complete
I admire.	I admire the art of Picasso and O'Keefe.
You believe.	
They consider.	
She demands.	
We were entering.	
They forwarded.	
He greeted.	
We hoped.	
She's inspecting.	

Figure 5.9   What Went Before?

Directions:

- In the Response column are nine responses that will only make sense if you have a "prior statement."
- Write a prior statement for these responses. The first prior statement and response provide an example.

Prior Statement	Response
I heard that Sara lost her job.	If only she had listened to me.
	To think that I once helped him.
	Why all the fuss?
	Serves you right.
	Just once in a while.
	Imagine that.
	What a lucky break.
	But if they don't show up?
	Well, well, well, my old friend Josh.

Teaching Sentence Sense Through Metacognition

While there are students who easily make the transition from spoken language to written language, many have great difficulty. Students are often *asked* to write without sufficient *instruction* about how to write. They are likely to say it "wrong" before they say it "right" and get back their papers with lots of "corrections." Beginning in the primary grades and through high school, students need to go through the metacognitive steps of comparing their spoken sentences with their written sentences. Metacognition means consciously thinking about one's own knowledge or responses, a thinking process that is essential to developing high level language, including sentence sense. We present four types of activities that can pleasantly develop and improve sentence sense:

- Sentence Expansion—Add, Delete, Substitute, Rearrange
- Sentence Stretchers
- Composing With Keywords
- Imitation Writing

In *Writing as Learning* (Rothstein et al., 2007a), we present the major ways to improve written sentences, which we call the "four improvers of writing" (p 211). These improvers are adding, deleting, substituting, and moving or rearranging and are called "improvers" because they provide the reader of the sentences with more information, greater clarity, or more vivid language. Figure 5.10 illustrates the use of these improvers by adding, deleting, substituting, moving, or rearranging.

Figure 5.10   Improve Your Sentences by Adding, Deleting, Substituting, Moving, or Rearranging

---

Directions: Follow these steps and learn how to turn good sentences into great sentences. Work with a partner.

1. Write this sentence on your paper. Leave lots of room in the margins on the sides, the top, and the bottom of your paper.

> **The dog went home.**

2. Discuss these questions with your partner: Does this sentence give the audience (reader) enough information about the dog?

   Does the reader know
   - What kind of dog?
   - How the dog got home?
   - When the dog got home?

3. Editing Solutions—Discussion: Would the audience get a better "picture" if we **substituted** the breed of a dog for the word "dog"? Think of a breed of dog to substitute.

   Cross out (do not erase) the word *dog* and substitute a breed (e.g., German shepherd).

   German shepherd

   The ~~dog~~ went home.

4. Discussion: A German shepherd definitely gives us a better image than the word *dog*. Now think of a verb that helps us imagine how this German shepherd "went" home. Think of a powerful or strong *verb of movement* or *locomotion* (e.g., raced, bounded, flew, drove, etc.).

   German shepherd bounded.

   The ~~dog went~~ home.

5. Discussion: Now the reader might want to know when this happened. You need to *add* a phrase or clause that tells "when."

   The German shepherd bounded home at the break of dawn.

   ~~dog went~~

6. Discussion: How could you be more specific about the word *home?* What could you *add* or *substitute?*

   The German shepherd bounded home to its master in the country at the break of dawn.

   ~~dog went home~~

7. Discussion: Does the sentence have "too many" words after the verb? Or are there any words that might be moved or rearranged to make the sentence "balanced?"

   The German Shepherd bounded home to its master in the country at the break of dawn.

8. Discussion: Move or rearrange some of the words. What must you do to fix the punctuation?

   At the break of dawn, the German shepherd bounded home to its master in the country.

   ~~dog went home~~

9. Discussion: What did you learn about improving a sentence?

In Figure 5.11, you can have your students write expansive sentences by writing about a dog and using a verb of locomotion.

Figure 5.11   Breeds of Dogs and Verbs of Locomotion

Write five (or more) sentences about five different dogs. Use a verb of locomotion for each dog. You can match any verb to any dog (e.g., The *English sheepdog danced* gracefully in the dog show and won first prize.).

	Breeds of Dogs (add others)	Verbs of Locomotion (add others)
A	Afghan	amble
B	Beagle	bound, bolt
C	Chihuahua	crawl
D	Dalmatian, Doberman Pinscher	drive, dance, dash
E	English Sheepdog	edge
F	Fox Terrier	fly
G	German Shepherd	gyrate, gallop
H	Husky	hop
I	Irish Setter	inch
J	Jindo	jog
K	King Shepherd	
L	Labrador Retriever	limp, lumber
M	Maltese	meander
N	Newfoundland	navigate
O	Otterhound	
P	Poodle, Pomeranian	prance
Q	Queensland Heeler	
R	Rotweiler	race, rocket
S	Schnauzer, Scottie	sprint, speed, scurry, soar
T	Tibetan Spaniel	trot
U		undulate
V		
W	Weimaraner	waddle
X		
Y	Yorkshire Terrier	
Z		zoom

In the strategy called Sentence Stretchers, the students are going to create an expanded sentence following the instructions in Figure 5.12. We start with a "plain sentence" as a model and take the students through these steps.

Follow-Up to Sentence Expansion Activity

- Have the students create two taxonomies or a dual taxonomy (as illustrated in Figure 5.11) in which they list breeds of dogs in Column A and verbs of movement or locomotion in Column B.
- Ask each student to select a breed and a verb and write a new sentence (e.g., The schnauzer skated home.).
- Have the students add their own time phrase and an expansion of "home."
- Ask the students to illustrate their improved sentences.
- Make a lovely bulletin board with a creative title (e.g., EDITORS AT WORK or FROM GOOD TO BETTER TO BEST).

This lesson combines using knowledge of a topic (e.g., dogs) with specific verbs and shows students the basic elements of edited sentence structures.

Sentence Stretchers

Sentence Stretchers is a lively activity for showing students how to expand sentences with a variety of words and syntax (Rothstein et al., 2007a, pp. 81–82). In addition, this activity clearly indicates the parts of speech by using word order slots rather than definitions. For example, students may have been told that an adjective is a "word that describes." However, when students do Sentence Stretchers, they observe that words that tell an amount (e.g., eight, many, both) always precede the "adjective" or descriptor as in *eight tall children* or *both brilliant students* and are not adjectives but a separate category called determiners (see Chapter 8, "Return to Parts of Speech").

Following is an example of a sentence created by using Sentence Stretchers, followed by the procedures for initiating this activity (Figure 5.12). Students will have now expanded their sentences beyond the one-word level and have created "information-bearing" statements that incorporate many parts of speech (e.g., *As the sun rose, twelve graceful cheetahs crawled silently through the jungle.*).

After students complete the template, have them share their sentences. Then ask them to repeat the process independently or in collaborative groups. Have the students create several of these Sentence Stretchers and illustrate one or two of them, putting in all the details in their illustration.

While the students are creating their sentences, set up three large taxonomy charts (ABCs). Head one ADJECTIVES, one ANIMALS, and one VERBS OF LOCOMOTION. Have each student contribute to each taxonomy so that you now have class lists of these categories as a "word wall." Encourage students to create new sentences from these words, adding phrases that tell when and where. Make a scrapbook of these sentences, or have them put on oak tag strips and display them with illustrations.

Figure 5.12   Sentence Stretchers

Directions:

- Using legal size or drawing size paper, fold the paper into eight slots. Number each slot.
- Write the "labels" as illustrated (e.g., When, Determiner, etc.)

1. When	2. Determiner	3. Adjective	4. Animal	5. Verb of Locomotion	6. Adverb	7. Where	8. Punctuation

Follow these instructions.

- Go to slot 4 and enter the name of an animal in the plural (e.g., giraffes, wolves).
- Go to slot 5 and put in a verb of locomotion. Keep the verb in the base form (e.g., race, leap).
- Go to slot 3 and enter an adjective (e.g., delightful, brilliant, elegant, etc.).
- Go to slot 2 and choose a determiner, which can be a definite number such as "three" or an indefinite form such as "several."
- Go to slot 6 and put in an -ly adverb (e.g., quietly, wildly, gently, etc.).
- Go to slot 1 and write a phrase that tells "when" (e.g., Late last night). Then return to slot 5 and "adjust" the verb if necessary to the past form (e.g., dance, danced).
- Go to slot 7 and write "where" this event took place (e.g., on top of a mountain).
- Go to slot 8 and put a period.

Here is an example of a completed sentence in the Sentence Stretcher template.

1. When	2. Determiner	3. Adjective	4. Animal	5. Verb of Locomotion	6. Adverb	7. Where	8. Punctuation
As the sun rose	twelve	graceful	cheetahs	crawled	silently	through the jungle	.

Follow Up With Other Verb Categories

By first having students set up a Taxonomy of Verbs of Locomotion, they can now build taxonomies of other verb categories and create different Sentence Stretcher arrangements. In addition, by having students collect these words, they have valuable synonyms for writing. Here are three other verb categories (see Figure 5.13), followed by examples of Sentence Stretchers (see Figures 5.14 and 5.15).

More Examples of Sentence Stretchers

Figure 5.13   Using Person and Verb of Vocalization

1. When	2. Determiner	3. Adjective	4. People	5. Verb of Vocalization	6. Adverb	7. Where	8. Punctuation
When the bell rang	many	restless	students	shouted	wildly	in the classroom	.

Figure 5.14   Using Person and Verb of the Mind

(note change of order and ellipsis for student completion)

1. When	2. Determiner	3. Adjective	4. Person	5. From Where	6. Verb of the Mind	7. Complete on Your Own
In 1998	twenty	brilliant	scholars	from the university	discovered . . .	

Figure 5.15   Using Person and Verb of Gesture or Body Language

(note change of order and ellipsis for completion)

1. Adverb	2. Adjective	3. Person	4. Verb of Gesture or Body Language	5. To Whom or What	6. Complete on Your Own
Quietly	the talented	musician	signified	to the orchestra . . .	

Composing With Keywords for Building Sentence Sense

Composing With Keywords is fully described in *Writing as Learning* (Rothstein et al., 2007a, Chapter 3) as a writing strategy that moves from words to syntax. It can be used as a writing strategy to make students aware of word order, parts of speech, and changes in the forms of words (morphology). This activity can be used with young students up through all the grades. Figure 5.16 provides a starting point.

Composing With Keywords is a powerful sentence-building strategy that allows students of all ages to create an infinite variety of statements by using a small number of words in all their morphological forms, in a variety of word orders. This strategy gives full credence to the Chomksy (1957) principle that "with a limited number of grammatical structures, we can create an infinite number of sentences."

Figure 5.16 Composing With Keywords

Complete this as a whole class activity with your students.

Begin with three lexical items—a name, a form of a verb, and a noun.

Example: *Humpty Dumpty   sat   book*

Set up the morphological elements of the verb (e.g., *sit*) and write the forms using this template.

Base	Verb -s	-ing	Past
Example: sit	sits	sitting	sat

Write both the singular and plural form of the noun (if possible):

book books

Compose three different sentences using the name, the verb, and the noun in different arrangements.

Examples:

1. As *Humpty Dumpy sat* reading a book, the king came by and waved.

2. I was *sitting* with a *book* in my lap when suddenly *Humpty Dumpty* came by.

3. Humpty Dumpty asked Little Bo-Peep to *sit* next to him and read their favorites *books* together.

Imitation Writing

Imitation Writing (Nessel & Graham, 2007) is a strategy to increase understanding of sentence structure and improve written versatility and expressiveness. The student reads a well-written model of a small piece of text, then copies the model word for word. After that, the student substitutes as many words as possible using a different topic. Figure 5.17 gives several examples from books for young children which can be used at any age level.

Figure 5.17   Imitation Writing

From: *I'll Teach My Dog a Lot of Words* (Frith, 1973)

1. **Copy:** The first words I will teach my pup are dig a hole and fill it up.

   I will teach him walk. I'll teach him run.
   I'll teach him catch a ball!
   We'll sure have fun.

2. **Substitute:** I'll Teach My **Chimp** a Lot of Words

3. **Imitate the pattern:**

   The first words I will teach my **chimp** are climb a tree and learn to swing.
   I'll teach her play. I'll teach her sing.
   I'll teach her words like moon and sun.
   She'll learn a lot and we'll have fun.

From: *The Ugly Duckling* (Andersen, 1855/1914)

1. **Copy:** It was lovely out in the country in the summer. The cornfields were yellow, the oats were green, and in the hay stood in the stacks in the meadows. All around the fields were great forests, and in the middle of these forests lay deep lakes.

2. **Substitute:** It was lovely in the city in winter.

3. **Imitate the Pattern:** It was lovely in the city in winter. The skyscrapers were a gleaming silver, the city lights glistened, and snow-covered cars stood like white mounds of soft marshmallow. All around the streets were food vendors hawking grilled meats on a stick and children tugging at the parents urging them to buy this succulent warming treat.

We hope that you can include these powerful sentence builders with your students and get the joy of praising them for their accomplishments.

INTERNET SITES

- http://www.everything2.com/index.pl?node=sentence

  This Web site offers an in-depth explanation of the relationship between syntax and semantics for further clarification of these aspects of language.

- http://www.eecs.umich.edu/~rthomaso/documents/general/what-is-semantics.html

  Here is a clear and interesting explanation of semantics as the core of meanings in sentences.

Introduction

Language and
Metalanguage

Builders of
Linguistic
Intelligence

Parts of
Speech and the
English Language

Syntax and
Semantics

**The Polyglot
of English**

The Polyglot:
Beyond Latin
and Greek

Return to Parts
of Speech

Sentences,
Paragraphs, and
Other Structures of
the Written
Language

Grammar for
Word Play

Reading, Writing,
and Grammar

Punctuation,
Spelling, Text
Messaging, and
Other
Consequences of
Grammar

Additional
Learning Activities

CHAPTER SIX

The Polyglot of English

In its full panoply of grammar, vocabulary, idiom, and nuance, English is both the world's key up-to-minute operational language and a kind of living classical language . . . .

(McArthur, 2002, p. 3)

Carnivores eat flesh and meat; piscivores eat fish; herbivores eat plants and vegetables; verbivores devour words. I am such a creature. My whole life I have feasted on words . . . .

(Lederer, 1994, p. 4)

We already know that English is one of the many Indo European languages (Chapter 2) and is currently the most widely spread tongue spoken in the world or what McArthur (2002) calls a "global lingua franca" (p. 1). As a result of its history and travels (via the British and later the Americans), it has picked up and incorporated a myriad of words from other languages. The triangle in Figure 6.1 gives an approximate visualization of the composition of the English language resulting from its widely traveled history. As we already know, the English language has developed from an Anglo-Saxon base of common words: household words, parts of the body, common animals, natural elements, most pronouns, prepositions, conjunctions, and numerous verbs. As a result of this base, children who learn English as their first (or only) language have a large command of these words which, assuming normal language development, they will use frequently and with fluency (e.g., "I lost my teddy bear because it falled/fell down in the hole and mommy is mad at me."). For the first five years, an English-speaking child will use mainly words of Germanic origin, which were transferred to the people of Britain.

Gradually the English-speaking child will incorporate Latin-based words depending on exposure from the home or community and the influence of

Figure 6.1   The Polyglot Composition of the English Language

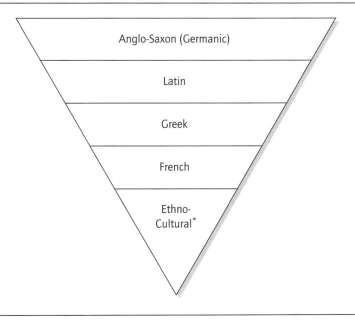

*Italian, Spanish, plus words from the vast numbers of indigenous and ethnic peoples who learned English and added their own lexicon (American Indians, East Indians, African Americans, Africans, Yiddish speakers, Australian Aborigines, Chinese, among others).

school vocabulary, as in an example of this dialogue between a parent and a child. The italicized words are Latin-based:

Child: I don't want to go to bed now. I want to stay up late like my sister.

Parent: You know you can't pay *attention* in school when you're tired.

Child: I do pay *attention*.

Parent: Remember when I had a *conference* with your teacher? We all *decided* that it's *necessary* for you to be in bed no later than 8:30 so you can *concentrate* on your work in school.

Child: I do concentrate.

Of course, school subjects will continue to add to the child's acquisition of Latin with words such as social studies, history, science, and eventually hundreds more. Soon, Greek words enter the child's lexicon, again depending on the social environment and the child's acquisition of subject area or academic vocabulary, as in the brief sample:

Parent: Hurry up. We have to get to the *pediatrician.* (Greek)

Child: Why do I need to see the *doctor?* (Latin)

Parent: Your school requires a *medical examination* (Latin) and needs to be sure that you have been *immunized.* (Latin)

Child: Will I get a shot?

Parent: Not today. But we'll have to stop at the *pharmacy* (Greek) to get some cough medicine.

You will notice that Anglo-Saxon words dominate in terms of numbers, but the Latin and Greek words add new substance to the language. Now, depending again on parent or community language, words of French origin come into the language, enhanced by school subjects:

Parent: I have to *chauffeur* (French) all of you kids to the soccer game and then run off to the *beauty salon* (French) to get a *manicure* (French).

Child: What are we having for dinner?

Parent: *Soup,* (French) *beef* (from the French boeuf) stew, and a *delicious* (French) *dessert* (French) which will be a *surprise* (French).

Finally, there are the words that come from Italian (*spaghetti, pizza, concerto,* and many more), Spanish (*adobe, sombrero, tortilla*), and other words that enter the child's language through ethnocultural exposure. But the structure of the grammar remains predominantly Germanic and Anglo-Saxon, with the Anglo-Saxon lexicon serving as the glue of the sentences.

THE LATIN "DNA"

As we mentioned previously, English grammar is only barely related to Latin grammar and, therefore, teaching English grammar through Latin is both faulty and inefficient. However, as we have previously seen, thousands of English words are the "offspring" of Latin words, making English a "kind of living classical language" (McArthur, 2002, p. 3). Hundreds of Latin words (e.g., *subtract, reject, interrupt,* etc.) consist of "roots and stems" (of words) that were once spoken in ancient Rome and at times in its conquered lands. When Latin "died out" as a spoken language, its offspring thrived as Spanish, Italian, Portuguese, French, Romanian, and "dialects" such as Catalan and Provençal. These languages are to this day called Romance languages from the word Roman.

Latin, however, traveled beyond the Mediterranean area because it had become the official language of the Roman Catholic Church, used in the Mass and the religious liturgy. But Latin, now in the form of "dialects" such as Italian and French, added to the Anglo-Saxon lexicon first through the Norman Conquest in 1066 when English became suffused with French words. In the next few hundred years, in the period called the Renaissance, there was a burst of literature, art, and music emanating from the western European continent that filled English with a plethora of new words born of Latin, as well as Greek. Students often study these Latin-based "roots" and may learn them as they prepare for the SAT or ACT tests. The training for these tests includes intensive work in the vocabulary of "Latin" and will generally pay off in improved scores.

The Study of "Latin" in the Classroom

We believe that learning the lexicon of Latin that has entered English is a worthy enterprise for building both an extensive vocabulary as well as providing an understanding of the English morphological system (or word structure). McArthur (2002) points out that Latin has been the "cultural and technical vocabulary" of the Western world and continues to be a resource for words related to the sciences, medicine, law, and even a certain amount of computer technology (e.g., *document, monitor, video, disk,* etc.). Helping your students build a Latin (and Greek) vocabulary will result in increased reading comprehension, higher level writing, and a greater knowledge of the relationship between words and grammar. We begin first with some definitions of terminology you will need, which have not always been consistent in traditional grammar books, followed by an organizational chart and an instructional activity.

TERMS FOR UNDERSTANDING THE STRUCTURES OF WORDS AND PARTS OF WORDS

The following four terms have often been taught, but without clear or stable meanings:

word, root, prefix, suffix

The clarification of these terms will help students build an extensive vocabulary, because they will see the related patterns of Latin-based forms that will enhance memory and the ability to generalize to new or unknown words. We begin by defining the word *word* in Figure 6.2 as the basis for understanding its synonym *vocabulary.*

Figure 6.2

What Is a Word?

• DEFINING FORMAT •

Question	Category	Characteristics
What is a word?		
A word is a	unit of language that	1. consists of one or more spoken sounds. 2. can be composed of one or more clusters of sounds called morphemes (e.g., jump-ing). 3. may be composed of sound clusters called syllables (e.g., hus-band). 4. is recognized by the speaker as having meaning, in contrast to a foreign or nonsense sound. 5. is understood by the speaker. 6. is usually part of a larger structure called a sentence, but may stand alone.

Many English words have "roots," which often indicate having an origin in another language (usually Latin or Greek). To better comprehend the concept of "root" in language, we must also understand the terms *morpheme, base,* and *affix.* Linguists call a word that has meaning by itself a *free morpheme* (e.g., port, meaning a harbor). An easier term for free morpheme is *base word* because it is the base that adds *affixes,* commonly called prefixes and suffixes. For example, when im- is affixed to "port" we get *import.* The affix is im- (written with a hyphen), and -port (now written with a hyphen) is the *root* to which affixes are attached.

The chart in Figure 6.3 illustrates how bases (free morphemes) can be affixed either preceding the base or following the base, using the example of words built upon the "root" -port. Note again, that when -port is written with a hyphen it indicates a root, as in these words:

> *deport, comport, export, import, purport, report, transport*

These words, metaphorically, belong to the same "family" or carry similar Latin "DNA." The form -port (in this family) means "to carry." When *port* is written without the hyphen, your students are likely to know that *port* is a harbor because it is a "word." Your students might be less likely to know that -port (a root) means *to carry.* Students as early as Grade 4 can be introduced to this chart and eventually create similar charts for other Latin root words. The APPLICATION TO LEARNING provides templates and activities to extend your students' knowledge of the Latin DNA in vocabulary and how it works in English grammar.

Figure 6.3   Chart of Common Latin Roots and Bases

-port	-ject	-tract	-rupt	-tain
deport	abject	abstract	abrupt	contain
export	deject(ion)	attract	corrupt	detain
import	eject	contract	disrupt	obtain
report	project	distract	erupt	retain
purport	reject	extract	interrupt	
transport	reject	protract		
	subject	retract		

GETTING MEANING BY SORTING AND CLARIFYING

As you will notice, students are likely to know or recognize many of the words or *bases* (free morphemes) that contain the roots (bound morphemes). But, unless there has been direct instruction, few, if any, students are likely to know that *-port* is to carry, *-ject* is to throw, *-tract* is to pull or draw, *-rupt* is to break, and *-tain* is to hold. By knowing the meaning of the roots, they can deduce or figure out the meanings of related "DNA" words. But first, students need to know the meanings of the affixes (bound morphemes). Here are examples of the literal meanings of several of the aforementioned words. Notice that for every Latin-based word, we need two or more Anglo-Saxon words to define it.

report—to carry back

project—to throw forward

detract—to pull down

interrupt—to break in

contain—to hold within

Once your students understand the patterns and organization, they can figure out the meanings of the related words and then check out their accuracy by looking them up in an unabridged dictionary that gives the full morphology and etymology.

The templates in Figures 6.4 and 6.5 can get your intermediate and secondary students started on building a Latin-based vocabulary and expanding their understanding of how this vocabulary fits into the grammatical structure of English.

APPLICATION TO LEARNING

Figure 6.4   Getting to the Roots

You can become a powerful writer and reader by learning Latin roots and English morphology. Here are seven Latin roots that have given English an enormous lexicon (or word bank): -tract, -port, -ject, -scribe, -mit, -duce, -fer.

Directions:

- Complete these charts with the morphological forms of the different words, all of which carry Latin roots or the "Latin DNA."
- Check out the meaning of the *front affix* or prefix. For example, a- means "to," re- means "back." The chart for the root -tract has been completed as a model.
- Complete the others by yourself or by working with others. You can use unabridged dictionaries and Internet sources to help you. (Not all of the words will have all of the parts of speech.)

Step 1. Read the words in the chart. Think of the Latin root -tract, meaning "to pull or to draw." Then think of how all the words with -tract mean *pull* or *draw*. Discuss your ideas with your partner.

Verbs (write all four forms)	Nouns	Adjectives	Adverbs	Related Words Using the Root
attract attracts attracting attracted	attraction attractions	attractive	attractively	tract (originally meaning a stretch of space) tractor traction tractable tractile
abstract abstracts abstracting abstracted	abstraction			

(Continued)

Figure 6.4 (Continued)

Verbs (write all four forms)	Nouns	Adjectives	Adverbs	Related Words Using the Root
contract contracts contracting contracted* *can serve as an adjective as in "contracted illness" contractor contractors	contract* contracts* *these are nouns when stress is on the first syllable contraction contractions	contractual	contractually	
detract detracts detracting detracted detractor detractors	detraction distractions			
distract distracts distracting distracted distractibility	distraction	distracting* *this is an adjective from the -ing form of the verb	distractingly	
extract extracts extracting extracted	extract* *this word can also be a noun by putting stress on the first syllable extraction extractability extractable			
protract protracts protracting protracted* *can serve as an adjective as in "protracted problems"	protraction protractor protractors protractedness	protractive protractible		
retract retracts retracting retracted	retraction retractions retractability	retractable		

Step 2. Write a "morphological paragraph" using as many of the -tract words as you can. Here is an example:

I recently received a **contract** for an **attractive** tract* of land and immediately called my **contractor.** I wanted to be sure that we **extracted** from the **contract** any statements that would cause a lengthy **protraction** of the job. I also wanted to be sure that there would be no **retractions** from the **contractor** that would **detract** from the **attractiveness** of the project. **Contracts** with **retractable** clauses are very dangerous and can result in serious **distractions** for getting the job done.

*What do you think is the difference between *tract* and *con-tract?*

Step 3. Set up and complete morphology charts for other Latin roots. Here is a taxonomy to get you started. All of these roots have formed English verbs. When you have a sizeable collection, write morphological sentences or paragraphs.

• TAXONOMY OF LATIN ROOTS •

	Latin Root	Meaning	Example		Latin Root	Meaning	Example
A				N			
B				O			
C				P	-port	carry	deport
					-pel	push, thrust	repel
D	-duct	lead, draw	conduct	Q			
E				R	-rupt	break, burst	corrupt
F	-fer	carry	transfer	S	-spire	breathe	inspire
G	-gress	march, go	regress	T	-tain	hold	obtain
H				U			
I				V	-vert	turn (back)	divert
					-volve	turn (around)	involve
J	-ject	throw	eject	W			
K				X			
L	-lect	gather, choose	select	Y			
M	-mit	send	remit	Z			

Figure 6.5 More Latin Roots for Nouns, Verbs, and Adjectives

By completing the following template you will enhance, enlarge, and magnify your vocabulary and grammatical ability. Different roots have formed different parts of speech, so sort the words carefully by checking an unabridged dictionary or the Internet. Add as many words as you can find for each root. Keep adding as you discover new words with Latin roots. Several examples are completed to get you started.

	Latin Root	Meaning	Verb	Noun	Adjective
A					
B					
C	-cide	kill		suicide genocide	suicidal
	-cred	believe	accredit	accreditation	credible
D	-duct	lead	conduct	conduction conductor	ductile
E					
F	-fract	break	fracture refract	fraction	fractious
	-flect, -flex	bend	reflect	reflection	reflective
	-fid	faith, trust	confide	confidant fidelity	confidential
G	-grat	thank	congratulate gratify	congratulation	
	-gress, -grad	go, walk	progress	progression	progressive gradual
H					
I					
J					
K					
L					
M	-mand	order	command	commandment	mandatory
	-mort	death		remorse mortuary	remorseful
	-mit	send	remit	remittance remission	
N					
O					
P	-ped	foot	impede expedite	impediment expedition	
	-prehend	grasp, seize	comprehend	comprehension	comprehensive prehensile
Q					
R					

	Latin Root	Meaning	Verb	Noun	Adjective
S	-strict	bind, draw tight	constrict	constriction constrictor	constrictive
T	-tor -ten, -tain -tact	twist hold, keep touch	contort retain contact	contortionist retention contact	retentive tactile
U					
V	-vor -viv	eat live	survive	carnivore survivor	carnivorous vivid
W					
X					
Y					
Z					

The Greek Connection

For those of you who would like to raise your students' vocabulary to the ultimate (Latin) or even penultimate (more Latin) levels, you have to go beyond Latin to the Greek source. From Greek, we get a *plethora* (Greek) of academic words filtered through literature, science, mathematics, and social science (McArthur, 1992). The epic writings of Homer in the *Iliad* and *Odyssey* have entered and enriched the English lexicon and continued this enrichment through the great dramas of Aeschylus, Sophocles, and Euripides, among others. Science and mathematics, also within the domains of the Greeks, exponentially added to the English word stock, especially during the Renaissance.

Figure 6.6 is a beginning chart of sources of Greek words with several examples in each category, followed by APPLICATION TO LEARNING (Figures 6.7–6.12). We recommend and urge that you guide your students as early as possible in collecting these words in as many creative ways as possible. The expansion of vocabulary is essential to the expanded use of grammatical structures. The Internet is a valuable resource for your students, and several sites are listed at the end of this chapter.

Figure 6.6   Chart of Sources of Greek Words (Add Other Terms)

Science	Mathematics	Social Science	Mythology and Literature	The Bible
anthropology	binomial	autocracy	atlas	bishop
biology	geometry	ethnology	mentor	Genesis
geology	matrix	philanthropy	psychic	Pentateuch

Figure 6.7   Selected Taxonomy of Greek Roots (Add Others)

Use this taxonomy as a beginning step for learning Greek roots.

Directions:

- Add to this list whenever you find or are told about Greek roots.
- Do the sentence activity which follows this taxonomy to help you create grammatically powerful sentences that can serve as prototypes (models) for your academic writing.
- Watch your vocabulary grow exponentially (Latin) and geometrically (Greek).

• TAXONOMY •

	Root	Meaning	Examples of English Words
A	anthro-	man	anthropology, anthropomorphic
B	biblio-	book	Bible, bibliography
C	cephal-	head	encephalogram, hydrocephalus
D	derm-	skin	epidermis, dermatologist
E	ethn-	nation	ethnic, ethnology
F			
G	gam-	marriage	monogamy, polygamy
H	hydro-	water	hydroelectricity, hydrotherapy
I	ichthy-	fish	ichthyologist
J			
K	klastes-	breaker	iconoclast, clastic
L	logos-	word, study	logogram, ecology
M	morph-	form, shape	morphology, metamorphosis
N	neuron-	nerve	neuroscience, neuritis
O	ornitho-	bird	ornithology, ornithopod
P	philo-	love	philharmonic, philanthropy
Q			
R	rrhea-	flow	logorrhea, diarrhea
S	seismo-	earthquake	seismology, seismic
T	theos-	god	monotheism, theology
U			
V			
W			
X	xeno-	stranger, foreign	xenophobic, xenobiotic
Z	zoo-	animal	zoology, zoogenic

Sentence Writing Activity Using Words With Greek Roots

There are 19 roots in the previous taxonomy.

Directions:

- Begin by selecting three English words with three different Greek roots.
- Then compose a sentence using all three words in the same sentence. You can use any form of the word you wish as in the example.
- Write six sentences.

    Example: *anthropology, xenophobic, philanthropy*

    A committee of scientific **philanthropists** voted to provide funding for **anthropologists** who were interested in studying the effects of **xenophobia** in early societies.

Greek Words From the Sciences

As many students of science have heard, "everything is Greek when it's not Latin." So for the logophiliacs, or word lovers, we present this start-up taxonomy of -ology words, followed by a syntax and semantic activity which we hope will entice your students to become well acquainted with Greek science and medical words (see Figure 6.8).

Figure 6.8   Know Your Greek morphology and Etymology

The Greek Etymology for Science and Medicine

Using the Taxonomy of Science and Medical Words, complete the text with different morphological forms so that it is "grammatically" appropriate. Here are some examples to get you going.

At a scientific conference in Athens, the following six physicians gathered:

a **cardiologist,** a _____, a _____, a _____, a _____, and a _____.

They met with the following six scientists:

a _____, a _____, a _____, a _____, a _____, and a _____.

Each physician paired up with a scientist, creating the following pairs (e.g., a dermatologist and an ichthyologist):

1. a _____ and a _____
2. a _____ and a _____
3. a _____ and a _____
4. a _____ and a _____
5. a _____ and a _____
6. a _____ and a _____

• TAXONOMY •

	Medicine or Science	Meaning of Root
A	archaeology	old
B	biology	life
C	cardiology	heart
D	dermatology	skin
E	ecology	nature
F		
G	geology	land
H	hematology	blood
I	ichthyology	fish
J		
K		
L	laryngology	larynx
M	meteorology	weather
N	nephrology	kidney
O	ophthalmology	eyes
P	paleontology	fossils
Q		
R	rhinology	nose
S	speleology	caves
T	toxicology	poison
U		
V		
W		
X		
Y		
Z	zoography	animal

Each pair had been studying a different problem related to their specialty in medicine or science. For example, the dermatologist (a skin specialist) and the ichthyologist (a specialist in fish) had been investigating problems that might be related to skin diseases that might be caused by fish. Each team has written an opening sentence for their research paper that they hope will attract interest in their findings. Write an enticing opening sentence for each pair of physicians and scientists that you have created. You can add a touch of humor if you wish. Here is an example:

Dr. U. R. Hyde, world renowned dermatologist and author of the best seller Under My Skin, *has recently produced a research study with his university colleague C. A. Fishman, PhD, a notable award-winning ichthyologist, indicating that the fish oils of the elongated elasmobranch, commonly know as the shark, can prevent wrinkles and other indicators of aging to people past the age of 90.*

Figure 6.9 Greek Words From Mathematics

As in science, we cannot do even the simplest *arithmetic* without Greek. Geometry would cease to exist without Greek, as would all the polygons. So here's a beginning taxonomy for budding Grecophiles and linguistic mathematicians, followed by an acrostic activity.

Mathematical Words From Greek Mathematicians

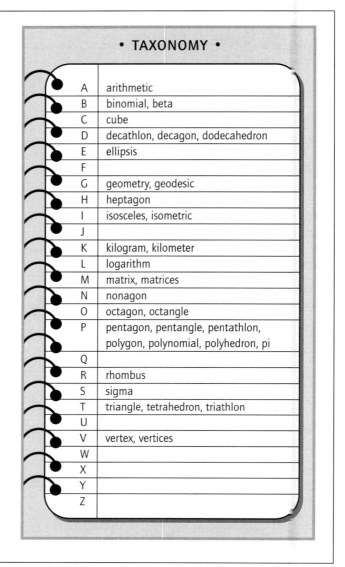

	• TAXONOMY •
A	arithmetic
B	binomial, beta
C	cube
D	decathlon, decagon, dodecahedron
E	ellipsis
F	
G	geometry, geodesic
H	heptagon
I	isosceles, isometric
J	
K	kilogram, kilometer
L	logarithm
M	matrix, matrices
N	nonagon
O	octagon, octangle
P	pentagon, pentangle, pentathlon, polygon, polynomial, polyhedron, pi
Q	
R	rhombus
S	sigma
T	triangle, tetrahedron, triathlon
U	
V	vertex, vertices
W	
X	
Y	
Z	

Greek Words From Mathematics

Imagine that you are a Greek mathematician who wants to explain a mathematical term using an *acrostic,* from the Greek form *acro-* meaning high and *stichos* meaning verse. Select one word from the taxonomy and write an acrostic that explains its meaning. Here is an example using the word *octagon.*

Only a polygon that

Can have eight sides is privileged to be

Termed an octagon and must also include eight

Angles which

Give it the

Octagonal shape and the

Name that means eight sides

Greek Words From the Social Sciences and Related Subjects

A visit to Greece today is not a visit without seeing the *Acropolis,* the ancient temple that sits high above the city overlooking today's Athens, a modern metrop*olis.* In the United States, we have the *-polis* of Minnea*polis,* Indiana*polis,* and Anna*polis* that celebrate their "citihood" in using a combined form. From -polis we also have *poli*tics and the related forms of *poli*tical and *poli*tician. The following template illustrates other Greek words or forms that are part of our social science vocabulary (see Figures 6.10–6.12) Activities to elevate your political, ethnic, and social awareness follow with the adage that "you can't know too much Greek." Figure 6.10 provides you with an overview of many of the Greek social science terms which you can introduce to your students. Figures 6.11 and 6.12 are templates with additional information and student activities.

Figure 6.10   Greek Vocabulary—Political, Ethnic, and Social

• TAXONOMY •	
A	anthropology, archaeology, anarchy, autocrat, autocracy, anglophile, archipelago, aristocracy, atheism, agnosticism
B	bibliophile
C	cosmology
D	democracy, democrat
E	ethnology, eugenics, euthenics
F	francophile
G	genealogy, geopolitics, geography
H	history
I	
J	
K	
L	
M	monarchy, matriarchy, macroeconomics, microcosm, macrocosm, metropolis, monotheism
N	numerology
O	oligarchy
P	philanthropy, philosophy, plutocracy, patriarchy, psychology, politics, polytheism, polyglot
Q	
R	
S	sociology
T	theocracy, technocracy
U	
V	
W	
X	xenophobia
Y	
Z	

Figure 6.11   Begin Your Greek With -polis -arch, -crat

Directions: See if you can figure out the meanings of words you may not know.

You can add other words that belong with this group to keep increasing your vocabulary and grammatical knowledge.

Noun Forms	Meanings of Roots	Adjectives
-polis	city, state	
politician, politics geopolitics cosmopolite metropolis, metropolitan	related to the city or state geo—land cosmo—world, universe metro—measure	political geopolitical cosmopolitan
-arch	high, top, chief	
monarch, monarchy oligarch, oligarchy anarchist, anarchy, anarchism matriarch, matriarchy patriarch, patriarchy	mono—one, single oli(g)—little, few lacking, missing maternal, mother paternal, father	matriarchal patriarchal
-crat	rule, ruler	
democrat, democracy autocrat, autocracy plutocrat, plutocracy theocrat, theocracy aristocrat, aristocracy	demo—people auto—self pluto (Latin)—wealthy theo—god, religion arista—the best, the top	democratic autocratic plutocratic theocratic aristocratic

Activity for "Arch-Achievement"

Complete the paragraph by putting in the appropriate word of Greek origin using the clues that define the words

   For several thousand years, almost all societies have had different _____ systems to govern their cities or states. Many of the early societies were under the rule of a religious leader and were known as a _____. Other societies had one ruler who ruled through hereditary power and was called a _____. Some societies were ruled by a few men in a system called an _____ and other societies were ruled by wealthy men known as _____ in a type of organization called a _____. All of these societies believed that only the "best men" should have the privilege of ruling and developed an _____ type of government. In ancient Athens (Greece), however, there was a group of men who believed that many people should have a voice in the rule of the city and that a _____ form of government was the best. These men considered their ideas to be universal and thought of themselves as _____ with the ability to make their city a true _____ for almost everyone. But even this society didn't include all people. As a _____ society, it excluded women as citizens, believing that only men were entitled to the rights of a _____. It also did not include slaves, foreigners, or people without property, so not everyone was privileged to participate in the _____ of the city or state.

Figure 6.12   Continue With -logo, -graph, -philo

Noun Forms	Meanings of Roots	Adjectives
-logo	means word and has come to mean "the study of"	
anthropology, anthropologist cosmology, cosmologist ecology, ecologist genealogy, genealogist	anthro—man, human cosmo—world, universe eco—nature gene—pedigree, heritage arista—the best, the top	anthropological cosmological ecologist ecological genealogical
-graph	write	
autograph biography, biographer autobiography, autobiographer monograph	auto—self bio—life mono—one	autographic biographical autobiographical
-philo	love of	
philosophy, philosopher philanthropy, philanthropist philology, philologist	-soph—wisdom	philosophical philanthropical

Activity: Choose a career with a Greek etymology. Use the following template organizer to write a summary of your work. Use the Internet to find more information about your "career."

For the past 10 years I have been a (e.g., philanthropist). In this career, I have become famous for three accomplishments.
First, _____
In addition, _____
Finally, _____
I was recently honored by _____ and hope to further expand my work by
_____.

Greek Words From Myths and Literature

Can poetry be studied without *metaphor*? Is our character *Apollonian* or *Dionysian*? What is a *titan*? And why are we *tantalized*? These words and many others are our gifts from the Greeks and their mythology. Students will be delighted to know their etymology, and fortunately the Internet is an excellent source for quick and easy research. Figure 6.13 is a start-up taxonomy that you can build with your students through material from their language or social studies subjects, followed by Figure 6.14 with student activities.

Figure 6.13 Get Started With the Wonderful World of Greek Myths and Literature

		• TAXONOMY •
	A	aphrodisiac, Apollonian, Achilles heel, Adonis, Amazon, ambrosia, atlas, aurora
	B	
	C	chimerical, cyclops
	D	Delphi
	E	Elysian, Europa, erotic, Echo
	F	
	G	griffin
	H	hector, hermetic, hygiene, hermaphrodite
	I	iris, iridescent
	J	
	K	
	L	lethal, lethargic, lesbian, laconic
	M	mentor, meander, music, morphine
	N	nemesis, narcissism
	O	odyssey, ocean
	P	procrustean, palladium, philippic, pyrrhic, paean, panic, protean, psychic, Pandora's box
	Q	
	R	
	S	siren, saturnine, stentorian
	T	titan, titanic, tantalize, thespian
	U	
	V	
	W	
	X	
	Y	
	Z	zephyr

The Greek Pantheon

Many of your students will know at least some of the Greek gods, and they might recognize the Roman version of these gods because of the names of the planets. These gods and goddesses and their role in Greek thought and history are often the underpinnings of Western literature—myths, plays, poetry, opera. In the words of the great mythologist, Joseph Campbell, "these bits of information from ancient times, with . . . themes that have supported human life . . . have to do with deep inner problems, inner mysteries [and] inner thresholds of passage (1988, p. 2).

But why include the Greek gods, or anything about the gods at all, in a book on grammar? One answer is that both are symbols of our knowledge. Myths constitute a large part of our literary knowledge; grammar (defined as morphology + etymology + syntax + semantics) represents our linguistic knowledge. Combining both—myth and grammar—can be truly mind-expanding, for "a myth is an explanation of something in nature" (Edith Hamilton, 1969, p. 18) and "grammar is an explanation of the structure of a language" (1972, Allen, 72). The template in Figure 6.14 shows (in part) this relationship, followed by Figures 6.15 and 6.16. This template lists the 12 gods and goddesses who, in Greek mythology, dwelt on Mt. Olympus. Next to the name of each god and goddess is their role or function in the family or pantheon and a descriptive quotation, using Latin or Greek vocabulary, taken from the great mythologist Edith Hamilton (1969), an author we recommend for middle and high school students. Use this template as an overview for having your students write about these deities and sharing the information with others.

Figure 6.14 The Greek Pantheon (etymology—pan + all; theon = gods) on Mt. Olympus

Olympian God or Goddess	Roman Name	Role in the Greek Pantheon	Quotation From Edith Hamilton (1969)
Zeus	Jupiter	supreme ruler, lord of the sky	Nevertheless, he was not omnipotent nor omniscient. (p. 27)
Hera	Juno	protector of marriage, wife of Zeus	. . . she was venerated in every home. (p. 28)
Poseidon	Neptune	ruler of the sea	. . . Zeus's brother and second only to him in eminence. (p. 28)
Hades	Pluto	ruler of the underworld	. . . the third brother among the Olympians . . . unpitying, inexorable, but just . . . . (p. 29)
Pallas Athena	Minerva	goddess of wisdom, reason, purity	She was pre-eminently the protector of civilized life . . . . (p. 29)
Ares	Mars	god of war	. . . murderous, bloodstained, the incarnate curse of mortals . . . . (p. 34)
Phoebus Apollo	(same)	god of light and truth	Apollo was a purely beneficent power . . . . (p. 31)
Artemis	Diana	goddess of the hunt	. . . she was protectress of dewy youth, but also fierce and revengeful. (p. 31)
Aphrodite	Venus	goddess of love and beauty	. . . the irresistible goddess who stole away even the wits of the wise. (p. 32)
Hermes	Mercury	messenger of the gods	He was graceful and swift of motion . . . the divine herald who led souls down to their last home. (p. 34)
Hephaestus	Vulcan	god of fire and the forge	. . . the workman of the immortals, their armorer and smith. (p. 35)
Hestia	Vesta	goddess of the hearth and home	. . . each city had a public hearth sacred to where the fire was never allowed to go out. (p. 35)

Figure 6.15   Building a Mega-Vocabulary From Edith Hamilton's (1969) *Mythology*

Use the information from The Greek Pantheon (Figure 6.14) with Mega-Vocabulary Taxonomy (Figure 6.15) to write your own mythical or imaginative story. You may change the morphology (forms) of the words to make them work in your story.

• TAXONOMY •

A	armor(er)
B	beneficent (beneficence)
C	civilized
D	divine
E	eminence
F	
G	graceful
H	
I	inexorable, incarnate, immortals, irresistible
J	
K	
L	
M	mortals, motion, murderous
N	
O	omnipotent, omniscient
P	pre-eminently, protector, protectress, public, power
Q	
R	revengeful
S	sacred
T	
U	unpitying
V	venerated
W	
X	
Y	
Z	

Greek Words From the Bible

Students in the upper grades can begin to make a compilation of Biblical words and study their etymological changes. For example, the book of Ecclesiastes is from the Greek word meaning *assembly* and is the basis of the Spanish and French word for church (*iglesia, eglise*). Deuteronomy, one of the books of the Pentateuch, carries the form "second" in "deu," referring to a second statement of the Mosaic law, found in the fifth book of the Pentateuch. Students who can make these connections can greatly increase their SAT scores as well as read and write with depth. Figure 6.16 is a start-up Taxonomy of Greek Biblical words, followed by a template of selected words related or "cognate" to these terms.

Figure 6.16   Taxonomy of Greek Words Related to the Bible

	• TAXONOMY •
A	Apocrypha, apostle, angel
B	Bible, bishop
C	Christian
D	Deuteronomy, Decalogue
E	Ecclesiastes, Epistles, Episcopal, evangelical, Exodus, epistemology, eucharist, epiphany
F	
G	Genesis
H	Heptateuch, hymn
I	
J	
K	
L	Leviticus
M	
N	
O	orthodox
P	Pentateuch, psalm, prophet
Q	
R	
S	Septuagint, synagogue
T	theology
U	
V	
W	
X	
Y	
Z	

Greek Biblical Word	Related or Cognate Words
Christian	Christmas
Decalogue	decade, monologue, dialogue, decathlon
eucharist	charisma
Genesis	genealogy
orthodox	orthopedic, paradox
Pentateuch	pentagon, pentathlon
Septuagint	septagon
synagogue	synthesis, syntax, pedagogue
theology	Theodore, theocracy
monotheism	monologue, polytheism

Activity: Webbing Words—Select a word from the list. Research its meaning and then search for as many related or cognate words as you can. Make a web (as illustrated in Figure 6.16c) with the word you have selected as the centerpiece. Then put as many related words as you can in the web "extensions," including morphological forms. When you have finished, write a paragraph including as many of these words as you can.

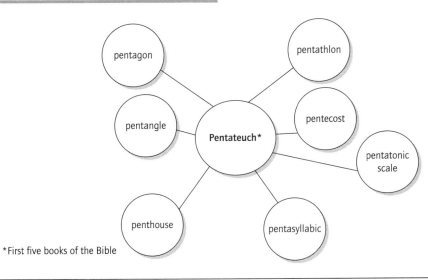

*First five books of the Bible

Greek Influence on English Spelling

chorus [1555–65; < L < Gk khorós a dance, band of dancers and singers]

In the National Spelling Bee competitions, the teenage contestants are allowed and encouraged to ask the origin or etymology of any word they have to spell. What these young contestants know is that the origin is often a determiner of English spelling. A most notable example of spelling origins is in words that begin with the letters or digraph of ch-. In elementary school, students quickly notice that ch- can be for *chair* and *charm* or for *Christmas* and *chorus*. By the upper grades they realize that ch- is also for *chauffeur* and *chaise*. Rarely (in our experience) are the students told why one digraph represents three "sounds" or phonemes. The answer is in the origin of the words and their history in finding their way into the English language. By organizing the words

Figure 6.17 English, French, or Greek—Organizing the Words With "ch"

Directions: Enter this template in your notebook and discuss the meanings of these words with your classmates. Then write a story in the English, French, or Greek *polyglot* (Greek for many tongues). Share your stories and there will be a *chorus* (Greek) of praise for the *cachet* (French) and *panache* (French) evidenced in your writing.

English	French	Greek
chair	chauffeur	charisma
chap	chaise	chorus
chase	chemise	choir
charm	chef	chasm
chip	charge d'affaires	chaos
chariot	chagrin	character
chubby	champagne	chemical
(and many others)	charlatan	chlorine
	chivalry	cholera
	chic	choreography
	cliché	Christian
	cachet	chronology
	chauvinism	chrome
	machine	chronology
	panache	stomach

as in Figure 6.16, students can see why we have these distinctions. By checking the etymology, they can discover where the words originated. For example, *chair* is related to the French word *chaise*, which was further derived from the French word *chaire* (pronounced in French as "sh"). Then there is *chorus*, which in Greek would have used

Figure 6.18   Add More Greek and Latin Words to Your Personal Thesaurus (Greek)

	Root	Meaning	Language Origin	Nouns (Examples)
				• TAXONOMY •
A	astro-	star	Greek	astronaut, astronomy, astrodome
	acro-	high, height	Greek	acrophobia, acrogen, acromegaly
	anthro-	man, human	Greek	anthropology, anthropoid
	avi-	bird	Greek	aviary, aviarist, aviation
	api-	bee	Greek	apiary, apiarist
	auto-		Greek	autoimmunity, autogamy
B	bio-	life	Greek	biology, biodiversity, biome
	bovi-	cattle	Latin	bovine, bovinity
C	cardi-	heart	Latin	cardiogram, cardiologist, cardiology
	cyto-	cell	Greek	cytoplast, cytologist, cytomembrane
	carni-	animal	Latin	carnivore, incarnate, carnival
	canis-	mean type of tooth (e.g., dog)	Latin	canine, canid
D	dent-	tooth, teeth	Latin	denture, dentist, orthodontist
	derm-	skin	Greek	dermatologist, epiderm, dermabrasion
E	eco-	environment	Latin	ecology, ecosystem, ecotype
	endo-	within	Greek	endomorph, endocardium, endocrine
	ecto-	outside	Greek	ectomorph, ectoplasm, ectoparasite
	entomo-	insect	Greek	entomology, entomologist, entozoan
	epi-	back, backward	Greek	epiphany
	equus-	horse	Latin	equestrian, equine, equinity
F	feli-	cat (family)	Latin	feline, felineness, felinity
G	gastro-	stomach	Greek	gastronomy, gastritis, gastrectomy
	gyno-	woman	Greek	gynecologist, gynepath, gynecocracy
	gamete-	reproductive cell	Greek	gametocyte, gametophore, gametogenesis
H	herbi-	plant	Latin	herbivore, herbologist, herbology
	hemo-	blood	Greek	hemophilia, hemorrhage, hemocyte
I				
J				
K	kine-	movement	Greek	kinesiology, kinesics, kinesiologist
L	lupi-	wolf	Latin	lupine, lupus
M	micro-	small	Greek	microbiology, microbe, microanatomy
	macro-	large	Greek	macrobiotics, macrodont, macrocosm
	mega-	great, large	Greek	megabytes, megahertz, megadose
	-morph	change, transform	Greek	metamorphosis, morphology, morphine

(Continued)

Figure 6.18 (Continued)

	Root	Meaning	Language Origin	Nouns (Examples)
			• TAXONOMY •	
N	neuro-	nerve	Greek	neuropathology, neuroses, neuralgia
	necro-	pertaining to death	Greek	necrobiology, necrotics, necromancer
O	ovi-	egg	Greek	ovulation, ovoviparism, ovule
	orni-	bird	Greek	ornithology, ornithologist, ornithopod
	ophtha-	eye	Greek	ophthalmology, ophthalmics, ophthalmia
	ortho-	straight, upright	Greek	orthodontist, orthotics, orthroscope
P	phobe-	fear	Greek	phobia, abiphobia, hemophobia
	pyro-	fire	Greek	pryomaniac, pyrotechnics, pyroxene
	paleo-	old, ancient	Greek	paleontology, paleozoology, Paleozoic
	-path	illness	Greek	pathologist, psychopath, pathomorphism
Q				
R	radi-	ray	Latin	radiologist, radius, radiality
S	seismo-	earthquake	Greek	seismologist, seismography, seismograp
	sangu-	blood	Latin	sanguinity, consanguinity, sanguinaria
T	taur-	bull	Latin	Taurus, tauromachy, taurobolium
	toxi-	poison	Greek	toxin, toxicology, toxicity
U	ursi-	bear	Latin	ursine, ursid, ursiform
V	vermi-	worm	Latin	vermicule, vermiculture, vermicide
	viri-	poison	Latin	virulence, viruloid, virus
	-vore	eat	Latin	herbivore, omnivore, voracity
W				
X	xeno-	stranger	Greek	xenophobe, xenolith, xenogamy
Y				
Z	zoo-	animal	Greek	zoography, zoogenesis, zooid

a K or kappa, and in the 1500s the "k" was changed to "ch," which may have seemed to the printers to be more in line with Latin spelling. This template can help your students understand why so much of English spelling is etymological rather than phonological. We can further see the Greek influence on spelling in Figure 6.17, which contrasts Greek with English and French spelling, using the same beginning letters, -ch.

Linking Latin With Greek

When students recognize the meanings of the Greek and Latin roots and stems of their science words, they have a mnemonic or "memory channel" that allows them to make connections within the different areas of science. For example look at the array of noun relationships that result from Greek and Latin roots and consider the vocabulary advantages that students have when they relate the meanings of

Figure 6.19   Alliterative Writing on the Theme of "It's Greek to Me"

Here is an example of an alliterative piece of writing using words of Greek origin (and also Latin origin) that begin with the phoneme [m]. After you have read this alliteration, write your own piece using a phoneme of your choice. If you want to further enhance your etymological power, check which of your high level vocabulary is Greek and which is Latin.

Megadoses of *macrobiotics* may result in *metamorphic malfunction* in creatures of the *macrocosm* that *manifest* changes in the *morphology* of the human body, possibly leading to *macrodontia* that might cost *megabucks* to repair and require *megadoses* of *morphine* to ease the *magnification* of human *misery*.

---

these roots to the multiplicity of science terms they encounter in their texts. We present this template (Figure 6.18) as a visual summary which you can use for your own background and also present, as appropriate, to your students. Following this template is an example of an alliterative activity (Figure 6.19) for your students to follow. We hope you and your students like having it.

INTERNET SITES

- http://www.kent.k12.wa.us/ksd/MA/resources/greek_and_latin_roots/transition.html

  A total listing of everything Greek and Latin your students need to know to build a powerful vocabulary.

- http://www.awrsd.org/oak/Library/greek_and_latin_root_words.htm

  An impressive collection of English words with Greek and Latin roots.

- http://www.biology.ualberta.ca/courses.hp/zool250/Roots/RootsMain.http

  Many technical terms and biological structures are formed from Greek and Latin roots. If your students become familiar with these roots, they can "translate" the technical terms into English. Great for the science classes.

- http://www.espindle.org/roots.html

  Another extensive etymological glossary for intermediate and secondary students.

- http://www.wordinfo.info/words/index/info/view_unit/4218/?letter=E&spage=4

  An excellent Web site for students in middle and high schools, this resource covers the historic development of English as a polyglot and the basis of Anglo-Saxon words in the history of the English language.

Introduction

*Language and
Metalanguage*

*Builders of
Linguistic
Intelligence*

*Parts of
Speech and the
English Language*

*Syntax and
Semantics*

*The Polyglot
of English*

**The Polyglot:
Beyond Latin
and Greek**

*Return to Parts
of Speech*

*Sentences,
Paragraphs, and
Other Structures of
the Written
Language*

*Grammar for
Word Play*

*Reading, Writing,
and Grammar*

*Punctuation,
Spelling, Text
Messaging, and
Other
Consequences of
Grammar*

*Additional
Learning Activities*

CHAPTER SEVEN

The Polyglot

Beyond Latin and Greek

Words are the skin of living thought.

(Justice Oliver Wendell Holmes,
Jr., cited in McWhorter, 1998, p. 86)

*English is the possession of every individual and every
community that in any way uses it, regardless of what any other
individual or community may think or feel about the matter.*

(McArthur, 2002, p. xi)

In addition to Greek and Latin, English contains a myriad of words from other languages: German or Anglo-Saxon (its basic origin), French from the year 1066 and the Renaissance, Italian through music and food, and other languages through geographic proximity and immigration. For example, in the United States we have numerous words from Spanish, Yiddish, American Indian, East Indian, and African American heritage. Nevertheless, the roots of English grammar (and its lexicon) are still predominantly "Anglo-Saxon" or Germanic, so that when we incorporate words from other languages, we conform them to the structure of English. For example, when English speakers use the French word *rendez-vous* (French spelling), they use it within the English noun and verb structure:

I am planning a *rendezvous* with my high school friends.

The spaceships will *rendezvous* beyond the Earth's atmosphere.

After the spaceships have *rendezvou'd* [sic], they will exchange materials and artifacts.

If you know something about French, these constructions would not work in French. First, the word *rendez-vous* has gender: le rendez-vous (masculine). Second, the word in French is solely a noun, never a verb. Third, were it to be a verb, it would not have the conjugational structure of English.

When your students learn and apply the richness of this polyglot of the words and phrases from other languages, they enter a world of cultural awareness as well as an understanding of the interrelationship between grammar and words. History, geography, and language begin to be viewed as humanity on the move—sometimes through war and greed, but other times through migration and the search for a better life. Language and its aspects of grammar and vocabulary are not a set of rules to be underlined or "looked up" in the dictionary, but a living force of communication and interpersonal relationships.

In the following section are taxonomies of words and phrases from the languages that have enriched the English lexicon, with activities and examples to provide your students with opportunities to write with humor and ever-expanding linguistic knowledge.

ICH SPRECHE DEUTSCH—THE GERMANIC CONNECTION

As mentioned previously, the base of English vocabulary is of Germanic or Anglo-Saxon origin and comprises the first words learned by children whose early language is English. Only students who are speakers of other languages need instruction in the basic core vocabulary of English. The "hurdle" for young English-speaking children is not the vocabulary or grammar, but in learning to read the archaic spellings of English, which are based on the pronunciations of Germanic and Anglo-Saxon speakers centuries ago.

By introducing your students to the cognate relationships of English with German, you can show them why English spelling, particularly of sight words, deviates so frequently from the sound-symbol rules expected of an alphabetic system. For example, when your students are studying the English words that begin with kn-, tell them that English speakers once pronounced the [k] that we now call "silent" and to this day, while English speakers say [nee], Germans say *k-nie* (German spelling). While we have changed the original word *k-necht* to *knight*, a German speaker to this day calls the medieval warrior a *knecht*, still pronouncing the [k] as well as the guttural [ch], with the original vowel [e] as in "bet." Figure 7.1, in APPLICATION TO LEARNING, provides a Dual Taxonomy of English words and the German cognates or related words followed by a writing activity that involves composing with keywords.

APPLICATION TO LEARNING

Figure 7.1   A Taxonomy of Related English-German Words

Here is a Taxonomy of related or *cognate* English-German words that can help you become a *linguistic detective* or an *expert in language.* Cognates are words that are descended from the same language but are likely to be pronounced and spelled differently (e.g., *brother* in English, *bruder* in German).

- Work with a partner. Compare the spellings and try to pronounce the German words based on *their* spellings. Notice the differences. For example, the English word *apple* is *apfel* in German.
    1. With your partner, read and talk about the similarities and differences in this vocabulary. Notice the differences and similarities in the English and German words.
    2. Take turns reading the English and "German" story that follows.

(Continued)

Figure 7.1 (Continued)

3. Then write your own story in English using as many of the words from the Taxonomy as you can.
4. When you have finished, draw a line through the English words you have used from the Taxonomy. Substitute the German words for the English words.
5. With your partner, read your stories aloud to each other, pronouncing the German words as you think they might sound. One rule for German is that the letters "ch" are pronounced like "k" with a breath sound. But "schule" and "schnee" are pronounced *shula* and *shnay*. The vowel combination "ei" in German is pronounced like the English word "I." The combination "ie" is pronounced "ee"
6. Have fun with your language creativity.

If you are interested in the German pronunciations, you can check them out in a German dictionary or on the Internet (see www.utils.ex.ac.uk/german/pronounce).

• TAXONOMY •

Taxonomy ICH SPRECHE DEUTSCH (I Speak German)

		English	German
	A	apple	äpfel
	B	bread, brother, blue, beer	brot, bruder, blau, bier
	C	cat, cheese, church, children, come	katz, kaese, kirche, kinder, kommen
	D	dance, daughter	tanz, tochter
	E	eat, eight	essen, acht
	F	fall, father, friend, free, fine, family	fallen, vater, freund, frei, fein, familie
	G	good, garden, glass	gut, garten, glas
	H	house, hound, help	haus, hund, helfen
	I	instead	anstatt
	J		
	K	know, knee, knight, kitchen	kennen, knie, knecht, küche
	L	laugh, love, light, long, learn	lachen, lieb, licht, lang, lernen
	M	make, mother, man, mouse, milk	machen, mutter, mann, maus, milch
	N	night, new, no	nacht, neu, nein
	O	old, open	alt, offen
	P	penny	pfenig
	Q		
	R	rain, red, right, rich	regnen, rote, richt, reich
	S	snow, stone, sun, storm, seven, school	schnee, stein, sonne, sturm, sieben, schule
	T	think, two	denken, zwei
	U	under	unter
	V		
	W	white, week, water	weiss, woche, wasser
	X		
	Y	year, young, yes	jahr, jung, ja
	Z		

Here is an example of an English story with German words which you can use as a model.

Original Story in English	Story With German Words
Eight year old Tommy was walking to his *house* with his *six year old sister* Gretchen. They were *laughing* about their *school* day. Usually it took them about *seven minutes* to walk to their *house* from *school*, but today *instead* they took a *long* route. They walked *under* the bridge and around Mrs. *Penny's garden*. The *garden* had many *apple* trees. The flowers in the *garden* were *red* and *white* and *blue*. Tommy and Gretchen each decided to *eat* one of the *apples*, when Tommy's *brother* suddenly appeared. He shouted. "Don't you *know* your *mother* is worried and your *father* is *out* looking for you?" The *two children* were so afraid that they began to run to their *house* so fast that they fell on their *knees*. But Tommy's *brother helped* them get up and made sure that they were *fine*. He took them into the *kitchen*, gave them each a *glass* of *water*, and told them to always *come* directly to their own *house* and be *good* to their *family*.	*Acht jahr alt* Tommy was walking to his *haus* with his *sechs jahr alt schwester* Gretchen. They were *lachen* about their *schule* day. Usually it took them about *sieben minuten* to walk to their *haus* from *schule*, but today *anstatt* they took a *lang* route. They walked *unter* the bridge and around Mrs. *Pfenig's garten*. The *garten* had many *apfel* trees. The flowers in the *garten* were *rote* and *weis* and *blau*. Tommy and Gretchen each decided to *essen* one of the *äpfel*, when Tommy's *bruder* suddenly appeared. He shouted. "Don't you *kennen* your *mutter* is worried and your *vater* is *aus* looking for you?" The *zwei kinder* were so afraid that they began to run to their *haus* so fast that they fell on their *knies*. But Tommy's *bruder helfen* them get up and made sure that they were *fein*. He took them into the *kuche*, gave them each a *glas* of *wasser*, and told them to always *kommen* directly to their own *haus* and be *gut* to their *familie*.

Source: Entela Kodra. With permission of the author.

THE FRENCH CONNECTION—THE YEAR 1066

The year 1066 was a watershed year for the English language. With William (the Conqueror) of Normandy defeating King Harold of England at the Battle of Hastings, the vocabulary of the English language became transformed, with almost 10,000 French words becoming part of the English lexicon (Bryson, 1990, p. 55). William, a speaker of Normandy French, usurped the English throne and for the next 100 years the English government was conducted in French, only gradually drifting back toward English. In fact, by 1362, the English parliament was still conducting business in French. However, the native Britishers kept talking *Anglo-Saxon*, but absorbed many of the French words, giving them the local English pronunciation. So *boeuf* became *beef*, *veau* became *veal*, and the French surname *Beauchamps* eventually transformed into *Beecham*. By 1415, the Norman French aristocrats were completely out of England, but had left behind a *corps* of French words that are now fully absorbed into English and counted as part of the English vocabulary as in Figure 7.2. The Taxonomies in Figures 7.3 and 7.4 contain only a portion of the numerous French words used in English with the rules of English grammar. Along with these Taxonomies are writing activities similar to the one for German words. However, because the French words presented are part of the English lexicon, the students can write directly in English-French, without making substitutions.

Figure 7.2 is a story that contains many French words that entered the English language beginning in the year 1066 and continued long after that year. Have your students follow the directions to write their own stories; each of them will not only learn many French-English words, but also compose an interesting and elegant bilingual story.

Figure 7.2   Je Parle Français—I Speak French

Read this English-French story and test your knowledge of French words in the English vocabulary. Go through the story and circle as many words as you already know. Look up the meanings of the other words. Write a story or a letter using as many French words as you can (the "Letter to William the Conqueror" is one example of how the French words have been included), using the words you have circled and the new words you have learned.

Share your story with friends, family, and anyone else you wish to impress with your language knowledge. And, of course, you can add other English-French words that you come across.

Example of a "French" Story—Letter to William the Conqueror

Dear William:

I am using my computer to write you a letter with as many *bon mots* as I can think of to tell you how grateful I am for your contribution to the English language. If it were not for you, I would buy only underwear instead of *lingerie*, never eat *fondue* or *quiche*, and never get to taste *bon bons* or *petit-fours*. Nor would I enjoy *nouvelle cuisine* or *croissants*. I would not have the *savoir-faire* to shop in a *boutique* or speak politely to my *chauffeur*. My friends and I would not be able to *rendezvous* or have our delightful *tête-à-têtes*. And what would literature be like without the many *genres* we have, including the great *roman a clef Les Misérables* or the theater without *ballet*?

Life without your contributions to English would be filled with *ennui*, lacking *objets d'art* for my home, *promenades* for strolling, *soirées* for entertaining conversation, and the laughter of *vaudeville* acts and comics. I would be considered *gauche, déclassé*, and totally without *chic*. So I say *merci* for the *souvenirs* of language you have left us and for the *potpourri* of words that permit me to do this *tour de force* of writing that gives me so much *joie de vivre* and is filled with so much literary *cachet* and *panache*. Please keep this letter in your *dossier* and *R.S.V.P.* as soon as you can.

Au revoir,

Source: Permission granted by the author, Leslie Chow-DeGeorge.

Adding More French Words to Your Vocabulary

Figures 7.3 and 7.4 are Taxonomies, organized by categories, of the many French words that have become part of the English language. Figure 7.3 includes food, history and government, the arts, and miscellaneous words. Figure 7.4 is for words related to persons, words describing persons, behaviors or feelings, and dress. Following these Taxonomies are activities that are *de rigueur* for knowing the many *bon mots* that come from French and for expanding your *dossier* of high level vocabulary.

Figure 7.3   French Words Used in English: Food, History and Government, the Arts, and Miscellaneous

		Food and Drink	History and Government	The Arts	Miscellaneous
		• TAXONOMY •			
A		à la carte apéritif			adieu au revoir au contraire
B		bons bons bouillon bouillabaisse buffet	bourgeois	ballet	bon voyage bon mots
C		crème brulée croissant coq au vin café café au lait	coup d'état	chanteuse	carte blanche coup de grace
D		demi-tasse dessert			déjà vu de rigueur dossier
E		escargots			entre nous
F		filet fondue		film noir	fête fait accompli
G		(au) gratin		genre	
H		hors d'oeuvres haute cuisine			
I					imprimatur
J					
K					
L		liqueur			legerdemain
M		menu		mise en scène	massage merci
N		nouvelle cuisine			
O			objet d'art		oblique
P		petit-fours prix fixe		pirouette pas de deux	potpourri parachute pièce de résistance parasol première
Q		quiche			rapport
R			régime	roman à clef	raison d'être R.S.V.P. (réondez s'il vous plaît)
S		sauté soup(e) du jour			soirée suite souvenir

• TAXONOMY •

	Food and Drink	History and Government	The Arts	Miscellaneous
T	table d'hôte			tête-à-tête tour de force
U				
V				vestibule vaudeville vogue
W				
X				
Y				
Z	zeste			

Activity: Prepare a menu of French foods. Organize your menu starting with an *aperitif* and ending with *dessert*. Write one or two sentences using French words what will entice people to come to your home or restaurant for this meal.

If you like this activity, write sentences or a story using the other words in this Taxonomy. Read your sentences aloud to anyone willing to listen.

Figure 7.4 French Words Used in English for Persons or to Describe Persons, Behaviors, Feelings, and Terms Related to Dress

• TAXONOMY •

	Persons	Words Describing Persons	Behaviors, Feelings, Events	Dress or Fashion
A	attaché			
B	bourgeoisie	blasé		bouffant boutique
C	chargé d'affaires connoisseur chauffeur corps de ballet	chic	cachet	chemise coiffure corsage cravat
D	debutante	debonair		
E	émigré entrepreneur envoy	déclassé	éclat ennui	
F	fiancé, fiancée		esprit de corps finesse	
G	gourmet gourmand		force majeure gauche	
H				
I	ingénue			haute couture

• TAXONOMY •

	Persons	Words Describing Persons	Behaviors, Feelings, Events	Dress or Fashion
J			joie de vivre	
K				
L			legerdemain	lingerie leotard
M	maître d' hôtel madame	maladroit		mannequin
N	nouveau riche	naïve nonchalant	noblesse oblige	
O				
P	protégé partisan	petite	panache	prêt-à-porter
Q				
R	raconteur		rapport raison d'être rendezvous	
S			sangfroid savoir-faire	
T			tête-à-tête tour de force	toupée
U				
V	valet		vaudeville	vogue
W				
X				
Y				
Z				

Follow-Up Activity

Here are the frames for five sentences that need to be completed with French words. In each sentence is a French word for a person. Complete the sentences by using the following:

- A French word to describe the person and French words that show behavior, feelings, events, or dress or fashion. The first sentence is done as an example.

    1. The petite *debutante* showed great *savoir-faire* in her choice of *haute-couture*.
    2. Giselle was the _____ in a play about a young woman whose _____ was missing in action.
    3. My neighbor Pierre is a _____ in the French embassy who is always _____ and shows great _____ in dealing with people.
    4. We called the _____ to make reservations in a _____ hotel where we could have a _____ with our friends.

If you enjoy this activity, write your own sentences with French words.

HABLO ESPAÑOL—I SPEAK SPANISH

On October 12, 1492, the day Columbus set foot on a land he mistakenly thought was close to India, the world was irrevocably changed—certainly, that part of the earth that came to be called the "New World," from Tierra del Fuego (Land of Fire) at the southernmost point of South America, to Mexico, the Caribbean, New Mexico, Texas, California, Arizona, Colorado, and Florida. Because Columbus had sailed for Spain, the Spanish language would replace and dominate the many indigenous languages of the existing population that Columbus collectively named Indians. Large areas of South and Central America, plus Mexico, the Dominican Republic, and Puerto Rico in the Caribbean would become predominantly Spanish speaking. Remnants of Spanish would remain in those U.S. states that were either purchased from Spain (e.g., Florida) or "won" from Mexico through the American policy of Manifest Destiny.

As the U.S. population grows to include increased numbers of native Spanish speakers, the inclusion of Spanish words in American English grows. English continues to benefit with an increased lexicon, so our earlier Anglo-Saxon linguistic heritage gets an additional dose of Latin, but through its offsprings of French and Spanish (and Italian, too, as we shall see subsequently). Not surprisingly, we absorb words of food (*tortilla, salsa*), clothing (*sombrero, serape*), shelter (*adobe, hacienda*), followed by other "personalized" categories (*amigo, mañana*). Following through on building fluency, we again suggest that your students collect the numerous Spanish words that abound in today's English, study their origins and history, and compose with them as they did in Figures 7.1 and 7.2. Figure 7.5 is a Taxonomy of Hablo Español, followed by Figure 7.6, a "Spanglish" story and an activity for your students.

Figure 7.5   Hablo Español—I Speak Spanish

• TAXONOMY •

Directions: Put a check mark next to the Spanish words you recognize. Put a question mark next to the words for which you need meanings. Add your own Spanish words, and then make new Spanish Taxonomies for the days of the week and numbers.

	Food and Clothing	Family and People	Colors	Places and Dwellings	Other
A	arroz (con pollo)	abuela, abuelo, amigo, amiga	amarillo azul	adobe	adios
B	burrito		blanco		buenos días, buenos noches bienvenido
C	cilantro, carne			casa	
D					dinero
E	enchilada				
F					fiesta, flores
G			gris		gusto, gracias grande

		Food and Clothing	Family and People	Colors	Places and Dwellings	Other
	H	huevos	hermano, hermana, hijo, hija		hacienda	
	I					
	J					junta
	K					
	L					
	M		muchacha, muchacho, madre, maestro, maestra	marrón		mañana, mucho
	N		niño, niña	negro naranja		noche
	O					
	P	papas fritas, paella, poncho	padre padres		pampas	
	Q					
	R			rojo, rosado	ranchero	
	S	salsa, serape, sombrero				señor, señora, señorita
	T	tortilla, taco	tía, tío			
	U					
	V			verde, violeta		vaquero
	W					
	X					
	Y					
	Z	zapatas				

Figure 7.6   Spanish-English Story

Directions: Read the following story with a classmate or friend. Add other Spanish words you know to the Taxonomy in Figure 7.5. Then write a "Spanglish" story with these and other Spanish words. The following is an example to help you create your own story.

Example of a Spanish-English Story

I finished my supper of *arroz con pollo* and *burritos* and went for a walk with my *hermana* and my *hermano* to visit my *abuela* and *abuelo* who would take us to a local *fiesta*. My *madre* told me to wear my new *zapatas* and put on my new *poncho* which my *tío* and *tía* had given me for my birthday. The sky was a beautiful *azul* color and was just changing to *rosado*, before the *noche* would set in. I took some *dinero* with me because my *hermana* and *hermano* liked to ride the *burros* that were always outside of the *adobes*.

When we got to the *casa* of my *abuela* and *abuelo*, we each ate a *naranja* and then left for the *fiesta*. As we walked through the town, we passed a beautiful *hacienda* with *flores* of *mucho colores—blanco, roso, violeta*, and *amarillo*. My *abuelo* and *abuela* greeted everyone politely: "*Buenos noches Señor Rodriguez, buenos noches Señora Gonzalez, buenos noches Señorita Perez*. Everyone greeted us with *bienvenido* at the fiesta. We all had a *bueno* time, and when we got back home we said *gracias* to our *madre* and *padre* for letting us have such a beautiful *noche*.

PARLO ITALIANO—I SPEAK ITALIAN

Almost all of us have some knowledge of Italian words. In addition, many Italian words are cognate with English, having come to English through Latin. The dialogue (see Figure 7.7) and the Dual Taxonomy (see Figure 7.8) contain the names of foods (*alimenti*) and other words (*parole*) that one might need in a *ristorante*.

Figure 7.7   Parlo Italiano—I Speak Italian

Following is an example of a dialogue that includes many Italian words. Read this dialogue with a classmate and see how many words you recognize.

Pronunciation clues: In Italian all vowels are pronounced (e.g., ris-tor-an-tay, ben-ay). The combination "ci" and "ce" is always "ch" (e.g., *cuchina, vermichelli*), and the combination "gi" is like in the English word *ginger*.

Maria and Alfredo were sitting at a *tavola* in a *ristorante* called *La Cucina*. They were talking about their *giorno*.

Maria:	What are you going to *ordinare?*
Alfredo:	I think I will start with *insalata fresca*. And you?
Maria:	I would like a tasty *zuppa*.
Alfredo:	I hear their *pasta e fagioli* is *deliziose*.
Maria:	No, I think I'll have some *legumi* in *brodo*.
Alfredo:	What kind of *vino* do you prefer *oggi?*
Maria:	*Oggi*, I prefer *acqua minerale*. And you?
Alfredo:	I will have some *vino blanco*.
Maria:	Here comes the *camariere* from the *cucina*.
Alfredo:	*Bene*. I am ready to *mangiare*.

Source: Entela Kodra. With permission of the author.

Figure 7.8   A Dual Taxonomy of Parole Italiani (Italian Words)

With a classmate or classmates, read the Italian words in the Dual Taxonomy. Use an Italian-English dictionary or an Internet Web site to get the meanings of words you don't know.

• TAXONOMY •
Alimenti e Altre Parole—Foods and Other Words

	Alimenti (Foods)	Altre Parole (Other Words)
A	aceto, agnello, acqua	arrivederci
B	brodo, bolognese	blanco, bene, buon appetito
C	cannoli, cappellini	cucina, casa, ciaò
D	dolci, deliziose	
E	espresso	
F	fagioli, funghi, fettucine	fresca, famiglia, fiori
G	gelato	giorno, grazie
H		
I	insalata	
J		
K		
L	linguini, latte	
M	macaroni, minestrone, minerale	mangiare, madre
N		
O	olio d' oliva	oggi
P	pomodoro, pasta, penne, pizza	piacere, prego, padre, porta
Q		
R	ragù	
S	spaghetti	sì
T		tavolo
U		
V	vino, vermicelli	
W		
X		
Y		
Z	zuppa	

Activity: With a classmate, create your own dialogue with Italian words.

YIDDISH OR YINGLISH

Beginning in the 1880s and throughout the 1920s, over 2 million Jews from Eastern Europe immigrated to the United States. The majority of them spoke Yiddish, a language with Germanic roots, interspersed with Hebrew and Slavic words. Although the children of these immigrants would almost immediately adapt English as their first language, they would also keep some of their Yiddish words. Many of these words would become part of the English lexicon, particularly in the areas where Jews settled (see Rosten, 1982.). Figure 7.9 is a Taxonomy of Yiddish words with their English meanings. An activity for your students follows.

Figure 7.9   Taxonomy of Yiddish Words for Speaking and Writing "Yinglish"

Directions: Add any other words you know.

• TAXONOMY •

		Yiddish Word	English Word or Meaning
A			
B		bar or bat mitzvah	religious ceremony for boy (bar) or girl (bat) at age 13
		bagel	bagel or a role with a hole
		borscht	beet soup
		bubbah	grandmother
C		challah	Sabbath bread
		chutzpah	nerve, audacity
D		dreidl	a spinning top used during Hanukah
E			
F			
G		gonif	thief
		gesundheit	bless you (after you sneeze)
H		Hanukah	a religious holiday in December
I			
J			
K		kibbitz	give unwanted advice
		kvetch	complain
		kvell	have great joy
		kinder	children
		kugel	pancake
		kosher	pure as related to food
L		lox	smoked salmon
		latkes	potato pancakes
M		mitzvah	religious deed or commandment
		mazel tov	good luck
		meshuga	crazy
		mezzuzah	door post icon containing commandments
		menorah	religious candelabra
		mensch	a person of character
		matzoh	unleavened bread
N		nosh	snack
O		oy vey!	woe is me!
P			
Q			
R			
S		schlep	drag or pull
		shabbos	sabbath
		schlemiel	a clumsy person
		shtetl	a small town (in Europe)
		schmooze	idly chit chat
		shmatte	rag
T		tush	backside
		Torah	first five books of the Hebrew Bible
U,V,W,X			
Y		yenta	nosy woman or gossip
		yarmulke	religious cap
Z			

Activity: Use as many of the words that you can from the Yiddish Taxonomy to write a story in "Yinglish." Here's a starting sentence if you need one, or you can use your own:

On Sunday morning, my family likes to sit around and *schmooze* while eating *bagels* with *lox* and cream cheese.

WORLDWIDE CONTRIBUTIONS— AFRICAN AMERICANS, AMERICAN INDIANS, EAST INDIANS

In addition to examples from German, French, Spanish, Italian, and Yiddish, the English language has incorporated hundreds of words from other sources, such as American Indians, East Indians, Africans, and wherever else English speakers have been in contact with indigenous peoples. The more a language travels, the more it grows, and the more it changes. Furthermore, the more diverse its population, the greater its lexicon. Languages borrow words and never return them!

In the ancient world, for example, Latin, the main language of the Roman Empire, was the *traveling* language, creating new languages that came to be known as Italian, French, Spanish, Portuguese, and Romanian, plus dialects within these languages, such as Catalan, Occitan, and Romansch, among others (McWhorter, 1998). Less than two centuries after Columbus, English would become the second most traveled language as the British, with their superior navy, brought or imposed English to places far removed from the roots of Anglo-Saxon, Latin, and Greek. As the British created settlements and colonial dominance in Africa, India, America, and Australia, they not only "deposited" the English language, but "took" words and expressions from the indigenous peoples they encountered. In addition, both the new settlers and the "already settled" peoples fashioned their own words and expressions from the "original" English they already knew or learned.

New words and expressions expand grammar and grammatical structures, giving further impetus to exposing our students to the numerous worldwide contributions to the English language melting pot. The following Taxonomies contain examples of words that come from African-Americans, American Indians, and East Indians (Figures 7.10, 7.11, 7.12), with activities that follow. The huge population of slaves brought to the English-speaking colonies would also enrich the English language both before and after slavery, as illustrated in Figure 7.10. Your students can add to these Taxonomies by searching the Internet or other materials. In addition, you can suggest that students research aspects of English spoken in the former British colonies such as Nigeria, Kenya, Ghana, South Africa, and others as an interdisciplinary activity.

Figure 7.10   Taxonomy of African American Words and Expressions From Different Parts of Africa

Here are African and African American words that come from several African countries and have enriched the English language. These words relate to music, food, places, and other topics. Also listed are the areas or languages of Africa where these words originated.

Do a research project which tells about a specific African language or area where African words that are used in English originate.

Find as many words as you can from this language that have become part of English.

Write a paragraph or statement in which you use these words.

Add other African words to this list.

(Continued)

Figure 7.10 (Continued)

• TAXONOMY •		
African Word	Language of Origin	Find Meanings of Words New to You
banana	Wolof	
banjo	Bantu	
chigger	Wolof and Yoruba	
chimpanzee	Wolof	
cola	Mandinka	
coffee	Amharic	
goober	Bantu*	
gumbo	Bantu	
jamboree	Swahili	
jazz	Mandinka	
juke(box)	Wolof	
Kwanzaa	Swahili	
marimba	Bantu	
merengue	Fulani	
okra	Igbo	
okapi	Congo	
safari	Swahili	
tango	Ibibio	
yam	Bantu	
zebra	Congo	

*Bantu languages are spoken in Cameroon, Gabon, Republic of the Congo, Democratic Republic of the Congo, Uganda Kenya, Tanzania, Angola, Zambia, Malawi, Mozambique, Zimbabwe, Namibia, Botswana, and South Africa.

The American Indian Influence on the English Lexicon

Most of us easily recognize place names that come from the indigenous peoples who already occupied the North and South American continents before Columbus. Although these indigenous peoples would be called "Indians" and would be swept out of their native habitats into new "colonies" or reservations, the white settlers were often willing to keep the original place names such as Mississippi, Idaho, Tallahassee, and hundreds of others. So today we have Indian names for many of our states, cities, rivers, and other sites. Of course, the pronunciation of these names today is only an approximation of how they were originally said or what they originally signified. In addition, many of the Indian names we use today (such as Arkansas) came through the French or Spanish explorers (McArthur, 1992).

Figure 7.11 gives a start-up Taxonomy of American Indian place names divided by states, cities, and rivers and other waterways which you can use to get your students started in this research. Your students can also create a taxonomy of other place names such as Appalachia, Allegheny, Shenandoah, and Manhattan, among others. Following the Taxonomy is an example of student research on Indian place names.

Figure 7.11   Start-Up Taxonomy of American Indian Place Names in the United States

- Use the Internet or other sources to research the name of a state, city, or waterway that has an Indian place name.
- Find or create a map showing its location and write three (or more) important details about this place.
- Share this information with a partner or your class.
- If you find more places, add them to this taxonomy.
- An example of a report follows this taxonomy.

• TAXONOMY •

	States	Cities	Rivers and Other Waterways
A	Arkansas, Arizona, Alabama, Alaska	Albuquerque	Alabama-Coosa, Altahma-Ocmulgee, Apalachicola, Chattahoochee
B		Biloxi	Brazos
C	California, Connecticut	Chattanooga, Cheyenne, Chesapeake	Chesapeake, Cimarron, Connecticut
D	Dakota (North and South), Delaware		Delaware
E			
F			
G			
H			Housatonic
I	Illinois, Iowa, Idaho		Illinois
J			
K	Kentucky	Keokuk, Kenosha	Kanawha-New, Koyukuk
L		Laramie	
M	Massachusetts, Minnesota, Mississippi, Missouri, Michigan	Miami, Missoula, Milwaukee	Mississippi, Missouri, Monongahela
N	Nebraska, (New) Mexico	Nashua	Narragansett, Neosho, Niobrara, Noatak
O	Oklahoma, Oregon, Ohio	Omaha, Oshkosh	Ohio, Osage, Ouachita
P		Pueblo, Pocatello, Pascagoula, Pawtucket	Pecos, Potomac
Q			
R		Roanoke	Raritan, Roanoke
S		Seattle, Sioux City, Sioux Falls, Shawnee, Schenectady, Skaneateles	Susquehanna, Stikine, Seneca Falls
T	Tennessee, Texas	Tallahassee, Topeka, Tuscaloosa, Tucson, Tampa, Tupelo, Tacoma	Tanana, Tombigbee
U	Utah		
V			
W	Wisconsin	Waukegan, Winnetka, Wichita, Wahpeton, Woonsocket	Wabash
X			Yukon
Y		Yakima	
Z			

I was curious about many of the Indian place names in the United States and checked out many sources on the Internet. I discovered that 27 states had names that came from different Indian tribes or words. For example, Wyoming comes from the Delaware Indian word, meaning "mountains and valleys alternating"; Ohio is from an Iroquoian word meaning "great river"; North and South Dakota are from the Sioux tribe, meaning "allies"; and Oklahoma comes from two Choctaw Indian words meaning "red people."

I find this information so interesting that I am now planning to research how cities such as Pascagoula (MS), Yakima (WA), and Tampa (FL) got their names. Finally, I will search out the stories of the rivers, including the Mississippi, the Yukon, and the Susquehanna.

English and the Indian Subcontinent

When the British began their extensive journeys to the Indian subcontinent in the 1600s, they had no way of knowing that they were bringing back elements of their language that they had long ago received from the earlier people of India. William Jones, the esteemed linguist, was yet to make his discovery of the linguistic connections on what would be called *Indo-European* languages, and the British were not particularly interested in exploring the languages of the newly conquered peoples. However, a British occupation of India for over 300 years was going to have a marked influence on the diverse peoples in this part of the world, resulting in what today is called *Anglo-Indian English* (McArthur, 1992). Today, with many countries carved out of the "sub-continent, the term Anglo-Indian can also include English spoken in Pakistan, Bangladesh, Sri Lanka, and Nepal" (McArthur, 2002, p. 315).

English, in this part of the world, has become either a first or second language and is used widely in schools, businesses, and in both the national and local governments. Languages are both borrowers and lenders. Not only did the British impart English, but the indigenous languages have added richly to the English lexicon, many of which we use without thinking of their origin. The Taxonomy of Anglo-Indian Words (Figure 7.12) contains many of the words now commonly used in English that are drawn from the languages of Bengali, Hindi, and Punjabi, among others.

Figure 7.12   Taxonomy of Anglo-Indian Words

- With a classmate or classmates, read the following words and try to divide them into categories of dwellings, clothing or cloth, places, people, food and drink, and other. Then using the Internet or other sources, add more words from India that have become part of English.
- You might also want to read about the British presence in India from the 18th century to the 20th century and why so many people from India now speak English.

• TAXONOMY •

A	
B	bungalow, bamboo, basmati, bandana
C	curry, cheetah, chintz, cheroot, chutney, cummerbund
D	
E	
F	
G	guru, ginger
H	
I	
J	jodhpurs, juggernaut, jungle
K	karma, khaki
L	
M	mulligatawny, maharajah, monsoon*, mogul, madras
N	
O	
P	pyjamas, pariah, pundit, purdah, polo**
Q	
R	rupee, rajah
S	sari, shampoo
T	tamarind, tambourine, toddy
U	
V	verandah
W	
X	
Y	yoga
Z	

*Through the Portuguese.

**From the Tibetan through Kashmir.

CONTRIBUTIONS FROM CHINA AND JAPAN

We may not be aware of all the words that entered English from China and Japan—food, clothing, sports, and other categories—but as you and your students look at Figure 7.13, you may wonder how we missed citing them. For the activity, your students can check the Web site (http://www.zompist.com/chinawords.html) and sort the words into categories for sharing and discussion.

Figure 7.13 Taxonomy of Words in English Contributed From China, Japan, and Other Places of Asia

- Work with two or three partners, and sort these words into foods, clothing, sports, and "other." Check to see which words are Chinese and which are Japanese.
- If you eat in Chinese or Japanese restaurants, bring some menus to your class and see which of the words in this Taxonomy are on the menu. Add the words from the menu.
- Then write a paragraph using as many of these words as you can.
- You can add others that you know.

• TAXONOMY •

A	
B	bok choy
C	chai, china(ware), chop suey, chopsticks, chow mein, chow
D	dim sum
E	egg foo young
F	futon
G	ginkgo, ginseng, gung ho
H	haiku
I	
J	judo, jujitsu
K	ketchup, kumquat, kung fu
L	lychee
M	mahjongg, miso
N	ninja
O	
P	pekoe
Q	
R	rickshaw
S	Shinto, shogun, silk, soy, sushi, sashimi
T	tofu, tycoon, typhoon, tempura, teriyaki
U	
V	
W	wok, wonton
X	
Y	yin, yang, yen
Z	Zen

INTERNET SITES

These links offer students excellent information related to the English polyglot and are good research resources for intermediate and secondary students.

- http://www.utils.ex.ac.uk/german/pronounce
- http://www.zompist.com/chinawords.html
- http://www.une.edu.au/langnet/definitions/aave.html#vocab-hce
- http://french.about.com/library/bl-frenchinenglish-list.htm
- http://spanish.about.com/cs/historyofspanish/a/spanishloanword.htm
- http://www.answers.com/topic/list-of-english-words-of-yiddish-origin

CHAPTER EIGHT

Return to Parts of Speech

Introduction

Language and Metalanguage

Builders of Linguistic Intelligence

Parts of Speech and the English Language

Syntax and Semantics

The Polyglot of English

The Polyglot: Beyond Latin and Greek

Return to Parts of Speech

Sentences, Paragraphs, and Other Structures of the Written Language

Grammar for Word Play

Reading, Writing, and Grammar

Punctuation, Spelling, Text Messaging, and Other Consequences of Grammar

Additional Learning Activities

This is the sort of bloody nonsense up with I will not put.

(Attributed to Winston Churchill when corrected by an editor critical of Churchill's use of prepositions. Cited in Crystal, 2006a, p. 112)

Is this the party to whom I am speaking?

(Lily Tomlin, actress, comedian, TV wit)

THE SMALL WORDS

In traditional or prescriptive grammar, the most troubling parts of speech for students (and possibly teachers) are the definitions and "rules" for those *small* words known as prepositions, conjunctions, demonstrative pronouns, and other connectors of verbs, nouns, and adjectives. Even more complicated than merely explaining the rules and functions of these words is the "correctness" of their usage. We know that "I am speaking to the teacher" is fine, but why do some grammar books have a problem with "This is the teacher I have been speaking to"? And why does Lily Tomlin's impeccably correct sentence, *"Is this the party to whom I am speaking?"* sound so funny? One answer to the split between usage and "correctness" can be summed up in the words of Crystal: "An unrealistic rule is bound to be broken, because it is not part of the language . . . ." (2006a, p. 100).

Yet we often need to teach students about the use of the *small* words because they are essential to clear expression, especially in written language. Written language must be clear to the reader who can't easily phone or even e-mail the writer and ask, "Just what are you trying to say?"

The purpose of this chapter is to offer some clarification of the words that resist easy parts of speech classification and provide activities with these words that are engaging, fun, and informative. We begin with the part of speech called the *preposition*, a much misunderstood term because of its ubiquitous and varied use in the English language. Following is a definition from

127

the *Random House Webster's Unabridged Dictionary* (2000) with an explanation of its usage, a definition that is likely to be challenging to any student:

> *Prep·o·si·tion.* any member of a class of words found in many languages that are used before nouns, pronouns, or other substantives to form phrases functioning as modifiers of verbs, nouns, or adjectives.

> *Usage.* The often heard but misleading "rule" that a sentence should not end with a preposition is transferred from Latin, where it is an accurate description of practice.

But English grammar is different from Latin grammar, and the rule does not fit English. In speech, the final preposition is normal and idiomatic, especially in questions: What are we waiting for? Where did he come from? You didn't tell me which floor you worked on. In writing, the problem of placing the preposition arises most when a sentence ends with a relative clause in which the relative pronoun (that; whom; which; whomever; whichever; whomsoever) is the object of a preposition.

Or as Lily Tomlin might have said if she hadn't wanted to be humorous: *Who am I speaking to?*

Many of us may have heard puzzling statements about prepositions undoubtedly similar to the statements from the dictionary. We may have learned that prepositions are "words," such as *to, in, on, under, above, up, out,* or *down,* which precede a noun, as in "down the steps." But then one might wonder if the word *down* is a preposition, as in "down and out." Then we are told that the word *up* is a preposition, as in "up in an airplane," which apparently "modifies" another preposition (in), and the definition of a preposition is now modified. But then what part of speech is the word *up,* as in "take *up* tennis" or "back *up* the car" or "give *up*"? And why indeed can't we end a sentence with a preposition, as in "The rain just didn't let *up*" or "I won't give *in.*" Go figure!

The answer to this puzzlement emerged one day when Evelyn was in Spain and a Spanish friend asked her what the word *up* meant in English. Her first response was a gesture with a finger in an upward direction. But her friend said that she meant the word *up* as in "back up" or "finish up" or "cheer up."

Someplace in the back of her head, Evelyn recalled a teacher telling her that these *up* words were adverbs and modified verbs. But what would that mean to a Spanish speaker?

From this simple question, we began to think about how these non-morphological words, termed *prepositions,* operate in *English* and not in Spanish or French or Italian or Portuguese and so forth, all of which are Latin-based languages and have their own complications. When we think of the numerous verbs that pair with *up* or *down* or *to* or *by* or *out,* we have to define grammatical terms by what they are or do, rather than what we *want* them to do or be.

In Figure 8.1 we have *set up* a taxonomy organizing what Robert L. Allen termed two-part verbs (1972). Using this taxonomy as a starting point, we can build insightful lessons for students that will allow even the least fluent writers to create lively and creative pieces of writing. With access to two-part verbs, the English speaker can easily write in a colloquial or informal register before or while moving on to the more formal styles that are often expected in school and business writing.

APPLICATION TO LEARNING

Two-Part Verb —Lessons for Students

Start by having your students collect their "UP" verbs and place them on a taxonomy as in Figure 8.1. Figure 8.2 shows how students may write an "UP" story. The next activity, Figure 8.3, shows how the same words can be functionally different or "prepositional."

As you look at the words in Figure 8.1, you probably notice that there are synonyms for many of these two-part verbs in the form of a single verb (e.g., *back up/reverse*). However, the synonym is not an exact replacement, but an alternate way to express the same idea.

Example: I backed up the car.

I put the car in reverse.

Or

The soldiers gave up.

The soldiers surrendered.

After the students have completed their "UP" Taxonomy, have them complete Figure 8.2, with two-part verbs that use "up" and have verb synonyms. The last step will be to have students write their "UP" story.

Other Two-Part Verbs

Several other words that have been loosely classified as prepositions are similar in usage to the word *up*. That is, they change or extend the original or main meaning of the verb, as in the distinction between *call* and *call out*, or *sit* and *sit by*, or *come* and *come out*. Use the template in Figure 8.4 to have your students write sentences or stories using these two-part verbs to give them an awareness of the idiomatic and colloquial aspects and the possible substitutions that might need to be used for formal writing.

Prepositions in the English Language

Your students will have a better understanding of the word *preposition* by defining prepositions as a class of words that relate to destination, position, or space, as in *the town, over a bridge, alongside the river, up the mountain, by an ocean*. A clear way for students to understand and use prepositions (especially in writing) is to have them create a template, as in Figure 8.5, using the prepositions, followed by a destination or position. Some prepositions are two-part words. The template has been set up to get your students started.

Figure 8.1 A Taxonomy of "UP" Verbs— When "Up" Is Not *Up*

• TAXONOMY •

A	add up
B	beat up, batter up
C	call up, cook up
D	dress up
E	eat up
F	freshen up
G	give up
H	hold up
I	inch up
J	join up
K	keep up
L	loosen up
M	make up
N	nose up
O	own up
P	pass up
Q	queue up
R	read up
S	stay up
T	tear up
U	use up
V	veer up
W	wise up
X	
Y	
Z	

Figure 8.2 Two-Part "UP" Verbs and Their One-Word Verb Synonyms

Directions: This taxonomy contains verbs that are composed of two parts as in "end up" and are paired with a single form verb that is its synonym. Write two sentences, one using the "UP" verb, followed by a sentence using its synonym. You may have to change the syntax or sentence structure for some of these verbs. Here is an example:

I need to *free up* some time to visit my friend.

I'll have to *allow* at least a weekend so we can really chat.

• TAXONOMY •

A	add up—calculate
B	beat up—attack
C	call up—telephone
D	dream up—imagine
E	end up—remain
F	free up—allow, spend
G	give up—surrender
H	hold up—rob, detain
I	inch up—crawl
J	join up—enlist
K	keep up—maintain
L	loosen up—relax
M	mix up—confuse
N	
O	own up—admit
P	put up—prepare
Q	
R	read up—study, research
S	split up—separate
T	tear up—destroy
U	use up—consume
V	veer up—prepare
W	wise up—learn
X	
Y	
Z	

Figure 8.3 Writing With "UP" Verbs

Directions: You can create a simple, fun-to-do piece of writing with "UP" verbs. Use as many words as you need from the Taxonomy of "UP" verbs. You can use the following story as a model.

An "UP" Story

"Wake up," mother shouted. "Hurry up and dress up in your new clothes. We have to be at your sister Meg's play early so I can do her make-up. In the meantime I will freshen up and cook up a good breakfast for you." Jane and Jack had stayed up late the night before and getting up wasn't easy. Jane's teacher had told her to look up 20 words in the dictionary for homework and Jack had been told to do 20 sit-ups by the football coach. Mother wouldn't let up. "I need to back up the car and go up to the gas station before we get to school. You've messed up the garage with all your stuff. There's no just way I can keep up with your carelessness. I just give up!"

Jane and Jack shouted down. "Loosen up, Mom. We don't want to hold you up. We'll be down in a minute, eat up our breakfast, gather up our stuff in the garage, help you fill up the gas tank, and sit up quietly in the car while you drive up to the school so you can make up Meg's face for the play."

"Thank you, kids. I am sorry I acted up this way. I know that sometimes I have to face up to how I behave. You have cheered me up and raised up my spirits. But you still have to get up, dress up, and hurry up or better yet, hurry down."

Figure 8.4 Taxonomy of Two-Part Verbs Using *OUT, BY,* and *DOWN*

Here are verbs that have a change in meaning when the words *out, by, or down* are added, as in *break out* compared to *break.* Add others as you hear them or find them in your reading. Then write a letter to a friend using as many of these two-part verbs as you can.

• TAXONOMY •

	OUT	BY	DOWN
A	act out		
B	break out	bring by	break down
C	call out	come by	come down
D	dig out	drive by	drop down
E	edge out	edge by	
F	force out	fly by	feel down
G	get out	get by	get down
H	hold out, hang out	hang by	hold down
I			
J	jut out		jump down
K	keep out		keep down
L	leave out		let down
M	miss out		mark down
N			
O			
P	pass out, print out	pass by	pass down
Q			quiet down
R	rule out	ride by	run down
S	stand out, sing out	stand by	simmer down, settle down
T	take out		take down, tone down
U			
V			
W	wait out	wait by	water down
X			
Y	yell out		
Z	zoom out	zoom by	

Figure 8.5   Prepositions Get You Located

The first four prepositions shown here illustrate a destination or position. Add your own destination or position to the other prepositions.

• TAXONOMY •

Preposition	Destination, Position, Space
at	at the lake
around	around the corner
alongside	alongside my friend
away from	away from the water
by	
behind	
before	
down	
from	
in	
inside	
into	
on	
over	
off	
out of	
under	

Conjunctions—Words to Connect

Once students move from spoken language to written language, the use of appropriate conjunctions becomes essential to expressing ideas coherently and sequentially. One function of conjunctions is to connect nouns, verbs, adjectives, and adverbs, as in "The girls *and* the boys were *with* their kind *and* helpful teacher who told them they could *either* read *or* write quietly."

The italicized words are called coordinating conjunctions, and most speakers of English can easily use them. However, there is the more complex group of coordinating conjunctions that join two parts of a sentence to relate sequence, alternatives, or contrast. These words are *or, while, but,* and *neither . . . nor.* They seem simple, yet they can often be complicated for students to use in writing, as in the following examples:

We are not sure if we will have rain *or* snow.

He will not go to the picnic, *nor* will he go to the movies.

The younger children drew pictures, *while* the older children studied their math.

Some people learn a second language easily, *but* others have difficulty.

Neither the soldiers *nor* the police could control the riots.

Students who seem to be limited to writing in "short, choppy, sentences" can benefit by composing sentences using a variety of conjunctions that sequence, express alternatives, and use contrast as a preliminary means of improving their writing. Figure 8.6 is an example of an activity for using *coordinating conjunctions,* followed by an explanation of words that are commonly called *subordinating conjunctions.* You will find a student activity in Figure 8.7.

Figure 8.6   Upgrade Your Sentences by Using Coordinating Conjunctions

---

Rewrite the following paragraph using the listed coordinating conjunctions to improve your writing. Coordinating conjunctions can join two sentences that are closely related. When you have finished rewriting your paragraph, read it aloud to a classmate. Then write your own paragraph using the same coordinating conjunctions.

Coordinating conjunctions

either . . . or, nor, while, but, neither . . . nor

Paragraph

I was standing in the garden. My friend Amy was inside painting. I was not interested in painting. I did not want to be inside. I felt like smelling the flowers. I thought about planting new flowers. But I did not want to go inside. Amy did not want to stop painting.

Figure 8.7   Upgrade Your Sentences Using Subordinating Conjunctions

---

Subordinating conjunctions include words such as

until, where, if, though, in order to, because

These conjunctions join two closely related ideas into one sentence: *until, where, if, even though, in order to, because.* Complete each starting sentence in your own words. Then write your own sentences that use the same subordinating conjunctions following the same model.

I played soccer with my friends **until** my mother _____.

Give me your address so I'll know **where** _____.

We'll have to cancel the party **if** _____.

We still went shopping **even though** _____.

The students worked very hard all year **in order to** _____.

I missed the celebration **because** _____.

Transitions—Words to Guide the Audience

Many words in the English language defy easy classification as a "part of speech." Students do not necessarily need to classify them to use them. One group of these words is commonly called transitions, which is a semantic, rather than syntactic, organizer. Transition words do just what the word *transition* means—move one idea or sentence to the next. Teachers know the importance of these words (*since, however, nevertheless, first, second,* and so forth) and teach their students to use them in their writing.

Transition words serve as a road map for the reader. So rather than attempting to decide which "part of speech" the words fit, in Figure 8.8 we have organized them by time, contrast or opposition, frequency, order or rank, result or outcome, and "other." These categories are not rigid, but by separating them semantically you can offer your students an organizational schema for using these powerful words effectively in their writing. You and your students may add other categories.

Figure 8.8 Transition Words Semantically Organized (Add Others)

Use these transition words in your writing to help your audience follow and clearly understand your ideas. Following the chart are model paragraphs using these transition words. Use these models to write similar paragraphs of your own.

Time	Contrast, Compare, or Oppose	Frequency	Order or Rank	Result or Outcome	Other
as soon as	although	frequently	above all	consequently	naturally
by and by	however	generally	first	despite	perhaps
during	meanwhile	often	finally	furthermore	quickly
eventually	nevertheless	occasionally	following that	moreover	quietly
immediately	otherwise	rarely	last	therefore	scarcely
just	since	usually	second		
lately	similarly				
suddenly	though				
while	yet				

Read the following paragraph. Then write your own paragraph using the transition words from any of the categories shown in the chart.

Transition Words Expressing Time

As soon as I walked into the room, I knew I was in for a surprise. **Immediately** I could sense that there was going to be a celebration. I waited patiently. **Eventually** every one from my family entered the room. **By and by,** all of my aunts, uncles, and cousins, as well as my parents and siblings, had arrived. **During** this whole time, I waited impatiently to find out why everyone was here. **Just** as I was about to explode from waiting, my best friend, who had been living in China for 10 years, opened the door and screamed "surprise!"

Determiners

This is a term that has traditionally been left out of the parts of speech lexicon in grammar books, yet is fully explained and detailed in the works of prominent linguists and language experts (Allen, 1972; Crystal, 2006b; McArthur, 1992; Pinker, 1999).

Words that express numbers (*one, two, three,* etc.) or indicate amounts (*each, every, several, many,* etc.) have been classified as adjectives even though they do not *describe* or even compare. They state amounts or they count. They are words that *determine* singular or plural (*one* dog, *two* dogs; *each* child, *all* children; *this* friend, *these* friends). They precede adjectives (*many* beautiful homes; a *few* good people).

The words *the* and *a* or *an* are determiners, with the word *a* determining singular and the word *the* being the only determiner that has evolved into determining both singular and plural. The words that are traditionally called possessive pronouns are determiners (*my* book, *their* books). Many of the mathematical words are determiners (*half* as many, *twice* as much, *few, least, more*). By classifying these words as determiners, you eliminate using the more cumbersome and often inaccurate terms such as *demonstrative* and *possessive* pronouns; you don't have to think about articles, and more importantly, you are separating determiners from adjectives. Figure 8.9 provides an arrangement of determiners and a student activity.

Figure 8.9   Determiners for Singular and Plural

This category of words, called *determiners*, determines if the word or words that follow are singular (one) or plural (more than one). Some determiners can be used for both singular and plural. Use these words to write a story that includes as many of these determiners as you can. Following the chart is an example for you to follow.

Definite Amounts	Indefinite Amounts (Singular and Plural)	This and That	Mine, Yours, and Whose
one	all	this	my, mine
two	any	that	his
three	none	those	her, hers
(and all other cardinal numbers)	each	these	your, yours
first	every		our, ours
second	enough		their, theirs
third	either		whose
(and all other ordinal numbers)	neither		which
double	some		what
triple	many		
half	most		
a quarter of	much		
	few		
	least		
	lots (of)		

Write With Determiners: Almost everything you write contains words classified as determiners. Here is a model story using determiners from each of the groups in the previous chart. Read this story; then write your own story using as many determiners as you can.

One fine day, my **three** best friends and I decided that **each** of us would have **a triple** ice cream soda. **None** of us, though, had **enough** money so we agreed that **all** of us **four** friends would help mow **each** other's lawns and earn **some** money. **All** of **our** parents agreed to **this** idea. In **a few** days, we had **more** money than we needed. So we invited **our** siblings and **every one** of us had **lots of** fun.

The "wh-" Words Plus *How*

The words *who, what, where, when, why,* and its related member *how* constitute a group traditionally called *interrogative pronouns* or "question" words, as in "*Where* are you going?". They are also called *relative pronouns,* as in the construction, "We saw the person *who* wrote the book." Students are not likely to have trouble constructing sentences that use these words to start a question. However, they can be troublesome as "relative pronouns" and very troublesome when asked to make a distinction between who and whom (Is this the party to whom I am speaking?). More difficult yet are the words *whoever, whomever,* and *whomsoever,* of which the last two are almost obsolete. This group of words, often called "wh-" words, also serve as linking words, as shown in Figure 8.10. Students for whom English is a second language often struggle in using some of these wh- words.

Figure 8.10   Use "wh-" Words as Linking Words

When you use wh- words (words that start with wh-) and the word *how* in the middle of a sentence, you are actually putting together two sentences into one sentence. You may know how to do this if you have learned a "deep structure rule." See how this works.

Step 1. Someone has asked a question:

Who is the leader?

Step 2. You think you know the answer, so you might say:

I know who is the leader.

Or you might also say:

I know who the leader is.

Notice that you started with your own sentence, which is "I know." Then you take the question sentence and you add it to "I know." You have now combined two sentences into one sentence through the linking word *who.* And it was probably easy to do, but just to be sure here is some practice with using wh- words for linking two sentences (or ideas) into one sentence.

Linking With "wh-" Words

Here are five wh- words plus the word *how* in starter sentences. Complete each starter, which should be about one famous person. Then share this information with a classmate, and ask your classmate to share her or his information. You can use the Internet to get the information you need. If all of your classmates complete these sentences, your class will have a lot to share about well-known people.

I know **who** _____.

I know **what** _____.

I know **when** _____.

I know **where** _____.

I know **why** _____.

I know **how** _____.

Here is an example of the completed sentences:

I know **who** invented the electric light bulb.

I know **what** the inventor of the light bulb knew about electricity.

I know **when** the light bulb was invented.

I know **where** the inventor lived and worked.

I know **how** he was able to invent this bulb.

In Figure 8.11, we show these words in simple sentences where they serve to link what would be perceived as two sentences into one sentence, hence the word *relative*, meaning *related*. By having your students link two parts of a sentence in the activity that follows, they are using conjunctions or "joiners."

Figure 8.11   *Who?* or *Whom?*

You probably use the word *who* almost every time you are having a conversation and don't even bother to think about using it. But then there is the word *whom*, which is related to *who*, but used differently. Here is an activity that will help you use the word *whom* should you need to use it either in speaking or writing. The first one is done as an example. Rewrite the other sentences using *whom*. What do you think is the difference in using *who* or *whom?*

WHO as you usually hear it or say it	*WHOM* as you might write it or wish to say it	Answer with *WHO* or *WHOM* or both
1. Who did you call?	Whom did you call?	I called my friend who I knew for many years. Or I called my friend whom I had known for many years.
2. Who did you give the book to?		
3. Who did you stay with?		
4. Who are you speaking about?		
5. Who do you need to help?		

English speakers rely on these words to ask questions; point out people, places, and objects; make exclamations; and, as we stated before, link ideas. Classifying by parts of speech is tricky and frequently unnecessary. But students often are puzzled when they are "corrected" or told to use or not use these words in certain constructions.

For example, students are commonly uncertain about using *who* and *whom*. In traditional grammar, the word *who* has been called a nominative pronoun and its "morphological buddy," *whom*, is the objective pronoun. We have the constructions "Who is in the room?" and "To whom did you give the book?" The use of *who* in the first sentence is the expected construction for all English speakers.

But what about the second sentence? Many of us are likely to hear "Who did you give the book to?" What do we tell our students? Is there an important or even an unimportant distinction? Many of us are likely to think of one construction as informal and the other as formal or academic. Or we can just ignore the question and say what we think "sounds right."

However, you might want to or need to present this distinction because it is still a part of the English language.

The Words Called *Modals—Can/Could, Will/Would, Shall/Should, May/Might/Must, Need, Dare*

The Oxford Companion to the English Language (McArthur, 1992) calls these words *modal* verbs, and morphologically they are verbs that (1) no longer have or use all the conjugational forms of the English verb, and (2) *now* function differently from conventional verbs. By keeping in mind that language changes, we *must* or *should* or *need* to also change our categorization of words and usage. By checking these words in the *Random House Webster's Unabridged Dictionary* (2000), we find the original verb structure of *can, will, shall,* and *may* as words that have a conjugation with two tense forms, present and past, as defined in Chapter 4.

Figure 8.12 illustrates their original structure, and for those of you who teach Shakespeare, there will be immediate recognition of these forms. You might want to share this chart with your students.

Figure 8.12   *Can, Will, Shall, May*—All You Need to Know

Can	Will	Shall	May
can (base present)	will (base present)	shall (base present)	may (base present)
canst (thou)	wilt (thou)	shalt (thou)	mayest (thou)
can (you, we, etc.)	will (you, we, etc.)	shall (you, we, etc.)	may (you, we, etc.)
cunning (we are)	willing (we are)	(no -ing form)	(no -ing form)
couldst (thou past)	wouldst (thou past)	shouldst (thou past)	mayst (thou past)
could (past)	would (past)	should (past)	might (past)

As you can see in Figure 8.12, these modal verbs, over time, became "reduced" or leveled to have just present and past tenses (which are the only tenses in English). They are used to express tentativeness (I might), possibility (I could), command (I should), willingness (I would), and other "conditional" behaviors, which is why these words have often been labeled *conditional*. In addition, there are the verbs *need* and *dare*, which still follow the standard conjugations of English (*need, needs, needing, needed; dare, dares, daring, dared*) but are often used to express tentativeness, possibility, command, or willingness. Examples of this usage occur in statements such as the following: (1) "I need to remember to take my ticket." (2) "Dare we make this attempt?"

Another feature of modal verbs is their formation of contractions. All of them can join with *not* as in *can't, couldn't, won't, wouldn't, shan't, shouldn't, mightn't, needn't, daren't*. Several of these contractions may sound archaic or perhaps "British," but they all carry this feature of contracting.

Finally, the word *will* has taken on various meanings or functions. In its base form, *will* can mean "to offer," as in "I will this to you." By adding -ing, the word comes to mean *volition*, as in "I am willing to do this." But its most widespread use is as a marker of what we think of as the future, which is why students are taught that English has three tenses—past, present, and future. Structurally, however, English uses the word *will* + *present* to express the future, as in "I will stop." Both verbs (will and stop) are in the present tense to refer to future time. Similarly, to express future, we can say "I am going to stop," where *going* has no tense and *stop* is still in the present.

Figure 8.13 presents activities for students that illustrate the structure and usage of the modal verbs *shall/should, can/could, may/might, need,* and *dare*. Students in previous

Figure 8.13   Use the Modal Verbs *Can/Could, Shall/Should, Will/Would, May/Might,* Plus *Need* and *Dare*

You probably use these words dozens of times each day in your speech without ever having to think about how or why you are using them. They are just a common part of everyday English. However, these words, which are a special kind of verb called *modal* verbs, express the following:

1. Being possible or not possible as in *could.*
2. Being required to do as in *should* or *need.*
3. Being willing to do as in *would.*
4. Being tentative or not sure as in *might* or *dare.*

Complete each starter with your own ending.

I could get high grades _____.

My teacher said we should _____.

I would be happy _____.

We might have to _____.

My parents said I need to _____.

He didn't dare _____.

Now use the contraction or negative of these words by completing the starters.

I couldn't get high grades _____.

My mother said we shouldn't _____.

I wouldn't be happy _____.

We might not have to _____.

The teacher said we needn't _____.

You dare not _____.

This time use the "paired forms" of these modal verbs by completing the question starters.

Can you _____?

Could you _____?

Shall I _____?

Should I _____?

Will we _____?

Would we _____?

May I _____?

Might I _____?

Here are more uses of the word *dare. Dare* can be used in many constructions and in all its verb forms. Complete each of these starters in your own words.

You wouldn't dare _____!

How dare you _____!

I dare not talk about _____.

I dare you to _____.

She dared her opponent to _____.

Daring everyone in the audience, the trapeze artist _____.

generations were taught to make a distinction between *shall* and *will,* as well as between *can* and *may.* These distinctions are not in use in American speech, and they are becoming less common in British speech as well. The traditional rule of usage dates from the 17th century and says that to denote future time, *shall* is to be used in the first person (*I shall leave. We shall go.*) and *will* in all other persons (*You will be there, won't you?*). Whether this rule was ever widely observed is doubtful. Today, *will* is used overwhelmingly and in all types of speech and writing, though we do find it in some specialized situations, such as "I shall return," "We shall overcome," and in the language of laws and directives: "All visitors shall observe posted regulations" (adapted from the *Random House Webster's Unabridged Dictionary,* 2000).

Similarly, the distinction between *can* as in "Can I leave the room?" in contrast to *may* as in "May I leave the room?" has become fairly obsolete. However, the word *may* continues to have its own uses as in these sentences:

- It may rain.
- You may enter.
- I may be wrong.
- Times may change.
- May you live to an old age.

The words *need* and *dare* are also part of the spoken speech of students, as in "I need some water" or "I dare you to beat me." However, they have some specialized uses, which you can point out to your students that can "upgrade" their written syntax.

INTERNET SITES

- http://grammar.ccc.commnet.edu/grammar/prepositions.htm

  An excellent extension for understanding prepositions and nonprepositions with good follow-up activities.

- http://www.cuw.edu/Tools/resources/lrc/writing_center/pdfs/could_would_should.pdf

  This Web site provides accurate detailed information that students might find interesting and helpful.

CHAPTER NINE

Introduction

Language and
Metalanguage

Builders of
Linguistic
Intelligence

Parts of
Speech and the
English Language

Syntax and
Semantics

The Polyglot
of English

The Polyglot:
Beyond Latin
and Greek

Return to Parts
of Speech

**Sentences,
Paragraphs, and
Other Structures
of the Written
Language**

Grammar for
Word Play

Reading, Writing,
and Grammar

Punctuation,
Spelling, Text
Messaging, and
Other
Consequences of
Grammar

Additional
Learning
Activities

Sentences, Paragraphs, and Other Structures of the Written Language

Language was made before grammar, not grammar before language.

(Thomas Hardy, cited in McWhorter, 1998, p. 86)

The race is not to the swift, but to the verbal.

(Pinker, 1994, p. 3)

In Chapter 5, "Syntax and Semantics," we discussed aspects of sentences that have often been given short shrift in traditional grammar, which has focused mainly on the concept that a sentence is "a complete thought," with little attention to the many different kinds of sentences (Allen, 1972; Crystal, 2006a). Even when different *kinds of sentences* are presented to students, these sentences are likely to be characterized as declarative, interrogative, or imperative or simple, compound, or complex. In addition, there are terms such as coordinate, subordinate, clauses, phrases, gerunds, participles (past and present), and others; which are of Latinate origin, and while they describe Latin fairly accurately, they often miss the mark for English. So what are teachers to do?

Our focus here is on the distinction between spoken sentences and written sentences, since this distinction is generally the basis of classroom instruction.

141

Almost always, spoken sentences are different from written sentences. Speech flows, in the words of Hamlet, "tripplingly on the tongue," whereas writing requires more reflection, revision, and polishing. Spoken sentences are necessary to human communication; written sentences occur only in literate societies and are produced in quantity only by a portion of those who are literate.

The joy of spoken sentences is that they do not require *punctuation;* the voice does the work. They do not require *paragraphing;* each person just responds and even interrupts; topic sentences are not necessary. They do not always follow the *rules* of written sentences; we split infinitives, substitute adjectives for adverbs, leave out subjects or predicates, use our voice to ask a question, and so forth.

Because of this distinction, this chapter focuses predominantly on how to help students better understand the "grammar of writing" in contrast to the "grammar of speaking." We also hope that they will find that these aspects of grammar are lively and meaningful. We have drawn from David Crystal's (1995) magnificent discussion in the chapter "The Structure of Sentences" in *The Cambridge Encyclopedia of the English Language*, as well as Pinker's *Words and Rules* (1999), to create these activities, and recommend that you go to these sources for an in-depth understanding of this topic, delightfully written by both authors.

CONVERTING SPOKEN SENTENCES TO WRITTEN SENTENCES

Crystal refers to two types of sentences, which he terms *major sentences* and *minor sentences* (1995, p. 216). Major sentences are the constructions we are likely to read in expositions or nonfiction writing and generally follow the *rules* of having a noticeable subject (noun, noun phrase, noun clause, pronoun), a predicate by which we mean a verb, and other parts of sentences that are known as objects (direct or indirect). Minor sentences are likely to be used in conversation, fiction, plays, e-mails, and notices such as labels, headlines, advertising, and similar formats. For simplicity for your students, you can use the terms *spoken* and *written,* although you may wish to expand on these terms and introduce *major* and *minor.*

WORKING WITH SENTENCE UNITS

Teachers have often told students that they have written an "incomplete" sentence, a term that can be puzzling if a sentence means a *complete* thought and someone has written an *incomplete* thought. However, by thinking of a sentence as any grammatical unit that conveys meaning to speaker and audience, we can help our students move more easily from the spoken to the written constructions. Begin with Figure 9.1, Converting Spoken Sentences to Written Sentences, so that students see these distinctions between spoken and written. Figure 9.2 has examples for students to change phrases (word groups that generally do not have a verb) and clauses (word groups generally with a verb) into written sentences. Point out to your students that phrases or clauses, which can be called "sentence units," do not normally get punctuated, although that *rule* is often ignored, as we have seen in headlines, directions, dialogues, and other structures.

Figure 9.1   Converting Spoken Sentences to Written Sentences

Directions: Here are 10 "sentences" that you may have heard or read on signs or posters. You may not think of them as sentences, but when you hear them or read them, you probably convert them to sentences in your head. For example, when you see the words BUS STOP, you are likely to think, "Here is the place where I get the bus." Some linguists or language specialists call these word constructions *spoken* or *minor* sentences. Change these spoken or minor sentences into *written* or *major* sentences. The first one has been done as an example. When you have finished this activity, collect other examples of minor sentences and convert them to major sentences.

Spoken or Minor Sentence	Written or Major Sentence
1. Exit	That's the **exit** I'm looking for.
2. Maple avenue	
3. No parking	
4. Entrance to the right	
5. Open 24 hours	
6. Free samples	
7. Closed till further notice	
8. Winner of 10 awards	
9. Flight cancelled	
10. 50% Off	

Figure 9.2   Working With Sentence Units (Sometimes Called Phrases, Clauses, or Simply "Fragments")

Directions: Here are 10 "sentence units" that you may have heard. Some of these units are called phrases and usually will not have a verb. Other units are called clauses and they do have a verb. Write a sentence in which you use or incorporate these units. You will have to start with a capital letter and end with punctuation—a period, a question mark, or an exclamation mark. The first one has been done as an example.

Phrases	Clauses	Punctuated Sentences
1. just in case		**Just in case** we had unexpected company, my family always had extra food.
2. for several minutes		
3. by the light of the moon		
4. six frightened puppies		
5. during the movie		
	1. whenever I have a test	
	2. the last time she saw her friend	
	3. by the time the rain stopped	
	4. who never stops talking	
	5. sitting in the park	

FINDING SENTENCE BOUNDARIES IN WRITTEN SENTENCES

When we speak we punctuate with our voices. However, when we write we must use punctuation marks as a courtesy or guide to the readers. Not only must students remember initial capital letters, but periods, question marks, commas, semicolons, colons, and exclamation marks. The rules of these writing "conventions" can be troublesome and elusive because they have been developed over time by humans in contrast to being a natural part of language. Furthermore, the boundaries of written sentences are often perceived differently by speakers of different languages. Anyone who has read French literature or French newspapers immediately becomes aware of what English teachers call *run-ons*. In French writing, the comma or the *virgule* is the sentence boundary of choice, and the period or *point* seems to come when the writer is exhausted from stringing an endless number of *sentences* together. Spanish writers, on the other hand, are very considerate when they place an upside down question mark (¿) or exclamation mark preceding an interrogative or exclamatory sentence to clue the reader.

In Figure 9.3 we present an unpunctuated text for students to punctuate. Chances are you will get a variety of responses from students of all ages. Use their responses for a discussion of why they chose the boundaries they did and whether they might have made other choices.

Figure 9.3   Find the Sentence Boundaries

Directions: The following story is written without any punctuation—no capital letters, commas, periods, or question marks. Read the story with a colored pen or pencil in hand and put in the punctuation you think you need. Then meet with a classmate and share your information, explaining your reasons for the punctuation you used.

in 1963 toni morrison won the nobel prize for literature she was awarded this prize for her books song of solomon tar baby and jazz toni morrison is an african american woman who grew up in the south she did not begin writing until she attended howard university and was working as a book editor for random house her first book was the bluest eye in 1970 after she had written many more books she left her job at random house and began to teach at the state university of new york at albany toni morrison is a powerful voice for not only african american women but for all women and all humanity

---

"DECONSTRUCTING" SENTENCES TO FIND THEIR DEEP STRUCTURE MEANING

In the 1960s, Noam Chomsky coined the terms "surface structure" and "deep structure" in his seminal analysis of grammar (1957). By these terms, he meant that what we say or the way say it is only the surface of what we mean. Underlying the words and the sentence structure carrying these words is a much deeper meaning than is stated by the actual words, as illustrated in the Speaker-Listener dialogue that follows.

Speaker	*Listener*
I am speaking to you.	I know (maybe).
I have something you can see.	I see it (or I don't see it).
It can't stay out.	I understand (or I don't).
It must be put in a place other than where it is now.	Where should I put it?

Chomsky (1957) calls this ability to understand "transformational," meaning that both the speaker and the listener transform the surface meanings. Steven Pinker, a linguist strongly influenced by Chomsky, explains the reason why surface structure has the appearance of simplicity, but carries within it deep meaning. He says "our thoughts are surely more complex [than syntax] and we are limited by a mouth that can pronounce a single word at a time. [We use our brains] to convey complex thoughts as words and their orderings" (1994, p. 117).

By understanding the distinction between surface structure and deep structure, we can help students develop comprehension skills, particularly when they are faced with sentences that have complicated or embedded constructions. For example, here are two sentences taken from a middle school social studies book written for students who are not reading up to grade-level expectations.

> When Thomas Jefferson became President, the western boundary of the United States was the Mississippi River. The region west of the Mississippi was under the control of Spain. (*United States History*, 2004, p. 104)

Aside from the need to know the geography and the time period being referred to, the student (reader) must internally and rapidly *translate* these *two* sentences into the following deep structure sentences (words in quotations indicate a reader's possible underlying ideas or thoughts). Here are the possible thoughts of a "deep structure" reader:

Text—Thomas Jefferson was President of the United States.

Deep structure thought—"I'm not sure when he was President."

Text—The United States had a western boundary called the Mississippi River.

Deep structure thought—"So the boundary is not land."

Text—To the west of the Mississippi was a region that was still unexplored.

Deep structure thought—"A region must be a type of land."

Text—The region was under the control of Spain.

Deep structure thought—"Spain must be something. Spain must be someplace. The word *under* must mean something. I don't think that *under* is the opposite of *over*."

Of course, when we have students read this type of text, we assume a certain amount of prior knowledge, which may or may not exist, and we also depend on our being able to explain to the students the deep or underlying meaning of these seemingly simple two sentences. By having some understanding of surface and deep structure, we can use syntactic strategies that can help our students comprehend better.

In Figure 9.4 we present a student activity relating surface structure with deep structure to make students aware of how they can comprehend sentences that may be more complex than their words.

Figure 9.4 What Does This Sentence REALLY Mean?

Directions: Many times you read a sentence and wonder what the writer of that sentence means. You may understand all or most of the words, yet you're still not sure of the meaning. Here are six sentences that appear simple on the surface. But what lies beneath their words? See if you can find the deep structure of these sentences so their meaning is totally clear. You might want to work with a partner so you can really go "deep." The first one has been done to get you started.

Surface Structure	Deep Structure
1. Just listen.	I'm not supposed to say anything while the person is talking.
2. That's what friends are for.	
3. Never mind the rain.	
4. I'd rather be in school.	
5. What a joke!	
6. My mother never forgets.	

SUBJECTS AND PREDICATES

Everyone who has been exposed to traditional grammar instruction learned that a sentence must have a subject and a predicate and that one way to make this determination is to underline the subject once and the predicate twice. Many of us also were told that the subject tells what the sentence is about and the predicate is the action. We were then likely to be given examples of sentences that proved these dictums.

As we have already stated, subjects and predicates, one of the mainstays of traditional grammar, has not always been clear to students and for good reason. Many types of "complete sentences" could not be presented to the students because, while they were complete, they did not follow the rules of the subject being what the sentence was about or the predicate being the action. Or their structure required some *excuse*. For example, we might have been told that there are special kinds of sentences where the "subject is *you*, which is understood." These sentences are called *imperatives* because they give a command and the listener/reader *understands* who the subject is. We were to imagine that the subject "you" existed. We were then given examples:

Run.

Go home.

Eat your vegetables.

Then there were the sentences that defied having a subject that was about anything or having a predicate that showed any action, as in the following:

It is raining.

Here are the apples.

There were six people in the room.

Sometimes we remember being told that these types of sentences were "exceptions," yet that answer was puzzling since we use these constructions constantly and in abundance. Once again, we refer to the concept of deep structure. When we hear sentences that begin with *it, here,* or *there,* our brains quickly (luckily) convert these statements to their deeper meanings. In the sentence "it rains," we know that *rain is falling!*

Figure 9.5 presents a student activity relating deep structure to surface structure by converting the "subject-predicate" construction into the shortened forms that don't have an obvious "subject."

Figure 9.5   Go From Deep Structure to Surface Structure

Directions: In the column labeled "Deep Structure," there are six sentences which can be shortened or reduced and still convey the same meaning. Rewrite each sentence in a shorter form or as a "Surface Structure." The first three sentences have been done for you. What changes do you make when you go from deep structure to surface structure? Why do you think you can understand surface structure?

Deep Structure	Surface Structure
1. The snow has been falling since morning.	1. It's been snowing all day.
2. We need to leave immediately.	2. Let's go now.
3. You can eat all the food you wish.	3. Help yourself.
4. You have to stop making so much noise.	
5. You should complete your homework before dinner.	
6. I hope you enjoy yourself from sunup to sundown.	
7. You can open the door and enter.	
8. I know you are thirsty.	
9. I would like you to stay.	
10. You must be tired from standing.	

TENSES AND AGREEMENT

A major frustration for teachers (and writers too) is the concept of tense and its use in written and expanded sentences. One problem is that tense, a grammatical term, is often confused with time, a phenomenon of nature. For example, as we've discussed before, English only has two tenses: present and past. Yet with this *simple* verb system, we can express an infinite range of time from the distant past to the unforeseen future. Unlike Latin, French, Spanish, Italian, Portuguese, and many other languages, English is reduced to "Today I walk and yesterday I walked." (For further confirmation of this concept, see Crystal, 1995, p. 224.) However, we are able express all the time we need using just four forms of the verb:

- *Thousands of years ago people walked* across the land bridge from Siberia to the North American continent. (past tense/past time)
- This morning I *was walking* down the path and this afternoon I *will be walking* back. (past time/was + -ing; future time/will + -ing)
- When I was young, I could *walk* great distances. (Past time/present tense)

Experienced writers recognize this distinction between tense and time and craft their writing by using the two-tense system of English that expresses time, as all of us must do. You will notice in the selections that follow, taken from children's literature, that all the verbs are either past, present, or -ing (which derives its tense from the "be" verb, a feature that doesn't exist in Latin.) Unlike French (or other Latin-based languages), English has no specific verbs for past perfect, imperfect, pluperfect, future, future perfect, historic past, subjunctive, conditional past, conditional future, and so forth. However, English can express time with its verbs and time-based words, as in these examples, with the verbs bolded for present and italicized for past. You might notice that "would" in the third selection is not conditional, but more like the future that is normally expressed by the word "will."

"I **know**"—she *was* getting excited—"it could **be** a magic country like Narnia, and the only way you *could* **get** in **is** by swinging across on this enchanted rope." Her eyes *were* bright. She *grabbed* the rope. "**Come** on," she *said*. **Let**'s **find** a place to **build** our castle stronghold." (From *Bridge to Terabithia*, Katherine Paterson, 1977, p. 50)

or

Stanley *got dressed*. The clothes *smelled* like soap.

Mr. Sir *told* him he *should* **wear** one set to **work** in and one set for relaxation. Laundry *was done* every three days. On that day his work clothes *would* be *washed*. Then the other set would **become** his work clothes, and he would **get** clean clothes to **wear** while resting. (From *Holes* by Louis Sachar, 1998, p. 13)

Perhaps you're thinking that "build" in the first selection and "wear" in the last sentence of the third selection are infinitives and therefore not part of the tense system. Once again, we must look at English as English and not as Latin and its derivative languages. In Latin-based languages, the infinitive is one word (*parler*—to speak in French; *comer*—to eat in Spanish; *scrivere*—to write in Italian). We can now see why English-speaking students were told to *not split* an infinitive! This difference between English and Latin means that English has no true infinitive, but a structure that mimics an infinitive and is combined with *to + present* or base (Allen, 1972; Crystal, 2006a; Pinker, 1999).

Figure 9.6 presents an activity which illustrates the two-tense system of English, followed by Figure 9.7, which presents some of the -ly adverbs that are likely to "split infinitives."

Figure 9.6   Write About Past, Present, and Future *Time* Using Two *Tenses*—Past and Present

---

Directions: Here are 10 words or phrases that "express time" in English, followed by the four forms of five verbs. Construct five sentences using words or phrases of time and any of the four forms of the verb. You will notice that the verbs are either in the past or present tense, while the other words or phrases can be used to tell the "time." The time words are in italics and the bolded words are the verbs. Here is a sample sentence to get you started. What do you notice about past, present, and future?

Last night as the sun **was setting**, I told my friends that *tomorrow* I **was going** to **build** a tree house where we **will** all **be** able to **play** make-believe games that **will expand** our imagination and **provide** us with hours of fun for *years* to **come**.

Words That Express Time	Five Verb Conjugations	Sentences With Words of Time and Verbs in the Past, Present, and -ing
as soon as by the time during the day early this evening for a long time in the next few weeks later this morning next summer someday time after time	decide decides deciding decided pretend pretends pretending pretended swim swims swimming swam buy buys buying bought visit visits visiting visited	1. 2. 3. 4. 5.

Figure 9.7   To Split or Not to Split

Directions: In the English language there is a construction which uses the word *to* before the verb as in *to sing, to add, to make,* and so forth and is called the *infinitive*. This infinitive or the *to +* *verb* construction of the English language is often used with an -ly adverb (e.g., frequently, magnificently, completely). Sometimes speakers and writers place the adverb between the word *to* and the verb as in "The student realized that *to completely finish* the task before dinner would give her time to relax later. "It's also possible to say " . . . *to finish the task completely."* It's the writer's choice. Here are six -ly adverbs and six verbs preceded by the word *to.* Construct three sentences in which you place an -ly adverb between the *to* and the verb, and three sentences in which you place the adverb after the *to + verb.* You can decide which arrangements you prefer.

(Continued)

Figure 9.7 (Continued)

-ly Adverbs	To + Verb	Sentences
absolutely	to walk	
brilliantly	to speak	
carefully	to drive	
energetically	to sing	
respectfully	to follow	
delightfully	to dance	

VERB AGREEMENT

A major concern with student writing is the problem of agreement between singular and plural and for good reason because of the English verb structure. As you know, all English verbs have the -s inflection as in *she eats, he sleeps, the dog barks.* Because the inflection -s can also mark the plural noun (dogs, boys, girls), students can have difficulty explaining the grammatical differences between the two uses of the symbol -s. We have *the dog barks; the dogs bark,* in which the second statement uses the verb inflection of -s and does not relate to plural. The other use of -s is as a noun inflection to indicate plural. This is not easy to explain. A second problem is the common construction using words that express *more than one* as one unit. For example, we have a *group of children* or *one group, but many children.* There is a *herd of horses* or *one herd with many horses.* A third problem is that the noun in a sentence can be separated by its verb with lots of other words in between, as in "the woman who lived on the top of the mountain with her dogs and cats and numerous other animals. . . ." Then there are the constructions that use a word such as *none* as in *none of us is right* when we'd like to say *none of us are right.* In Figure 9.8 there are five sentences with noun-verb combinations that can require deep thought.

Figure 9.8   *Making Your Nouns and Verbs Agree*

Directions: Here are five sentences that need either the base form of a verb or the -s form of the verb. The base form of a verb is the verb without any endings or inflections as in *walk, speak, jump, imagine.* The -s form is simply adding -s as in *walks, speaks, jumps, imagines,* and so forth. In writing a sentence, we use the term "agree" to mean what form of the verb must be used with which noun. Sometimes you may have to think twice before you know which verb form to use before you complete the sentence. Meet with a partner to make your decision.

Make Your Nouns and Verbs Agree

1. One of the girls in the room _____ the answer. (know/knows)
2. All of my friends from school _____ to the drama club. (belong/belongs)
3. In our school assembly, first the band members _____, then the director of our two singing groups _____, and finally the lead singer with two back-up singers _____. (enter/enters)
4. Everyday of our lives _____ (bring/brings) new adventures.
5. None of us in this class of 25 children _____ (has/have) special privileges.

THE PARAGRAPH

Many of us were told or taught that a paragraph must start with a topic sentence, or if we can't start with a topic sentence, then we must end with one. Another idea was that a paragraph should have a certain number of sentences—at least three but not more than five or six. Then, traditionally, paragraphs have to start with an indentation (in writing, of course!). Would that it were so easy.

Historically, the extensive use of paragraphs began with the advent of the printing press, when printers felt that the presentation of text was an essential aspect of writing. Forming paragraphs would make reading lengthy text easier, and indeed that seems to be the case. As stated by McArthur (1992, p. 749), "Paragraph construction is as much a matter of layout and visual balance as of content and visual relationship. . . ." For students to understand and then master this writing convention, they need to read and observe text structure, write extensive pieces of nonfiction, and reread, revise, and get a "second opinion" or more. Figures 9.9 and 9.10 provide activities that you can use as starting points for paragraph writing.

Figure 9.9   Divide Into Paragraphs

Directions: Here is a piece of text that appears very long to the eye. You might find it easier to read if you divide it into two or more paragraphs. Read the entire piece, then put in a paragraph mark (¶) where you think you need a break. Meet with a partner and discuss why you made the paragraph break or breaks where you did.

Birds need a safe place to lay their eggs. Most birds build their nests in trees and bushes, but some birds find unusual places such as chimneys, in gardens, and even in watering cans. Hummingbirds often use walnuts as their nests and hornbills build their nests in the hollow of a tree. The mallee fowl builds its nest on a huge mound of earth covered with plants. Birds build their nests from many different materials. Some birds build their nests with twigs and leaves. Other birds, like the tailorbird, use their beak as a needle and sew leaves together with strands of cobwebs. The village weaver bird makes a frame from branches and weaves leaves and grass strips to make its nest. All birds want their eggs to be safe so that they will hatch and there will be new baby birds.

Figure 9.10   Create Your Own Paragraph

Directions: Here are five sentences that need to be put into an order to make it a good paragraph for the reader. Read each sentence, then number the order that you think will work best. Compare your order with a classmate's.

> **Create Your Own Paragraph**—Put these sentences in the order you think will form a good paragraph.
>
> _____ The animals in these lakes and swamps had to find a way to survive the dry season.
>
> _____ Every year some of the lakes and swamps would begin to dry up.
>
> _____ Millions of years ago, a long period of droughts began.
>
> _____ They might completely dry out.
>
> _____ There would only be a few small pools and puddles.

THE GRAMMATICAL VOICE

The grammar we use often depends on our audience. The term for that differentiation of grammar is _voice_ and encompasses many terms or metalanguage. We speak of language that is formal and informal, academic, idiomatic, colloquial, slang, jargon, argot, patois, or dialect. Those of us fortunate enough to "become educated" can use all aspects, although we might choose to limit ourselves to only a few. But all of us recognize when we "switch codes," as when we prepare for an interview, deliver a talk, chat in the teacher's room, meet family members, hang out with friends, talk to children, send an e-mail, and so forth. Having a range of grammatical voices gives us linguistic and social power, allowing us to mingle, get jobs, read widely, and write more effectively. For students, developing a variety of "voices" is essential to their future.

In Figure 9.11 there are two letter-writing activities, one titled "Formal to Friendly" and the other "Friendly to Formal." The task for the student is to rewrite each letter and change its voice. Use this activity as a starting point for your students in learning how to "switch voices."

In the last chapter of this book (Chapter 13), we have added a variety of sentence and paragraph activities which you can use as is or adapt as needed. We have tried to make them lively, content-area oriented, and helpful in expanding both the spoken and written language of your students.

Figure 9.11 Go From "Formal to Friendly" and "Friendly to Formal"

Directions: Here are two different letters, each written in a different "voice." One is from Harriet Beecher Stowe, an abolitionist fighting slavery and a believer in women's rights who is writing to Susan B. Anthony. The letter by Harriet Beecher Stowe is probably too formal, since both women were working for the same causes and would probably be on very friendly terms. Rewrite Ms. Stowe's letter to Ms. Anthony letter in a much friendlier or informal style.

June 1873

Dear Ms. Anthony:

We have recently received the news that you have been placed on trial for attempting to vote and for advocating the rights of women's suffrage in national and state elections. Your cause is indeed noble, but as you are undoubtedly aware, the political establishment is totally opposed to any such legislation. However, you have my complete support for your endeavors and rest assured that I and my colleagues will do all in our power to prevent any action taken that will dispute your innocence.

Most cordially,

Harriet Beecher Stowe

Now rewrite this informal note to John Adams from Edmund Burke, a member of Parliament in England, just before the start of the American Revolution.

May 1773

Dear John:

I've just heard that a bunch of you in the Colonies are hopping mad over the tea tax. I can understand your feelings, but thinking about dumping tea in the harbor won't get you anywhere. You know George (our king) just isn't that smart, but he'll back down. In a couple of years, he'll forget the tax, which isn't much anyway. In the meantime, switch to coffee. Let me hear from you by the next packet steamer from Boston to London. Give my best to the wife and kids.

Regards,

Ed

INTERNET SITES

- http://books.google.com/books?id=4DwjAAAAMAAJ&dq=history+of+ paragraphs&printsec=frontcover&source=web&ots=ul0Q9xCpRw&sig=e_7z pVUXFlLkrYAhwq8an7WHJbY#PPA5,M1

  This is an 1894 dissertation about the paragraph from the University of Chicago, and it is fascinating.

- http://englishplus.com/news/news0300.htm

  This is the history of English grammar rules that found their way into school textbooks and who made up these rules and why.

Introduction

*Language and
Metalanguage*

*Builders of
Linguistic
Intelligence*

*Parts of
Speech and the
English Language*

*Syntax and
Semantics*

*The Polyglot
of English*

*The Polyglot:
Beyond Latin
and Greek*

*Return to Parts
of Speech*

*Sentences,
Paragraphs, and
Other Structures of
the Written
Language*

**Grammar for
Word Play**

*Reading, Writing,
and Grammar*

*Punctuation,
Spelling, Text
Messaging, and
Other
Consequences of
Grammar*

*Additional
Learning Activities*

CHAPTER TEN

Grammar for Word Play

MAKING GRAMMAR REALLY FUN

*You have committed the following crimes . . sowing confusion, upsetting
the applecart, wreaking havoc, and mincing words.*

(from the police officer Short Shrift in
The Phantom Tollbooth, Juster, 1989, p. 62)

*"Mine is a long and sad tale!" said the Mouse turning to Alice and
sighing. "It is a long tail, certainly," said Alice, looking down with
wonder at the Mouse's tail; "but why do you call it sad?"*

(from *Alice's Adventures in
Wonderland*, Carroll, 1861/1995b, p. 30)

Playing with words is fun. That's why we do it. But it is also more than
fun. Word play gives joy to language, making us laugh and making us think.
Word play is the gift we get from language that allows us to tell jokes, describe
people and events succinctly, feel included in a conversation, and smile,
chuckle, grin, and guffaw. This chapter offers word-play activities that
students will enjoy while gaining deeper meanings from words and sentences.
All of these word-play activities help students reflect on the meanings, the
humor, and the etymology of these terms and offer opportunities for class discussion, illustration, and lots of joyful writing. We include the following:

- metaphors, similes, and idioms
- oxymora
- eponyms
- colorful words
- affixes awry
- comedic characters

Many of the items in the previous list are likely to be taught by language
arts or English teachers rather than in the "content areas." Yet, as you will

see, all of the humorous and unusual aspects of words in our language are an integral part of our speech and writing. George Lakoff, for example, has stated that " . . . metaphor is pervasive in everyday life, not just in language but in thought and action," adding that "our conceptual system is largely metaphorical" [and] . . . the way we think, what we experience, and what we do every day is very much a matter of metaphor" (Lakoff & Johnson, 1980, p. 3). Richard Lederer, a master of word play, hooks us into his language books with titles such as *Adventures of a Verbivore*, (1994) and *Crazy English* (1998). And then there are *Mad Libs* (Macrone, 2005), which use simplistic definitions of parts of speech to produce laughable stories that students love to create. Bringing the ideas from the world of word play will easily engage your students, while expanding their linguistic knowledge.

APPLICATION TO LEARNING

We begin with metaphors, a figure of speech in which a term or phrase is applied to something that is not literal, but suggestive, such as "the heart of the matter." In Figure 10.1 there is a collection of expressions that use foods to provide images and metaphoric meanings, followed by activities.

Figure 10.1   Eat Your Words

Directions: Here is a taxonomy of metaphors that uses foods for expressing an idea that is not about food. These metaphors are figurative expressions, which means that the words don't literally mean what they say. For example, when someone butters you up they say nice things about you to get you to do them a favor. This doesn't mean they will put butter all over you!

Select five of these metaphors that "tickle you." Then write two sentences for each metaphor, one of which uses the metaphor and one sentence which explains its figurative meaning.
Then are three examples to guide you. Then illustrate your paragraphs, showing both the figurative and literal meanings of these expressions or metaphors. You can also add other food metaphors to the taxonomy.

Sample Sentences Using Food Idioms

Jamie knew that if she didn't finish school she would end up *working for peanuts*. She decided to study hard so that she would get a *high-paying job*.

The moment Shawn saw his mother's frown, he knew he was *in the soup*. Only an apology now would get him out of *trouble*.

Everyone agreed that Wanda was a *good egg*. All you had to do was ask and she was *ready to help*.

• TAXONOMY •	
A	apple of my eye
B	butter me up
C	cool as a cucumber
D	my little dumpling
E	eat your heart out
F	fine kettle of fish
G	good egg
H	hard-boiled
I	in the soup
J	
K	know your onions
L	long drink of water
M	milk it dry
N	nutty as a fruitcake
O	out to lunch
P	pleased as punch
Q	
R	rub salt
S	salt of the earth
T	top banana
U	
V	
W	work for peanuts
X	
Y	
Z	

Another type of figure of speech is a simile, which is used to compare one idea or word with another, as in "slippery as an eel." Figure 10.2 illustrates a collection of similes using animals, followed by activities.

Figure 10.2   Similes Using Animals

Directions: A simile is a figure of speech that compares a word or action in an imaginary way with another word or idea. Here are similes that use animals to illustrate behaviors or actions of humans. Select five similes and write a short statement for each one that will help a reader understand the meaning of the similes. There is an example following the list of similes.

Example Using an Animal Simile

Although Patty was only 10 years old, she was *as wise as an owl*. She always gave *good advice* to her friends about food, school, and being kind to others.

BAT—as blind as a bat

BIRD—as free as a bird

BEE—as busy as a bee

BULL—like a bull in a china shop

DOG—as faithful as a dog

EEL—as slippery as an eel

FOX—as sly as a fox

LAMB—as gentle as a lamb

LOON—as crazy as a loon

LION—as strong as a lion

MULE—as stubborn as a mule

MOUSE—as quiet as a mouse

OWL—as wise as an owl

In addition to metaphors and similes, there are also idioms. Figure 10.3 uses words from our bodies that give us images and imagery in a variety of ways.

Figure 10.3   Body Language

Directions: Here are examples of idioms that use body words to give an image of something different from the actual or literal words. For example, "to have eyes in the back of the head" means you know what is going on all around. Select five of these idioms, and write a story using all five idioms in the same story. There is an example following the list. Illustrate your story if you wish.

BONE—cut to the bone, bare bones, bone of contention
EYES—eyes in back of the head
EARS—all ears, bend someone's ear
EYEBROWS—raise one's eyebrows
FACE—face up, do an about face
FINGER—at one's fingertips, have a finger in the pie, cross your fingers
FEET—feet of clay, put one's foot in one's mouth, get one's foot in the door
HEAD—head and shoulders above the crowd, come to a head
HEART—have a warm heart, take heart, heart in my mouth
LIPS—her lips are sealed, button your lips
MOUTH—put your money where your mouth is
MIND—read my mind
MUSCLES—flex your muscles
NECK—stick out one's neck
NOSE—a nose for news
PALM—grease one's palm
SHOULDER—get the cold shoulder, cry on my shoulder
TEETH—grit one's teeth, armed to the teeth, by the skin of my teeth, fight tooth and nail, gnash one's teeth, cut one's teeth
TONGUE—at the tip of my tongue, get a tongue lashing

Example of a Story Using "Body Language"

By knowing idioms you will be *head and shoulders* above the crowd. You will have numerous phrases *at your fingertips* and will be able to get your *foot in the door* for many good jobs.
In discussions, you will be able to *cut to the bone* when it comes to ideas and *put your money where your mouth is*. So don't worry about *sticking your neck out* on these words. Just *flex your [linguistic] muscles* and *become all ears* so that you can learn these phrases.

Oxymora

The oxymoron is a phrase with contradictory words (e.g., a small fortune) that comes from two Greek words that are semantically opposite, meaning *sharply dull.*

Word play with oxymora (the plural) is not only fun for students, but makes them think about how words with opposing meanings can still provide us with an image or a meaning. Figure 10.4 offers a sampling of the numerous oxymora in English and also offers your students opportunities for humorous composing and illustration. Students across a wide spectrum of grades can try explaining these.

Figure 10.4 A Taxonomy of Oxymora

Directions: Oxymora are phrases which use two words with opposite meanings, such as a "clever fool." Select six of these oxymora and write a statement explaining why these words say what is "impossible" or contradictory. Examples follow the taxonomy.

• TAXONOMY •

A	almost always, almost never, almost impossible
B	big sip, baby grand (piano)
C	calm winds, clever fool
D	down elevator
E	exact estimate
F	false facts, fresh frozen foods
G	good grief
H	half empty, half true
I	ill health, inside out
J	junk food, just war
K	
L	lesser evil, loud whisper
M	minor disaster
N	near miss, nearly complete
O	old news, open secret
P	partial silence, perfect idiot
Q	quiet revolution, quiet scream
R	restless sleep, random order, rules of war
S	second best, sad clown
T	terribly good, tense calmness
U	unwelcome recess, unbiased opinion
V	vaguely aware, voluntary taxes
W	whole half, working vacation
X	
Y	young sixty
Z	zero defects

Examples of the Contradiction (Opposites) in Oxymora

Minor disaster—A disaster means a terrible event or tragedy. Minor means small or trivial. So how could a disaster be minor?

Working vacation—When we take a vacation, we don't expect to work. So how could we have a working vacation?

Eponyms

Eponyms are words that come from people's names, such as Boycott and Fahrenheit. By learning eponyms, students get to know about famous (and infamous) people and the inventions or stories related to their names. Figure 10.5 gives a list of famous

Figure 10.5   A Taxonomy of Eponyms

The people listed in this taxonomy have become famous as words in our language. For example, John Montagu, the Fourth Earl of Sandwich in England, wanted to have more time to gamble and needed a quick way to eat. One day his servant put some meat between two pieces of bread and soon people everywhere were eating a "sandwich." Research the story of three or four of the people in this taxonomy, and write the story of how their names became eponyms. Then write a statement telling how you might become an eponym yourself by making some contribution to humanity. An example follows the taxonomy.

• TAXONOMY •	
A	Arachne
B	Boycott (Charles), Braille (Louis)
C	Chauvin (Nicholas),
	Celsius (Anders)
D	Diesel (Rudolph), Dobermann (Ludwig)
E	Eiffel (Alexandre Gustave), Echo
F	Fahrenheit (Gabriel Daniel)
G	Guppy (Robert J.L.)
H	Hygeia
I	Iris
J	Janus, Juno
K	Kelvin (William
	Thomson)
L	Leotard (Jules)
M	Morpheus
N	Nicot (Jean)
O	Ohm (George Simon)
P	Pasteur (Louis)
Q	(Don) Quixote
R	Richter (Charles)
S	Silhouette (Etienne de)
T	(the) Titans
U	
V	Volta (Alessandro)
W	Watt (James)
X	
Y	
Z	Zeppelin (Count Ferdinand Von)

Name of Person—Louis Pasteur

Eponym—pasteurize, pasteurization

Event or Story—Louis Pasteur was a scientist in the 1800s who observed that many people became very ill from drinking cow's milk. In searching for the cause, he discovered that milk and milk products such as cheese often contained harmful bacteria. He experimented with heating the milk to a temperature that could destroy the bacteria without changing or spoiling the test. His experiments were successful, and to this day we still *pasteurize* milk and milk products.

Be an Eponym

Think of a product that you might make or an invention that you will develop. Then name that product or invention after your first or last name or use some part of your name. For example, if your name is Andy, you might develop a highly nutritious fruit bar that provides lots of energy and vitamins. Soon people will be calling these bars "Andys" or "Andy Bars." Use the frame to help you.

Your first or last name _____

Your invention or contribution to society _____

How your name has become "eponized" _____

eponyms. We suggest that students research how these words came into our language and, as a class or group, have them create a Book of Eponyms. Then students can make their own name into an eponym by doing a positive deed or creating an important or useful product or invention.

Colorful Expressions

We might say that English is a colorful language. It certainly has a vast amount of colorful words, such as *in the pink* to express health, *black sheep* for character, *red carpet* for hospitality, and many more expressions that use color to give meaning. As your students become familiar with these phrases, they can again write, illustrate, and make delightful personal or class books. Figure 10.6 provides a Taxonomy of Colorful Expressions and their meanings. Have fun with them.

Figure 10.6   A Taxonomy of Colorful Expressions

Directions: Contribute to a class book in which you write two or three sentences using "colorful phrases." Then illustrate each phrase. An example follows the Taxonomy. Share the book with other classes.

Colorful Phrase	Meaning
black sheep	person who causes shame or embarrassment in a family
true blue	loyal
feeling blue	down-hearted
bolt from the blue	an unexpected event
once in a blue moon	rarely or seldom
singing the blues	feeling or acting sad
good as gold	a safe investment
green thumb	good at gardening
gray matter	brains
in the limelight	being the center of attention
in the pink	feeling healthy
red-carpet treatment	being considered important or royal
rose-colored glasses	seeing the world as kind and good
red-letter day	getting good news
paint the town red	have a wonderful, wild time
red as a beet	showing embarrassment
silver lining	the inside of a cloud that tell us that life is better than it looks
white elephant	an item that is more expensive than it's worth
white lie	a minor falsehood
yellow-bellied	a coward
yellow journalism	news reporting that exaggerates

Here is an example of a "colorful" statement: I have a *true blue* friend who is *as good as gold* and always gives me the *red-carpet treatment.*

Affixes Awry or Missing

Have you ever wondered why we can be *uncouth* but not couth, *ruthless* but not ruthful, *toothless* but not toothful, or *truthf*ul but not truthless? There are numerous words in the English language that can be affixed to have a meaning that is either negative or positive. But often these very words don't "accept" both affixes, as in helpful and helpless or happy and unhappy. Interestingly, these words that do not seem to have opposite affixes may have started out as opposites (as in ruthless and ruthful), but over time one survived and the other became disused. By studying the etymology of these affixed and "affixless" words, your students can gain much information and insight about how vocabulary grows, changes, appears, and disappears. Figure 10.7 has a compilation of the words in which the "affixes have gone awry, followed by a question for you to answer."

Figure 10.7   Taxonomy of Affixes Awry

Directions: The words in this taxonomy have either a front affix (prefix) or an end affix (suffix). However, we might expect that because of their prefix or suffix, they should also have an opposite affix. For example, we have the word *timeless*, yet we don't have *timeful*. Why not? Work with a partner and select 10 words from this taxonomy. Then answer the questions beneath each word. Check an unabridged dictionary to find out the history (etymology) of the words and why only one form is in use.

A	Aimless What would happen if your behavior was *aimful?*
B	Blissful What would you feel like if you were *blissless?*
C	Childless Describe a family that is *childful.*
D	Discombobulated Describe what you would be doing if you were *combobulated.*
E	Eventful What would be a life that is *eventless?*
F	Fretful Tell what it is like to be *fretless.*
G	Grateful How would someone *grateless* behave?
H	Hapless What is the difference between a hapless person and *a hapful* person?

(Continued)

Figure 10.7 (Continued)

I	Impunity What would be the difference between being treated with impunity compared to being treated with *punity*?
J	
K	
L	Listless How might you change from listless to *listful*?
M	Masterful What would happen to a *masterless* horseback rider?
N	Nonchalant What would be the difference between someone who is nonchalant and someone who is *chalant*?
O	
P	Plentiful How might one's life go from plentiful to *plentiless*?
Q	
R	Respectful What are some characteristics of being *respectless*?
S	Sorrowful What might change a sorrowful mood into a *sorrowless* mood?
T	Truthful How might you treat a person who is *truthless*?
U	Unruly How might we make some unruly students *ruly*?
V	Vengeful What would someone *vengeless* be like?
W	Wonderful What might change a wonderful day into a *wonderless* day?
X	
Y	Youthful How might a *youthless* person act youthful?
Z	Zestful Describe a person who is constantly *zestless*.

Comedic Characters

One of the games our family would play on rainy days was a game we named "Comedic Characters." We would make up characters with names such as Al Cohol, Ben Evolent, Ella Phant, and so forth, and then do little playlets or scenes. Not only was the game fun, but it became a great vocabulary builder, and soon the whole family (four children plus parents) was searching for words that could become characters. When we introduced Comedic Characters into the classrooms, we found that students not only laughed, but they too, like our family, went on a search and soon discovered Greg Arious, Cara Smatic, Phil Anthropic, and a host of "Latin and Greek personalities." Figure 10.8 represents some of our characters. Following the taxonomy is a character profile for developing the "character" and other suggestions for building semantic superiority in all your students. (Spellings may vary!)

Figure 10.8 Taxonomy of Comedic Characters

Directions: These "characters" get their names from words that mostly have Latin and Greek origins. Select one of the characters and complete the character profile that follows. Then meet with three or four of your classmates and share the information you have gathered. Try to write a story with your classmates using these characters.

• TAXONOMY •

A	Ann Onymous, Ann Tonym, Al Gebra, Al Gorithm, Ali Mentary
B	Ben Evolent, Ben Efactor, Ben Eficent
C	Cara Smatic, Cal Cium
D	D. Pendent, Dan Dee, Di Agram, Di Aphanous, Di Gest
E	Ella Phant, Evan Escent, Etta Kett
F	Frank O. Phile, Fran Chise
G	Greg Arious
H	Hugh Manity, Hy Gene
I	I. Sosceles
J	Jo Cular
K	Kit Tennish
L	Lu Cent, Leo Tard
M	Mag Nitude, Mel Ifluous, Martin Ett, Moe Beel
N	N. Velop
O	O. Bey
P	Phil Harmonic, Phil Anthropic, Phil Osophy, Phil Ander, Polly Gon, Polly Morphic, Polly Glot, Pat Ronize, Penny Less
Q	Quint Essence
R	Ray Venn
S	Sue Pine, Stu Pendous, Sal Ubrious, Sal Amander
T	Tim Idd
U	Una Verse, Una Form
V	Val Liant, Vic Torious
W	Wanda Ring
X	Xena Phobic
Y	Yugo Slav
Z	Zig Zag

Figure 10.8 (Continued)

Using Comedic Characters to Create a Character

- An example might be the comedic character "Wanda Ring."
- **Check the dictionary:** Research the word in an unabridged dictionary or on the Internet. Look up the word by base (wander, not wandering).
- **Copy the entry or entries as in the following example** (e.g., wandering [wan-der-ing]):
  1. moving from place to place without a fixed plan; roaming; rambling: *wandering tourists.*
  2. having no permanent residence; nomadic: *a wandering tribe of Indians.*
  3. meandering; winding: *a wandering river; a wandering path.*
  4. an aimless roving about; leisurely traveling from place to place: *a period of delightful wandering through Italy.*
  5. Usually, **wanderings.**
     a. aimless travels; meanderings: Her wanderings took her all over the world.
     b. disordered thoughts or utterances; incoherencies: mental wanderings; the wanderings of delirium.
     [bef. 1000; ME (n., adj.), OE *wandrigende* (adj.). See WANDER, -ING2, -ING1]: to ramble without a definite purpose or objective; roam, rove, or stray: *to wander over the earth.*
     [bef. 900; ME *wandren*, OE *wandrian* (c. G *wandern*), freq. of *wendan* to WEND; see -ER6]
     wanÆderer, *n.*
     Syn. 1. range, stroll. 2. saunter. 6. swerve, veer. 8. ramble, rove. (*Random House Webster's Unabridged Dictionary*, 2000)
- **Complete a character profile.**

Here is an example of a completed character profile on *Wanda Ring:*

Name of character: Wanda Ring

Age: 15 (note: about an age when someone might start to wander)

Family background or character: Germanic, Anglo-Saxon; family goes back to the time of Middle English

Habitat: England, United States, and other English-speaking countries

Wishes of character:
- To see the world
- To meander along the rivers and highways
- To meet people from everywhere

Fears of character:
- To be cooped up
- To get lost
- To be alone

Positive character traits: adventurous, curious, open-minded

Negative or weak character traits: may be aimless, forgetful, inattentive

Paragraph based on previous information: Wanda Ring is an interesting character for many reasons. She is an explorer who always wants to know what is happening in other parts of the world. In addition, she has had a long history in our language, going back to the Anglo-Saxon days. Finally, she is associated with the nomadic peoples of the earth who travel constantly to find food, water, and better places to live.

Other information: Wanda Ring has been part of the lives of Bedouins, Berbers, Roms, and many other nomadic peoples in different parts of the world who have always welcomed her into their homes.

INTERNET SITES

- http://www.oxymoronlist.com
- http://www.whonamedit.com/azeponyms.cfm/A.html
- http://members.tripod.com/~foxdreamer/page2.html
- http://www.saidwhat.co.uk/spoon/metaphors.php
- http://www.saidwhat.co.uk/spoon/similes.php
- http://thinks.com/words/index.htm

Introduction

*Language and
Metalanguage*

*Builders of
Linguistic
Intelligence*

*Parts of
Speech and the
English Language*

*Syntax and
Semantics*

*The Polyglot
of English*

*The Polyglot:
Beyond Latin
and Greek*

*Return to Parts
of Speech*

*Sentences,
Paragraphs, and
Other Structures of
the Written
Language*

*Grammar for
Word Play*

**Reading, Writing,
and Grammar**

*Punctuation,
Spelling, Text
Messaging, and
Other
Consequences of
Grammar*

*Additional
Learning Activities*

CHAPTER ELEVEN

Reading, Writing, and Grammar

Using grammar, we can think about our ideas, because our ideas are captured in the amber of sentences.

(VanTassel-Baska, Johnson, & Boyce, 1996, p. 152)

The last thing we want to do is to make people uptight about the epicenter of their identity—the way they communicate.

(Lederer, 1991, p. xviii)

COMBINING READING WITH GRAMMAR

While the teaching of grammar has often been justified as a means for improving reading and writing, students have not necessarily seen the connection between these language areas. The grammar exercises have been isolated from "real" language and reading, while writing instruction often only makes reference to "correct grammar" without specific activities that show the relationships.

In the book *Developing Verbal Talent*, VanTassel-Baska and her colleagues (1996) refer to grammar as a "rigorous method of higher-order thinking" (p. 152) that provides us with the meaning of speech and written text. Teachers of reading and language are likely to agree with this premise, yet they have often found a serious gap between what they have to teach about grammar and what they have to teach to help their students comprehend the text or write an acceptable essay. An example of the gap between common schoolbook grammar and the sentences of great writers noticeably widens when students have to read deep or powerful literature. Even the grammar of nursery rhymes and stories for young children is far more complex than grammar book exercises, as in the examples that follow.

From the famous Mother Goose we have

One misty, moisty morning when cloudy was the weather,

I chanced to meet an old man clothed all in leather.

He began to compliment

And I began to grin,

"How do you do? And how do you do? And how do you do again?"

Imagine how complex parsing this poem would be even to a middle school student. If the subject is "I" and the predicate is "chanced," do we really know what the sentence is about? And why does "cloudy" precede "weather"? Shouldn't the writer have said "when the weather was cloudy?"

Your answer might be, "Well this is a poem and a poet can 'break the rules,'" as in the lovely line of "Mending Wall" by Robert Frost (1916): "Something there is that doesn't like a wall."

Yet good writing, poetry or prose, results from an author's deep and intuitive understanding of the many transformations of language and makes use of its registers, such as conversational, informal, and formal, and its written genres that include fairy tales, myths, novels, plays, essays, journalism pieces, and dozens of other formats. By making students aware of the grammar of these genres through reading and writing, we give students the ability to use a wide range of language, appropriately and creatively.

Sources From Literature for Teaching Grammar

The Fairy Tale

We can begin, for example, by introducing to students of almost all ages grammar as illustrated in this version of the fairy tale *Snow White.*

> *Poor Snow White! She ran till she dropped from weariness and fell asleep. When she awoke, she saw a little house in a clearing. The door was open. Inside everything looked a mess. In the kitchen were seven little bowls and seven little chairs, some of them overturned.*

What is the grammatical structure of these sentences that allows an English speaker to get meaning? One answer comes from Noam Chomsky (1957), who refers to language as an instinctual system in which children learn the complex grammar of their (first) language rapidly and without formal instruction. But even more impressive about this instinctual learning is that children understand and compose sentence structures that they have never previously heard (Pinker, 1994).

With this postulation of Chomsky, a five-year-old English-speaking child (without any developmental difficulties) easily understands the total gist of the Snow White paragraph. "Poor Snow White," a group of words without a verb, is internalized as "Snow White is in trouble," or something like that. The total sentence, "She dropped from weariness and fell asleep," is understood by most children to mean that Snow White was so tired that she fell down and fell asleep. The words "dropped" and "fell" are used as idioms, and through the total context the child recognizes or understands that "dropped" means to fall, but "fell asleep" involves no real "falling." Of course, all of this understanding comes when we are operating in our native or first language. People who learn English as a second language are likely to have trouble with these literal and figurative words that are not similarly used in their first language (Gardner & Davies, 2007).

How might a five- or six-year-old child know what weariness means if the word is not used in the household? We call this *context learning*, whose meaning is triggered by the phrase "fell asleep," another example of what Chomsky calls *deep structure understanding*.

Now comes the next challenge in this passage—"When she saw a little house in a clearing." Even without knowing the precise meaning of *clearing*, we can expect our young child to imagine a little house in a place. Perhaps the exact nature of the place is not yet clear (pun intended), but the child knows that this house is in some type of place and most likely this place is different from the place of the house. If the text happens to be matched by an illustration of a house set apart from other houses, the child can intuitively understand the word *clearing* to know that there are no other houses around.

You might ask if there is any grammar to teach for this type of text. By thinking of grammar as a higher order of thinking, you can teach the "grammar of restating," which brings about interpreting and clarification (VanTassel-Baska et al., 1996, p. 155). By asking the students to retell this segment of the story in "one's own words," usually known as paraphrasing, you provide the opportunity for moving from deep structure (internalized understanding) to using surface structure or one's own natural grammar. Here is an example from a second grader:

> *Snow White was very scared. She ran as fast as she could. But she got so tired that she fell down and went to sleep right on the ground. Then she got up and ran some more. Soon she saw a little house that was all by itself. She got to the house and knocked on the door. But the door opened by itself. Yuck. The kitchen was a mess. All the chairs were knocked over and the whole place was yucky.*

APPLICATION TO LEARNNG

After paraphrasing, you can ask the students to compare their grammar with the story grammar. In this type of comparison, students will begin to clarify their understanding of the words, phrases, and sentences and express this clarification to others. Figure 11.1 shows how this comparison looks.

Figure 11.1   Comparison of a Text Version With a Restatement Version

Text Version	Restatement Version
Poor Snow White!	Snow White was very scared.
She ran till she dropped from weariness and fell asleep.	She ran as fast as she could. But she got so tired that she fell down and went to sleep right on the ground.
When she awoke, she saw a little house in a clearing.	Then she got up and ran some more. Soon she saw a little house that was all by itself. She got to the house and knocked on the door. But the door opened by itself.
The door was open. Inside everything looked a mess.	
In the kitchen were seven little bowls and seven little chairs, some of them overturned.	Yuck. The kitchen was a mess. All the chairs were knocked over and the whole place was yucky.

From Children's Literature

One of our most successful strategies has been to use books for young children to include grammar lessons, without compromising the joy of reading these books. A favorite book is *I'll Teach My Dog a Lot of Words* (Frith, 1973). If your librarian can get at least five copies, you can arrange to have all your students read the book in preparation for this activity. We have also included an example of a text suitable for middle or high school students in Figures 11.8, 11.9, and 11.10. After you and the students have read this book together, move on to showing the relationship between grammar and reading as illustrated here. This activity can be done over several days or several weeks. We have included a portion of the text of this book so that you can better understand how we have developed the lesson.

I'll Teach My Dog a Lot of Words (Frith, 1973)

> The first words I will teach my pup are . . . :
>
> dig a hole!
>
> And fill it up!
>
> I'll teach him walk.
>
> I'll teach him run . . .
>
> then catch a ball!
>
> We'll sure have fun.
>
> Then I'll teach him bark
>
> and beg
>
> wag your tail
>
> and
>
> shake a leg . . .
>
> wash your ears
>
> and
>
> wash your toes!
>
> Scratch your head
>
> and
>
> blow your nose.

Instruction Sequence for *I'll Teach My Dog a Lot of Words* (Frith, 1973)

1. First, have the students simply read the story aloud without any interruptions. Then follow this plan or script.
2. Have students set up a Taxonomy of Verbs from *I'll Teach My Dog a Lot of Words* in their notebooks. Figure 11.2 shows the Taxonomy of Verbs from the book.
   - Tell the students that they can determine if a word is a verb simply by using the word *I* with the verb as in "I teach," "I dig," "I fill." Students can work in groups or as a whole class.

Figure 11.2

A		
B	bark, beg, blow	
C	catch, chase, climb, cut, clean	
D	dig, do	
E	eat	
F	fill, follow	
G		
H	have	
I		
J		
K	kiss, know	
L	learn	
M		
N		
O		
P	paint	
Q		
R	run	
S	shake, scratch, shine, sing, stand	
T	teach, think, toot	
U		
V		
W	walk, wag, wash	
X		
Y		
Z		

• TAXONOMY •
Taxonomy of Verbs From
I'll Teach My Dog a Lot Of Words (Frith, 1973)

3. Then ask the students to find the words they think are adjectives. Most of the adjectives are on the fourth page. Have the students set up a template of the adjectives as in Figure 11.3. This template will show a specific type of adjective that has a base, an -er inflection, and an -est inflection, all of which are adjectives of comparison. Then have them set up a template of adjectives of color as in Figure 11.4. They will notice that only some of the color adjectives use the -er, -est inflections and that five of the six words can use the inflection -*ish*.

4. Now go through the book and list words that the students think are nouns. List them in a template of nouns (Figure 11.5) organized by categories of person, place, animal, object, and other. Expect some discussion of what is an "object" and what is "other."

5. Finally, have the students list all the other words as a taxonomy called "unclassified," as in Figure 11.6. These words have traditionally been classified as pronouns, articles, conjunctions, and so forth, which we have discussed in other chapters. Linguists called most of these words (with the exceptions of pronouns) function words, which serve to "glue" the other words together. There is very little reason to have students classify these words grammatically at this beginning stage.

6. When the students have finished this classifying, have them create a Morphology Template of Verbs (Figure 11.7) using the verbs from Figure 11.2. Remind the students of the definition of a verb as a word in the English language that has a conjugation with four forms and an occasional fifth form (see Chapter 4). Have them complete the Morphology Template, and when they have entered all the verbs and their inflections, have a discussion focusing on what is the same for all words and what are the variations. We urge the use of the word variations rather than "irregularities," because a language is always based on rules and variations. Have the students underline the verbs in the past that have variations (e.g., vowel-changing verbs (blow-blew; vowel-changing + t as in caught; null or no change as in cut). Then have the students complete the Observation Checklist that is part of Figure 11.7. (You might find it interesting to know that all of these verbs, in a book for young children, are of Anglo-Saxon origin.)

Figure 11.3   Template of Adjectives of Comparison

base	-er	-est
big	bigger	biggest
small	smaller	smallest
fat	fatter	fattest
thin	thinner	thinnest
short	shorter	shortest
tall	taller	tallest
dark	darker	darkest
light	lighter	lightest

Figure 11.4   Adjectives of Color

base	-er	-est	-ish
red	redder	reddest	reddish
blue	bluer	bluest	bluish
green	greener	greenest	greenish
orange			
purple			purplish
pink			pinkish

Figure 11.5   Nouns by Categories

Persons	Places	Objects*	Parts of a Body	Animals	Other
	hole	ball	tail	pup	words
	zoo	food	leg	cat	fun
		chair	ears	dog	day
		road	toes	goose	night
		underwear	head	birds	lot
		grass	nose		
		shoe	thumb		
		bugle			
		drum			

*Objects can be further categorized, such as furniture, clothes, etc.

Figure 11.6   Unclassified Words (for a Future Time)

A	are, a, and, all	N	never, not
B	but	O	on
C	can	P	
D		Q	
E		R	
F	first	S	sure, still, some, someone's
G		T	the, then, this, there, to, that's
H	him, here, he'll	U	up
I	I, it	V	
J		W	will, we'll, with
K		X	
L	like (this)	Y	your, you've
M	my, me, more	Z	

Figure 11.7   Morphology Template of Verbs From *I'll Teach My Dog a Lot of Words* (Frith, 1973)

Base	Verb -s	-ing	Past	-n Past
bark	barks	barking	barked	
beg	begs	begging	begged	
blow	blows	blowing	blew	blown
catch	catches	catching	caught	
chase	chases	chasing	chased	
clean	cleans	cleaning	cleaned	
climb	climbs	climbing	climbed	
dig	digs	digging	dug	
do	does*	doing	did	done
eat	eats	eating	ate	eaten
fill	fills	filling	filled	
have	has*	having	had	
kiss	kisses	kissing	kissed	
knowl	knows	knowing	knew	known

Base	Verb -s	-ing	Past	-n Past
learn	learns	learning	learned	
paint	paints	painting	painted	
run	runs	running	ran	
scratch	scratches	scratching	scratched	
shake	shakes	shaking	shook	shaken
shine	shines	shining	shone	shone**
sing	sings	singing	sang, sung***	
stand	stands	standing	stood	
teach	teaches	teaching	taught	
think	thinks	thinking	thought	
toot	toots	tooting	tooted	
wag	wags	wagging	wagged	
walk	walks			
wash	washes	washing	washed	

*What has happened here?

**What do you notice?

***Can you explain this?

Observation Checklist

Upon completing this template of verbs, I noticed that

1. all the verbs in the first column _____.
2. all the verbs in the second column _____.
3. all the verbs in the third column _____.
4. the verbs in the fourth column mostly _____, but some verbs _____.
5. there are only a few verbs _____.

The information and activities in Figures 11.8 to 11.10 are particularly suitable (and important) to middle and upper grade students.

Lewis Carroll and the Teaching of Grammar

Richard Lederer refers to the "word magic of Lewis Carroll" in the two great classics: *Alice's Adventures in Wonderland* (1861/1995a) and *Through the Looking Glass* (1872/1995b). If you work with students from fifth grade and above, please introduce them to these books for their imagination, humor, wisdom, and unrivaled word play. As a sample for your students, you can begin with "Jabberwocky," which is in the first chapter of *Through the Looking Glass* when Alice finds a book that belongs to the White King. As she turns the pages to find a section she can read, the thinks, "It's all in some language I don't know" (p. 17). When she finishes reading "Jabberwocky," she says to the White King, "It seems very pretty, but it's rather hard to understand" (p. 19).

What Alice hadn't realized is that there are grammatical clues in this poem, and once these clues are perceived, the poem is, well, easy. In Figure 11.9 we present "Jabberwocky" and its grammatical clues.

Figure 11.8   Making Grammatical Sense Out of Lewis Carroll's Poem "Jabberwocky"

This poem comes from Lewis Carroll's great story *Through the Looking Glass and What Alice Found There* (1995b). After you have finished reading the poem and doing the activities, discuss what you learned about language and grammar with your classmates.

1. Read this poem with a partner or in a group. Read it with expression and don't worry about its meaning.

    Jabberwocky

    Lewis Carroll

    (from *Through the Looking Glass and What Alice Found There*, 1995b, pp. 18–19)

    'Twas brillig, and the slithy toves
    Did gyre and gimble in the wabe:
    All mimsy were the borogoves,
    And the mome raths outgrabe.

     "Beware the Jabberwock, my son!
    The jaws that bite, the claws that catch!
    Beware the Jubjub bird, and shun
    The frumious Bandersnatch!"

    He took his vorpal sword in hand:
    Long time the manxome foe he sought—
    So rested he by the Tumtum tree,
    And stood awhile in thought.

    And, as in uffish thought he stood,
    The Jabberwock, with eyes of flame,
    Came whiffling through the tulgey wood,
    And burbled as it came!

    One, two! One, two! And through and through
    The vorpal blade went snicker-snack!
    He left it dead, and with its head
    He went galumphing back.

    "And, has thou slain the Jabberwock?
    Come to my arms, my beamish boy!
    O frabjous day! Callooh! Callay!"
    He chortled in his joy.

    'Twas brillig, and the slithy toves
    Did gyre and gimble in the wabe;
    All mimsy were the borogoves,
    And the mome raths outgrabe.

2. Now here is the same poem, but with many of the "nonsense" words left out. Working with your partner(s), put your own words in the empty spaces. Think about the "clues" you are using for your words.

    'Twas _____ , and the _____ _____
    Did _____ and _____ in the _____:
    All _____ were the _____
    And the _____ _____

"Beware the Jabberwock, my son!
The jaws that bite, the claws that catch!
Beware the _____ bird, and shun
The _____ !"

He took his _____ sword in hand:
Long time the _____ foe he sought—
So rested he by the _____ tree,
And stood awhile in thought.

And, as in _____ thought he stood,
The Jabberwock, with eyes of flame,
Came _____ through the _____ wood,
And _____ as it came!

One, two! One, two! And through and through
The _____ blade went snicker-snack!
He left it dead, and with its head
He went _____ back.

"And, has thou slain the Jabberwock?
Come to my arms, my _____ boy!
O _____ day! _____ !"
He _____ in his joy.

3. Now use the template that follows. Put in the words you (and your partner) used next to a nonsense word. Decide if the replacement word is a noun, verb, adjective, or exclamation. How can you tell? The first word is done as an example.

Lewis Carroll's Words	Replacement Words	Noun	Verb	Adjective	Exclamation
brillig	sunny			✓	
slithy					
toves					
gyre					
gimble					
wabe					
mimsy					
borogoves					
mome raths					
outgrabe					
jubjub					
frumious					
bandersnatch					
vorpal					
manxome					
tumtum					
uffish					
whiffling					
tulgey					
burbled					
galumphing					

Figure 11.8 (Continued)

Lewis Carroll's Words	Replacement Words	Noun	Verb	Adjective	Exclamation
beamish frabjous callooh, callay chortled					

4. How do you think Lewis Carroll came up with these words? Well, he created what he called *portmanteau* words, meaning he put two words together to get one word, as in *brunch,* which is breakfast and lunch. The word *portmanteau* comes from two French words meaning to carry a cloak or a coat. Select five words from Lewis Carroll's list and research on the Internet or in an unabridged dictionary what two words he put together to get the portmanteau. For example, *mimsy* came from *flimsy* and *miserable.*

The Phantom Tollbooth—When Language Is Really Fun

Every student deserves to travel through Norton Juster's lands of Dictionopolis and Digitopolis so vividly described in *The Phantom Tollbooth* (1989). In this book, for fourth grade through high school, your students will travel through The Sea of Knowledge, climb the Mountains of Ignorance, and find themselves Beyond Expectations. This modern version of Carroll's "Wonderland" is a treasure of language learning with laughs. We suggest that you use this book as an ongoing read-aloud with younger students and a "read-and-discuss" book with older students. Figure 11.9 provides a lively activity based on a section from this marvelous book.

Figure 11.9 "Scheduling" Idioms

In the book *The Phantom Tollbooth* (Juster, 1989), Milo, the main character, has arrived "in the Doldrums" and meets its inhabitants called the "Lethargarians." These Lethargarians tell Milo that they have a very busy schedule and then describe that schedule. Here's your task.

1. Check out the meaning of *Doldrums* and write what you think this place is like.
2. Check out the meaning of the word *lethargic* and write a brief description of the Lethargarians.
3. Read the following daily schedule of the Lethargarians and notice the bolded words. Then use the bolded words to write your own description of these characters, telling whether you think they are as busy as they say.

   "There's lots to do; we have a very busy schedule—
   "At 8'o'clock we get up, and then we spend
   "From 8 to 9 **daydreaming**.
   "From 9 to 9:30 we take our daily **mid-morning nap**.
   "From 9:30 to 10:30 we **dawdle and delay**.
   "From 10:30 to 11:30 we take our **late morning nap**.
   "From 11:30 to 1:00 we **bide our time** and then eat lunch.
   "From 1:00 to 2:00 we **linger and loiter**.
   "From 2:00 to 2:30 we take our **early afternoon nap**.
   "From 2:30 to 3:30 we put **off for tomorrow what we could have done today**.
   "From 3:30 to 4:30 we take our **early late afternoon nap**.
   "From 4:30 to 5:30 we **loaf and lounge** until dinner.
   "From 6:00 to 7:00 we **dillydally**.
   "From 7:00 to 8:00 we take our **early evening nap**, and then for an hour before we go to bed at 9:00 we **waste time**." (Juster, 1989, pp. 26–27)

Here is a passage from *Narrative of the Life of Frederick Douglass, an American Slave* (Douglass, 1845–2003), with the verbs shown in bold. Use the template that follows to organize the conjugation form of each verb. There is an example for you to follow. When you have finished, write your own passage using these verbs. You can write the verbs in any form you need. Underline or bold them and then share your writing with a partner.

Figure 11.10 Verbs From *Narrative of the Life of Frederick Douglass, an American Slave* (Douglass, 1845/2003)

Colonel Lloyd **kept** from three to four hundred slaves on his home plantation and **owned** a large number more on the neighboring farms **belonging** to him.... The overseers of these and all the rest of the farms... **received** advice and direction from the managers of the home plantation.... All the disputes among the overseers were **settled** here. If a slave was **convicted** of any high misdemeanor, **became** unmanageable, or **evinced** a determination to **run** away, he was **brought** immediately here, severely **whipped**, **put** on board the sloop, **carried** to Baltimore, and **sold** to Austin Woolfolk... as a warning to the slaves **remaining**. (pp. 22–23)

Base	Verb -s	-ing	-d or -ed Past	Vowel Changing Past	"BE" Verb Present and Past
					were was
keep	keeps	keeping		kept	

Source: Excerpt from *Narrative of the Life of Frederick Douglass, An American Slave* (Originally published in 1845).

ABC BOOKS FOR BUILDING LANGUAGE AND GRAMMAR LITERACY

Throughout this book we have used alphabetic taxonomies to illustrate various ways to organize and categorize words. By using the alphabet, students develop a system for adding to their "word stock" and for retrieving words they need. Students can then create ABC books on different parts of speech and categories as ways to understand the structure of the English language. These ABC books can be done as a class project, by individual students, or by teams of students. Older students can make these books for younger siblings or for sharing with lower grade students. Here is a suggested list of ABC books which your students can make, followed by two examples. (You can add your own titles.)

- My ABC Book of Plural Nouns
- My ABC Book of Verbs of Locomotion
- My ABC Book of Verbs of the Mind
- My First Book of Adjectives
- My Second Book of Adjectives
- My Book of Adjectives and Adverbs
- An ABC Book of Nouns That End in -ion
- An ABC Book of Nouns That End in -ment
- My ABC Book of UP Verbs
- My ABC Book of French (Spanish, Italian, etc.) Words

Figures 11.11 and 11.12 are examples to get your students started. You will notice that in Figure 11.11 there are a variety of noun plurals to illustrate the variations. From this example, students can observe the following:

- Many nouns change from singular to plural by adding -s.
- A few nouns change their vowel (e.g., mouse-mice, woman-women). These are called vowel-changing nouns.
- A few nouns change their consonant (e.g., knife-knives, wife-wives). These are consonant-changing nouns.
- A few nouns stay the same (e.g., deer-deer, sheep-sheep). These are null-changing nouns.

Vowel changing, consonant changing, and null changing nouns are of Anglo-Saxon origin. The book is arranged as a panel book for ease of viewing.

In Figure 11.12 we give an example of My First Book of Adjectives. This book should contain only those adjectives that inflect with -er and -est.

Figure 11.11   My ABC Book of Plural Nouns in the English Language

A	B	C	D
One apple Two apples	One baby Two babies	One child Two children	One deer Two deer
E One elephant Three elephants	**F** One friend Three friends	**G** One gift Three gifts	**H** One house Three houses
I One island Many islands	**J** One jellybean Many jellybeans	**K** One knife Many knives	**L** One lady Many ladies
M One mouse Lots of mice	**N** One neighbor Lots of neighbors	**O** One onion Lots of onions	**P** One pet Lot of pets
Q One queen A pair of queens	**R** One rooster A pair of roosters	**S** One sock A pair of socks	**T** One ten A pair of tens
U One unicorn Six unicorns	**V** One vegetable Six vegetables	**W** One woman Six women	**X** One xylophone Six xylophones
Y One yard Three yards	**Z** One zebra Three zebras		

Figure 11.12 My First ABC Book of Adjectives That Compare With -er and -est

A	B	C	D
My neighbor was **angry** when someone picked his flowers. He became **angrier** when a dog ran on his lawn. He was the **angriest** man I had ever seen when someone broke his car window.	This dog is **big**. This dog is **bigger**. This is the **biggest** dog I have seen.	My sister has a **cute** kitten. My brother's kitten is even **cuter**. But I have the **cutest** kitten of all.	A river can be **deep**. Some lakes are **deeper** than rivers. An ocean is the **deepest** body of water.
E	**F**	**G**	**H**
Adding three-digit numbers is **easy**. Adding two-digit numbers is even **easier**. Adding one-digit numbers is the **easiest** adding of all.	A tiger runs **fast**. A jaguar runs **faster** than a tiger. A **cheetah** is usually the **fastest** feline in the jungle.	"I think you're **great**," said my Mom. "I think you're **greater** than anyone I know," said my Dad. "I think you're the **greatest!**" said my Grandma.	Here are my three best faces: **Happy** **Happier** **Happiest**
I	**J**	**K**	**L**
	"Be **jolly**," said the clown, because the **jollier** you are, the **jolliest** you'll be."	**Kind** is good. **Kinder** is better. **Kindest** is the best.	**Long** days, **short** nights. **Longer** days, **shorter** nights. The **longest** days, the **shortest** nights.
M	**N**	**O**	**P**
Smile and be **merry**. Chuckle and be **merrier**. Laugh and be your **merriest**.	Share your books. That's very **nice**. Share your food. That's even **nicer**. Share your love. That's the **nicest**.	I am eight years **old**. I am **older** than my six-year-old sister. I am the **oldest** child in my family because my little brother is only three years old.	I think Snow White is **pretty**. I think Cinderella is **prettier** than Snow White. Who do you think is the **prettiest** character in all of the fairy tales?
Q	**R**	**S**	**T**
"Sh. Be **quiet**." "Sh, Sh. Get **quieter**." "Sh, Sh, Sh. Be the **quietest** you can be."	Roses are **red**. Apples are **redder**, and beets are the **reddest** red I know.	I can draw a **silly** face. I can draw a face that's **sillier** than the silly face I just drew. I can draw the **silliest** face in the whole world.	If I grow to six feet **tall**, I will be **taller** than my Mom and will probably be the **tallest** in the family.
U	**V**	**W**	**X**
		"I'm **wise**," said the squirrel. "I save for a rainy day." I'm **wiser**," said the tortoise. "I am slow and steady." "I'm the **wisest**," said the owl. "I just look and listen."	
Y	**Z**		
The **young** student told the **younger** student to take care of the **youngest** students.	"I'm a **zippy** zebra. No zebra can be **zippier** than me, not even the **zippiest** of zebras."		

INTERNET SITES

- http://www.alice-in-wonderland.net
- http://www.lpl.arizona.edu/~bcohen/phantom_tollbooth
- http://www.luminarium.org/contemporary/alicew

CHAPTER TWELVE

Punctuation, Spelling, Text Messaging, and Other Consequences of Grammar

Introduction

Language and Metalanguage

Builders of Linguistic Intelligence

Parts of Speech and the English Language

Syntax and Semantics

The Polyglot of English

The Polyglot: Beyond Latin and Greek

Return to Parts of Speech

Sentences, Paragraphs, and Other Structures of the Written Language

Grammar for Word Play

Reading, Writing, and Grammar

Punctuation, Spelling, Text Messaging, and Other Consequences of Grammar

Additional Learning Activities

More important things than grammar? Yes, according to some— punctuation.

(Crystal, 2006a, p. 131)

Commas really do make a difference. The student, said the teacher, is crazy. The student said the teacher is crazy.

(Jill Murphy in reviewing *Eats, Shoots & Leaves*— www.thebookbag.co.uk/trusseats.htm)

As you read your students' writing, you probably have said these things to yourself:

"If I can just get my students to start their sentences with a capital letter and end with punctuation."

"Why can't they understand the difference between a run-on sentence and two separate sentences?"

"They just seem to sprinkle commas like so many seeds or they leave their text barren."

"They either hate apostrophes or love them."

"Why is learning or teaching punctuation so difficult for so many students? Why is it possible for some students to write fairly well, with few "grammatical" errors, yet not understand punctuation?"

The first thing to realize is that writing predates punctuation. Second is that punctuation has developed and changed over time. Third is that different languages "perceive" punctuation differently and have different rules for sentence boundaries, capitalization, and apostrophes (if they even use apostrophes). Finally, the original purpose of punctuation (in Latin, then in English) was to approximate the oratorical cadences of the language for the orator, not the reader (Crystal, 2003, p. 278).

Today, writers and student writers are often judged by their ability to use punctuation "correctly" and to keep up with the changing rules. For example, do we put a comma before "and" in a series (often called the Harvard comma or the Oxford comma) or follow the *New York Times* and omit it? This topic of punctuation has been so bothersome to so many teachers that it has resulted in Lyne Truss's book on punctuation, *Eats, Shoots & Leaves* (2003), with over a million copies sold in the United Kingdom and the United States.

For this vast topic which fills school grammar books and has produced thousands of worksheets, we offer a starting point with several learning activities and many references from the Internet which you may want to explore. To put you at ease, we begin with a statement on punctuation from *The Oxford Companion to the English Language* (McArthur, 1992, p. 824):

> There are two extremes in use: heavy punctuation and light punctuation. In the 18th and 19th centuries, people tended to punctuate heavily, especially in their use of commas. Currently, punctuation is more sparing, but individuals and house styles vary in what they consider necessary: the same writer may punctuate more heavily or lightly for some purposes than for others.

As you can see, punctuation is not absolute, but conventional, and often depends on the writer's or the publisher's points of view. Nevertheless, there are some requirements for *standard* prose writing, with certain "exemptions" for poetry, advertising, public signs, and other nonprose writing. The conventions of punctuation are based on grammatical structure and serve both a linking function and a separating function (McArthur, 1992, p. 824). When we use commas in a series, the commas link as in "We have carrots, peas, and string beans." Commas (and other punctuation marks) also separate as in "We have carrots and peas, but no string beans." Furthermore, punctuation conventions are essential if your students are to be *marked as literate*. We have listed them in relative order of developmental usage, meaning that some punctuation conventions are easier for students to understand or perceive:

- capitalization
- periods
- question marks
- commas
- exclamations

- quotation marks
- apostrophes
- colons
- semicolons
- dashes
- parentheses

LEARNING ABOUT PUNCTUATION

Begin by telling your students that punctuation has a history and that the punctuation we are using today was not always the same and is very likely to change over time (as in text messaging and e-mail). Nevertheless, the point you want to make is that "punctuation counts," first because the reader depends on it for getting meaning and second because the writer is often judged as an "educated" writer by using current punctuation rules. Figure 12.1 is an informal pretest for students, which provides you (and them) with a starting point for discussion and instruction. We put discussion first because students need to fully understand the reasons for punctuation and know how to *remember* the plethora of rules, some of which are *absolute* (begin your sentence with a capital letter) and others which are *optional* (you can use a colon or a dash). When your students have completed the first part of Figure 12.1, have them complete the second part, Organizing Punctuation, and state or discuss the rule for the punctuation (e.g., We capitalize the names of people and their titles).

Figure 12.1   Personal Punctuation Assessment

Here are 10 sentences that need punctuation—capitalization, periods, commas, apostrophes, and exclamation marks. By hand or on the computer, add the punctuation you think is correct. The computer may give you some hints, but you will need to know more than the computer. Then meet with a partner and compare your changes. Discuss why you made them and why you and your partner might not have used the exact same punctuation. The first sentence has been done as an example.

1. i would love to go to camp summerfield this summer (Edited: I would love to go to Camp Summerfield this summer.)

2. my best friend abigail is going because she won a vermont state scholarship

3. the green mountains in vermont and the white mountains in new hampshire have some of the best camps

4. there is swimming water skiing and tennis

5. mr marshall the camp director is great so is ms. redstone the tennis coach

6. dad said we dont have enough money to go

7. mom said you can start saving the birthday money you get from grandma evelyn

8. i also decided to babysit every saturday and sunday

9. mom and dad were proud of me because i earned 100 dollars for my camp tuition

10. wow I cant believe my good luck and abigails good luck too

(Continued)

Figure 12.1 (Continued)

Organizing Punctuation

After your have finished your Personal Punctuation Assessment, use the grid to organize what you did and then complete the Punctuation Rules section.

Sentence	Capitals	Periods	Commas	Quotation Marks	Apostrophes	Exclamation Marks
1	I, Camp Summerfield					
2	My, Abigail, Vermont State Scholarship	.				
3	Green Mountains, Vermont, White Mountains, New Hampshire	.				
4	There	.	swimming, water skiing, tennis			
5	Mr. Marshall, Ms. Redstone	.	Mr. Marshall, the camp director, Ms. Redstone, the tennis coach			
6	Dad, We	.	said,	"We don't have enough money"	don't	
7	Mom, Grandma Evelyn	.	said,	"You can start saving the money you get from Grandma Evelyn"		
8	I, Saturday, Sunday	.				
9	Mom, Dad, I	.				
10	Wow, I	.			can't, Abigail's	Wow!

Punctuation Rules—Complete each sentence and give an example.

- We always use capital letters _____
- We always use periods _____
- We need to use commas _____
- We need to use quotation marks _____
- We need to use apostrophes _____
- We usually use exclamation marks _____

APPLICATION TO LEARNING

Commas, Quotation Marks, and Apostrophes

The Comma

We have selected these three punctuation items to expand on because they are heavily related to grammatical structures, their use can vary with writers' and editors' styles, and they can be difficult for students to fully understand. The word comma, from the Greek *komma,* which means a piece cut off, is probably one of the most difficult punctuation markers for students to use. In addition, writers, grammarians, and publishers often dispute or disagree with their usage. For those of you who wish to deepen your knowledge of the comma and its disputations, we are citing two (of several) Web sites on this topic: *When Is a Comma Splice NOT an Error* (Blue, 2000, http://www/grammartips.homestead.com/spliceok.html) and *Using Commas* (http://owl.english.purdue.edu.handouts/print/grammar/g_comma.html).

Figure 12.2 gives examples of using commas for the types of word separations where the comma is used to

- mark off a sequence of words, often called commas in a series, as in *dogs, cats, gerbils, and other household animals,*
- separate words that are called parenthetical or might also be marked off by parentheses, as in Ms. Benjamin, *a brilliant English teacher,* won the prize as Teacher of the Year,
- separate clauses or groups of words in sentences where the groups of words contain a noun and a verb or verbs, as in If *you need help* with your homework, *I'll be glad to work* with you, and
- separate words that mark time, connect, affirm, or negate, as *in From time to time,* we visit our relatives in Costa Rica. *Lately however,* we have been seeing them less and less. *Unfortunately,* my mother has not been well. *Nevertheless,* they know we miss them.

Figure 12.2 Commas for Clarification

Here are sentences that need commas. Work with a partner and put in commas where you think they belong. Then discuss with your partner why you think these commas are needed to make the sentences clearer for the reader.

1. Sara wished that for her birthday she would get a new coat a puppy and a book of crossword puzzles.
2. She knew that the new coat would keep her warm the puppy would give her love and the book of puzzles would keep her busy when she had nothing to do.
3. Five students all of whom were 11 years old won a trip to Japan.
4. Eliza a student from Georgia was one of the five students.
5. Josh knew that if he wanted to get high grades he had to study every night to reach his goal.
6. Even though the books he had to read were difficult he worked patiently to understand them.
7. As the sun rose in the east the travelers began their voyage. However the waves were high and dangerous. Nevertheless the travelers were skilled and brave. Several months earlier they had made the same voyage. Being brave and hardy they had confidence in their ability as sailors.

More Comma Practice With Parenthetical Phrases

Parenthetical phrases are word groups that are included within a sentence and set off by commas, as in "the man from Haiti." The phrases often seem to be an "aside" or provide additional of information. Another term for these phrases, which are included in the main sentence, is *apposition*. Parenthetical or appositional phrases allow the writer to add details without the need to write a full sentence. Figure 12.3 will get your students started in using these handy written forms.

Figure 12.3   Commas and Parenthetical Phrases

Here are two activities that will help you become a skilled writer. In activity A are a set of two sentences that can be combined into one for providing the reader with expanded information. In Activity B there are parenthetical phrases that need to be included in sentences. Write your own sentences using these phrases. Make sure you have used commas to "set off" the phrases. Then compare your sentences in A and B with one of your classmates. Contribute your favorite sentences to the class for a bulletin board of "Sentences With Parenthetical or Appositional Phrases." The first sentences in A and B have been done as examples.

A. Sentences to Combine

Two Sentences	Combined Sentences
1. Zeus was the lord of the sky, the rain god, and the cloud gatherer. Zeus was the son of a Titan.	Zeus, the son of a Titan, was the lord of the sky, the rain god, and the cloud gatherer.
2. Hera was Zeus's wife. Hera was the protector of marriage.	
3. Poseidon was Zeus's brother. Poseidon ruled the sea.	
4. The other brother was Hades who ruled the underworld. Hades was a dark, somber god.	
5. Pallas Athena was Zeus's daughter. Pallas Athena was the goddess of wisdom, reason, and protector of the city.	
6. Apollo had a chariot to drive the sun across the sky. Apollo was the god of truth and light.	
7. Artemis was the protector of woodland animals and plants. Artemis was Apollo's twin sister.	

B. Parenthetical Phrases in Search of a Sentence

Parenthetical Phrase	Sentence With Parenthetical Phrase
1. the youngest student in the class	1. Angela, the youngest student in the class, was also one of the most intelligent.
2. for many years	
3. while living in Africa	
4. as lifelong friends	
5. in the midst of a war	
6. from that moment on	
7. an adorable puppy	
8. having only few dollars in her pocket	
9. barely able to walk	
10. free at last	

Quotation Marks

Fewer punctuation marks give students more trouble than quotations because of their absolute rules and their optional roles. They are absolute when we want to use "direct speech" and quote someone's speech or written words:

She said, "The pot is on the stove."

Then there are double quotes and single or inside quotes:

I like when Little Red Riding Hood says to the Wolf, "I don't know what you mean when you say, 'Better to eat you with, my dear.'"

They can be optional when we put quotes around a word for highlighting or to indicate sarcasm or emphasis:

When he whispered words of "love," what did he really mean?

There are also ways to *quote* someone without using quotation marks, called indirect quotes:

Brutus asks forgiveness of the crowd when he tells them it's not that he *loved Caesar less,* but that he *loved Rome more.*

As you undoubtedly know, students need to read a lot to observe the different uses of quotation marks. They need lots of direct instruction. And they need editorial patience.

Figure 12.4 will give your students a starting point for building their understanding of this important, but elusive, punctuation form.

Figure 12.4   Quotes and Quotation Marks

Here is a conversation between Stanley and his friends from the book *Holes* (Sachar, 1998, p. 97), with the quotation marks missing. Work with a partner and put in the needed marks. Discuss why you need quotation marks and what problems a reader might have when they are left out.

Do you know the alphabet? Stanley asked.
I think I know some of it, Zero said. A,B,C,D.
Keep going, said Stanley.
Zero's eyes looked upward. E. . . .
F, said Stanley.
G, said Zero. I've heard it before. I just don't have it memorized exactly.
That's all right, said Stanley. Here, I'll say the whole thing just to refresh your memory,
then you can try it.

Quotation Marks for Emphasis or to Highlight Words or Phrases

Figure 12.5 (see page 188) illustrates an activity in which quotation marks are used to make the reader aware of particular words or phrases and are often used based on the writer's choice or decisions. For example, a writer might choose to use "quotation marks," *italics,* **bold,** or underline, the last three of which are part of the tool bar on the computer.

Figure 12.5   Highlight Your Words

Here are activities for which you will need a computer. Copy these nursery rhymes as they are written. Then decide which words or word groups you would like to "highlight" with "quotations marks," *italics,* **bold,** or underline. Then meet with a partner and discuss the reasons for your choices. How differently would you read these rhymes by *highlighting* the words?

Little Bo-Peep

Little Bo-Peep has lost her sheep,

And doesn't know where to find them.

Leave them alone and they will come home,

Wagging their tails behind them.

One Misty, Moisty Morning

One misty, moisty morning.

When cloudy was the weather,

I chanced to meet an old man clothed all in leather.

He began to compliment,

And I began to grin,

How do you do and how do you do,

And how do you do again?

Now try highlighting the words you think should be emphasized in the poem "The Charge of the Light Brigade" by Alfred, Lord Tennyson (1874):

Half a league, half a league,

Half a league onward,

All in the valley of Death

Rode the six hundred.

"Forward, the Light Brigade!

"Charge for the guns!" he said:

Into the valley of Death

Rode the six hundred.

"Forward, the Light Brigade!"

Was there a man dismay'd?

Not tho' the soldier knew

Someone had blunder'd:

Their's not to make reply,

Their's not to reason why,

Their's but to do and die:

Into the valley of Death

Rode the six hundred.

The Apostrophe

The *apostrophe* is a word from the Greek—apo/strophos—meaning a mark that *turns away*. This mark, common in English and rarely used in other languages, is often confusing to writers, especially student writers, because it serves several grammatical and vocabulary purposes with many "exceptions." It was introduced in the 16th century (McArthur, 1992) to indicate the loss of letters (as in o'er for over and 'tis for it is). Today the apostrophe is also used for

- omissions as in contractions (couldn't).
- omissions as in numbers (the '90s for the 1990s).
- word clippings as in huntin,' fishin' singin,' 'fraid, 'gator.
- possession for singular nouns as in the boy's hat.
- possession for plural nouns as in the girls' coats.

But while these uses seem fairly straightforward, complications occur because of complexities in English grammatical structure and idiosyncratic usage. For example, we have the men's, women's, and children's clothing in which the already pluralized noun is perceived as a *mass singular noun.* Then there are the nouns that already end in s (boss, Ms. Harris) which result in writing "the boss's computer" or "Ms. Harris's worksheets." In addition, advertisers and publishers often keep some possessive apostrophes and omit others as in Men's and Ladies Watches, Keats Poetry, Old Wives Tales. And above all there is the confusion of "its" and 'it's,' as in "*It's* a good day" for "*It is* a good day" or "*It's* been a good day" for "*It has* been a good day," followed by "The cat looked for *its* bowl." So what's a teacher or student to do?

The Apostrophe in Contractions

Figure 12.6 can be a starting point for helping your students sort out the confusing world of apostrophes and possibly enjoy the challenges. Figure 12.7 provides an activity with contractions with the word *Not.*

Figure 12.6 Sorting Out the Contractions of English

English has many words which are called contractions because they have been "contracted" or shortened. Contractions are formed by

- putting two words together,
- leaving out a letter or letters, or
- replacing the letter or letters with an apostrophe, as in *"let us go"* to *"let's go"* or *"she does not"* to *"she doesn't."*

Here are examples of English words that form contractions. Write the contraction and then write a short sentence using that contraction. The first contraction has been done as an example. Work with a partner and compare and discuss your work.

(Continued)

Figure 12.6 (Conitnued)

Separated Words	Contracted Words or Contractions	Sentence Using Contraction
I will	I'll	I'll see you in the morning.
I have		
I might have		
We could have		
I would		
He will		
They will		
She is		
Let us		
We are		
They are		

Figure 12.7   Contractions With the Word *Not*

Here are words that have been *contracted* with the word *not.* Separate the words. Then write a sentence with the separated words. Discuss with your partner or class when you might use contractions and when you would use the separated words.

Contractions	Separated or Noncontracted Words	Sentence With Noncontracted Words
isn't	is not	The teacher is not here today.
aren't		
wasn't		
weren't		
hasn't		
haven't		
hadn't		
can't		
couldn't		
wouldn't		
shouldn't		
doesn't		
don't		
didn't		
won't		

The Apostrophe for Singular and Plural Nouns

Figure 12.8 is an activity for making students aware of the variations in using apostrophes in singular and plural nouns. As we mentioned earlier, some rules are absolute, others are optional. Welcome discussion on this difference with your students.

Figure 12.8   The Apostrophe for Singular and Plural Nouns

In this activity you have to decide whether to place an apostrophe before the letter *s*, after the letter *s*, or not use the apostrophe at all. This use of the apostrophe is called "The Possessive" or "The Genitive" and signals the idea of *ownership* or *belonging to*. Work with a partner and discuss your choices and reasons. The answers can be tricky. The first two are done as examples.

Missing Apostrophe	Add Apostrophe or Leave Blank (there may be more than one answer)	Reason for Decision
Sylvias home	Sylvia's	The house belongs to Sylvia or is where Sylvia lives.
her sisters homes	sister's or sisters'	Sylvia's sister has many homes or Sylvia has more than one sister and they have homes.
Mr. Charles bookstore Maxs notebook the fifth graders work Chelsea Lanes gardens my best friends brothers and sister		

The Apostrophe for Clipped Words in Literature

Most people are likely to "clip" words when they speak conversationally or informally, dropping the [-ng] sound (rushin' around) or saying *yeah* instead of *yes* or *how'd you do* or *what's a matter?* When these clipped words are written, the custom is to use an apostrophe to indicate the loss of sounds. Bret Harte, Mark Twain, and Joel Chandler Harris are among American writers who have written dialogue in what is called the *vernacular* or *indigenous speech*, to provide the audience with a sense of realism. To give the audience a "visualization" of this speech, they have made extensive use of the apostrophe as well as other punctuation and spelling devices. In fact, there is the Greek word *apheris*, which means the dropping or clipping from a word as in 'cept for except, s'pose for suppose, and many others. Students may already be aware of them if they have been reading Mark Twain's *The Adventures of Huckleberry Finn* (1885) or *The Adventures of Tom Sawyer* (1876).

Figure 12.9 is a collection of sentences using clipped words which students can "unclip" and then discuss why authors might use them.

Figure 12.9 Clipped Words and Apostrophes

Many writers, most notably Mark Twain, have use "clipped words" to try to accurately write the way their characters speak. For example, in the *Adventures of Tom Sawyer* (1876), Mark Twain has Tom Sawyer "saying," "A body can't be too *partic'lar* how they talk *'bout* these-yer dead people" (p. 10). You will notice that the single apostrophe shows that when Tom speaks he leaves out certain sounds or syllables. Here are sentences which contain clipped words. "Unclip" the words and write them in what is called "standard spelling" (e.g., *'bout* for *about*), in contrast to spelling that is used to imitate speech. The first one is done as an example.

Sentences With "Clipped Spellings" Using Apostrophes	"Unclipped" Standard Spelling
It's *'bout* time you came home.	about
Everyone came to the party *'cept* my brother.	
No one move *'til* I tell you.	
I *'most* passed the test, but I forgot the last answer.	
I was *goin'* to call you, but the phone was dead.	
We can't *'low* them to stand *'round* in the street.	
When the waiter asked the customer if he wanted water, he said, "*O' course* I do."	
We always answer "*Yes'm*" to be polite.	
'Cause he was sick, he couldn't go to school.	

Colons, Semicolons, and Dashes

These three forms of punctuation are often elusive to young writers, and for good reason. While they represent separateness, they are not quite periods or as the British say, "full stops." The colon has several conventional uses which students can recognize:

1. In a salutation of a formal letter:

   Dear Dr. Hoffman:

2. In the introduction as in item 1 or to a set of ideas as in this example:

   These are the main points for understanding economics:

3. To lead from one point to another as in:

   I want to emphasize my position: all students have the ability to learn.

The semicolon is more complicated because it is closely related to the period as well as the comma (which is why it has both a period and a comma). The best explanation to students for its use is that it links statements that are very close in meaning or ideas. And while these statements could be separated by periods, their closeness is better revealed by the semicolon. Here's an example: *Their situation was desperate; retreat was the only alternative.*

Dashes are often an alternative to semicolons because many writers feel less secure about the semicolon (McArthur, 1992). The dash, while sometimes a substitute for the semicolon, has its own uses:

1. For emphasis—*She became a lawyer in spite of her poverty—and a good lawyer indeed.*

2. To indicate a pause—*There is only one way out—through the tunnel.*

3. As an afterthought—*He couldn't imagine what he would do—when suddenly a brainstorm.*

In Figure 12.10 are activities for colons, semicolons, and dashes.

Figure 12.10   Upgrade Your Punctuation With Colons, Semicolons, Commas, and Dashes

Here is part of a speech made by Susan B. Anthony in 1871 after she was arrested for casting an illegal vote in the presidential election. The colons, semicolons, commas, and dashes are missing. Work with a partner and decide which of these punctuation markers you would use and why you would use them.

It was we the people not we the white male citizens nor yet we the male citizens but we the whole people who formed the Union. And we formed it not to give the blessings of liberty but to secure them not to the half of ourselves and the half of our posterity but to the whole people women as well as men. And it is a downright mockery to talk to women of their enjoyment of the blessings of liberty while they are denied the use of the only means of securing them provided by this democratic-republican government the ballot. (see www.quotedb.com/quotes/324)

The Parentheses

This word, from the Greek *parenthesis,* means "a placing between." Parentheses are used to qualify, explain, or place into apposition words that interrupt a construction or idea, but are also related to that construction or idea. The use of parentheses may seem optional or may often be replaced by commas or dashes. As writers mature, they make use of these punctuation options, but also avoid overusing them. Figure 12.11 illustrates a passage that might need parentheses, commas, or dashes.

Figure 12.11   Missing Parentheses, Commas, Colon, Semicolons, and Dashes

This passage is from Toni Morrison's book *Beloved* (1987). Some of the punctuation has been removed. There are two places where she uses parentheses and other places where she uses commas, dashes, and semicolons. Work with a partner and decide where you might put these punctuation markers. Following this passage is a copy of how Toni Morrison punctuated the passage. Compare your punctuation with Toni Morrison's.

124 WAS SPITEFUL. Full of a baby's venom. The women in the house knew it and so did the children. For years each put up with the spite in his own way but by 1873 Sethe and her daughter Denver were its only victims. The grandmother Baby Suggs was dead, and the sons Howard and Buglar had run away by the time they were thirteen years old as soon as merely looking in a mirror shattered it that was the signal for Buglar as soon as two tiny band prints appeared in the cake that was it for Howard. Neither boy waited to see more another kettleful of chickpeas smoking in a heap on the floor soda crackers crumbled and strewn in a line next to the doorsill. Nor did they wait for one of the relief periods the weeks months even when nothing was disturbed. No. Each one fled at once the moment the house committed what was for him the one insult not to be borne or witnessed a second time. (p. 3)

(Continued)

Figure 12.11 (Continued)

Beloved **Book Excerpt**

124 WAS SPITEFUL. Full of a baby's venom. The women in the house knew it and so did the children. For years each put up with the spite in his own way, but by 1873 Sethe and her daughter Denver were its only victims. The grandmother, Baby Suggs, was dead, and the sons, Howard and Buglar, had run away by the time they were thirteen years old—as soon as merely looking in a mirror shattered it (that was the signal for Buglar); as soon as two tiny hand prints appeared in the cake (that was it for Howard). Neither boy waited to see more; another kettleful of chickpeas smoking in a heap on the floor; soda crackers crumbled and strewn in a line next to the doorsill. Nor did they wait for one of the relief periods: the weeks, months even, when nothing was disturbed. No. Each one fled at once—the moment the house committed what was for him the one insult not to be borne or witnessed a second time. (Morrison, 1987, p. 3)

SPELLING AND GRAMMAR

We have already touched on the relationships between spelling and grammar in our discussion on morphology and etymology (Chapters 3 and 4), where we have seen that the spelling of many words in English is related to its history, as in the continued use of "silent" letters (g in sign) , in its contraction system (as in they're for they are), and the many homophones that "sound" the same but signal different meanings (to, too, two).

These aspects of English spelling can be troublesome to many students, and because "spelling counts," students often "lose points" even on good writing. By understanding and explaining the complexity of spelling, we can give our students historic information and also help them remember the "rules" for what appears to be inconsistent spelling.

Figure 12.12 shows the original or earlier spelling of many of the words that have a "silent gh," followed by an activity that requires the student to write the current spellings. You will notice that in all of these words, the hard [g] was pronounced. This sound only became "silenced" as generations began to "clip" the [g] phoneme. In addition, there are a few words in which the *gh* became the phoneme [f] as in *cough, rough, tough,* and *enough.*

Figure 12.12 The *gh* Words in the English Language

You may have wondered why there are so many words in English that have the spelling *gh*, yet you do not pronounce what should be the *sound* for these letters. You probably think of these letters as "silent." In most of these words with *gh.* Yet, a long time ago, in a period now called Old or Middle English, the *g* (or *gh*) was pronounced. Over time, people stopped pronouncing this sound or "clipped" it. And in some words, they changed the sound of [gh] to [f] as in *cough.* In the following activity are earlier spellings of words where the *gh* is no longer pronounced or is pronounced as [f]. Next to these words are sentences with a missing *gh* word. Fill in the missing words with their modern spellings. Compare your answers with a partner and try pronouncing the original Old English words to each other. The first one is done as an example.

Old or Middle English Phonetic Spelling With Sounded [g] or [k]	Sentence to Complete (example is given)	Modern Spelling
baug	When the <u>bough</u> breaks the cradle will fall.	bough
coghen	When I get a cold, I always start to _____ .	
daug	We prepared the _____ to make our bread.	
genug (clue: first letter is now silent also)	I hope I have _____ money to get home.	
acht	After the number seven, comes the number _____ .	
tochter (the first letter will also change)	My grandma had a son and a _____ .	
thaug	Even _____ this lesson is hard, I understand it.	
slagter	To get meat, we have to _____ animals.	
heg	The explorers had to climb a _____ mountain.	

Homophones

Many languages have homophones (sometimes called homonyms), meaning that the words are pronounced the same, but have different meanings and are distinguished in reading by different spellings (e.g., sail, sale). Homophonic spelling errors are perceived both as spelling and vocabulary errors especially, as in "I saw *there* houses where *their* living with *they're* friends" or "*Its* time to tell *it's* name." Activities with homophones can be made humorous and lively. In Figure 12.13 there is an example of a homophonic exercise that students can enjoy and be the basis of discussion and further lessons.

Figure 12.13 Homophony

Homophones are words that have the same sound but with different meanings and spellings. Following are sets of homophones for composing homophonic sentences, such as "The *knight rode* on a dusty *road* through the *night* in order to give the *maid* a necklace he had *made* for her." Write five sentences combining as many homophones as you can into one sentence. Then work with a partner and collect your own list of homophones.

Homophonic Pairs

guest—guessed

prints—prince

groan—grown

hoarse—horse

some—sum

tow—toe

Sunday—sundae

ceiling—sealing

soared—sword

knows—nose

roomer—rumor

tail—tale

we—wee

mail—mail

Text Messaging—The New Grammar

Many of your students are undoubtedly far ahead of teachers and parents in their ability to text message, which is today's new language tailored to current technology.

How this new "grammar" will develop and what its consequences will be is uncertain, but we can certainly predict that its use will grow and expand and certainly change styles of writing, spelling, and punctuation. Figure 12.14 is a starting point for acknowledging this communication and for acknowledging the messaging skills that your students may already have.

Figure 12.14   Numbers and Symbols for Text Messaging (Add Others)

You might want to add these text messaging "words" to your own text messaging vocabulary. One group is made up of the numbers 2, 4, 8, and 10. The other group comes from mathematical symbols and icons (signs) on your computer. Send a message to a classmate using these symbols. Here is an example:

*2bad the 4cast 4 2morrow neg8s any chance of 10is. There will b a # of *s who will lose lots of $ and make < they hoped 4.*

2	4	8	10
2day	4most	b8	10der
2morrow	4tune	cr8	10is
2night	4head	d8	10tacle
2n	4ce	f8	10t
2t	4father	gr8	10sion
2th	4cast	h8	10ant
2lip	4go	l8	10d
2tor	4man	m8	10ement
2–2	4sight	pl8	10or
2zday	4give	r8	10th
	4midable	s8	10acious
	4ward	st8	10derloin
	4close	appreciat8	10fold
	4bid	negoti8	10tative
	4go	investig8	
		initi8	
		hesit8	
		cooper8	

INTERNET SITES

- http://grammar.ccc.commnet.edu/grammar/marks/semicolon.htm

- http://owl.english.purdue.edu/handouts/grammar/g_overvw.html

- http://www.kidskonnect.com/content/view/346/27

- http://www.webopedia.com/quick_ref/textmessageabbreviations.asp

- http://www.e-speec.com/index.htm

Introduction

Language and Metalanguage

Builders of Linguistic Intelligence

Parts of Speech and the English Language

Syntax and Semantics

The Polyglot of English

The Polyglot: Beyond Latin and Greek

Return to Parts of Speech

Sentences, Paragraphs, and Other Structures of the Written Language

Grammar for Word Play

Reading, Writing, and Grammar

Punctuation, Spelling, Text Messaging, and Other Consequences of Grammar

Additional Learning Activities

CHAPTER THIRTEEN

Additional Learning Activities

For this final chapter, we have added student activities based on the information in many of the previous chapters. Use as many of them as you need, and adapt them to based grade and student levels. Included are activities for sentence development, paragraph writing, vocabulary building, and other aspects designed to build "linguistic intelligence" for high level language achievement. If you need the rationale or explanation for these activities, use the table of contents or the index to find the references. We hope your students enjoy including them in their language studies and apply what they have practiced in their reading, writing, and content area learning.

BUILDING SENTENCE POWER

APPLICATION TO LEARNING

The following activities will get you started writing sentences that will help you become a master of spoken and written language in just about every subject area. Work with a partner or a small group of classmates so that you can share and discuss what you wrote and why you think what you wrote is so "masterful."

- Figure 13.1—Plan to Expand
- Figure 13.2—People in Apposition
- Figure 13.3—Verbs of Locomotion for Getting Places
- Figure 13.4—To + Verb = One Great Sentence
- Figure 13.5—Past Tense Openers

Figure 13.1   Plan to Expand

Following is a Taxonomy of Adjectives that can make your sentences informative and powerful. Use the words from this taxonomy to give your readers expanded information in the four sentences that follow. You can add your own adjectives if you wish and check the meanings of adjectives you do not yet know. Submit two of your favorite sentences to your teacher for posting on a wall or bulletin board. If you like this activity, write your own sentences using these adjectives.

Sentences in Search of Adjectives

1. Twenty _____ children from my school decided to share their _____ adventures with a group of _____ visitors from Mexico.

2. Prowling through the _____ jungle, a pride of _____ lions attacked the _____ zebras.

3. Standing on the top of the _____ mountain, we looked up at the _____ sky and were thrilled to feel so _____ and _____.

4. My best friend is not only _____, but he/she is also _____, _____ and _____.

• TAXONOMY •
Adjectives for Information and Power

A	angry, appreciative
B	bold, brilliant
C	courageous, careful
D	dependable, daring
E	energetic, entertaining
F	fierce, friendly
G	generous, graceful
H	honest, huge
I	innocent, intelligent
J	joyful, jocular
K	kind, knowledgeable
L	likeable, loving
M	miserable, magnificent
N	noble, needy
O	overbearing, obedient
P	polite, pleasant
Q	quiet, quick-witted
R	reasonable
S	sympathetic, spectacular
T	timid, thoughtful
U	useful, understanding
V	valiant, victorious
W	warm-hearted, wild
X	xenophobic
Y	youthful, young
Z	zealous, zestful

Figure 13.2   People in Apposition

You can often improve your writing by combining two sentences into one sentence. One way to do this is by writing a parenthetical sentence, which is also called an appositional sentence. Follow these directions, and you will have spectacular sentences that give lots of information to your audience.

- Read these two sentences about Harriet Tubman:
  Harriet Tubman guided hundreds of slaves to freedom via the Underground Railroad.
  Harriet Tubman was a dedicated leader.

- Combine them using apposition. Notice where you have to put commas.
  Harriet Tubman, *a dedicated leader,* guided hundreds of slaves to freedom via the Underground Railroad.

(Continued)

Figure 13.2 (Continued)

Now combine these five pairs of sentences about people of accomplishment:

1. Susan B. Anthony fought tirelessly for women's right to vote.

   Susan B. Anthony was a determined social activist.

2. Mary Cassatt was honored by the French government for her outstanding works of art.

   Mary Cassatt was an American impressionist painter.

3. Andrew Z. Fire and Craig C. Mello won the Nobel Prize for physiology and medicine for their discovery of RNA interference—gene silencing by double-stranded RNA.

   Andrew Z. Fire and Craig C. Mello are medical school professors.

4. Lewis Latimer (1848–1928) was an African American who invented an important part of the light bulb—the carbon filament.

   Lewis Latimer worked in the laboratories of both Thomas Edison and Alexander Graham Bell.

5. Maria Tallchief became a world-renowned ballet star.

   Maria Tallchief was the daughter of an American Indian.

If you like this activity, research other people of accomplishment, and write sentences using apposition to provide your audience with information.

Figure 13.3 Verbs of Locomotion for Getting Places

By starting your sentences with the -ing form of the verb, you can create interesting images and ideas that will entertain and entice your audience. Here are five pairs of sentences to get you started. Read the first sentence in the pair. Then complete the second sentence in your own words. Here is an example:

The astronaut was flying at 20,000 miles per hour in space.

Flying at 20,000 miles per hour in space, the astronaut knew she was breaking all speed records.

1. The monkeys were swinging from tree to tree.

   Swinging from tree to tree, _____.

2. The sponge collectors from Greece were diving into the clear waters of the Aegean Sea.

   Diving into the clear waters of the Aegean Sea, _____.

3. The sky divers were gliding gracefully over the Rocky Mountains.

   Gliding gracefully over the Rocky Mountains, _____.

4. The mother kangaroos were hopping along with their joeys in their pouch.

   Hopping along with their joeys in their pouch, _____.

5. The Olympic team was skating peacefully on Lake Placid.

   Skating peacefully on Lake Placid, _____.

If you think this activity can make you a better writer, compose five more sentences that begin with the -ing form of verbs of locomotion.

Figure 13.4   To + Verb = One Great Sentence

Another way to write great sentences is to know how to start with the word *to* plus a verb as in *to understand* or *to imagine*. Some books call this construction the *infinitive*. Here are five sentence pairs. Read the first sentence in the pair. Then complete the second sentence that begins with the word *to* followed by a verb. Here's an example:

The counselor told the students **to prepare** for their final tests.

To prepare for the final tests, the students met together every afternoon for three weeks.

1. Mr. Harris tried **to be** a good father.

   To be a good father _____.

2. The fifth graders decided **to help** the retired citizens.

   To help the retired citizens _____.

3. Francine wanted **to please** her grandfather.

   To please her grandfather _____.

4. Kevin wanted **to win** a scholarship.

   To win a scholarship _____..

5. My mother taught us how **to answer** the telephone properly.

   To answer the telephone properly _____.

Figure 13.5   Past Tense Openers

Here are five sentence pairs. The second sentence begins with the past tense of a verb. Finish each sentence with your own ideas related to the story of King Arthur. Here's an example:

Through Merlin's teachings, Arthur was **determined** to rule Camelot wisely.

Determined to rule Camelot wisely, Arthur gathered brave knights from all over the kingdom.

1. Arthur was **destined** to be a great king.

   Destined to be a great king _____.

2. Merlin **prepared** Arthur to understand the world from different points of view.

   Prepared by Merlin to understand the world from different points of view _____.

3. Merlin was **delighted** with Arthur's intelligence and sense of humor.

   Delighted with Arthur's intelligence and sense of humor _____.

4. At times, Merlin was **angered** by Arthur's lack of attention.

   Angered by Arthur's lack of attention _____.

5. At other times, Merlin was **amused** by Arthur's pranks and jokes.

   Amused by Arthur's pranks and jokes _____.

PARAGRAPHS AND TRANSITIONS

Writing paragraphs can be tricky, because there is no exact formula. Writers often experiment with what sounds like a paragraph and looks like a paragraph. The following activities will give you practice in putting together separate sentences that seem to make up a whole.

- Figure 13.6—Transitions for History
- Figure 13.7—Transitions for Greek Gods
- Figure 13.8—Transitions for Comparing and Contrasting
- Figure 13.9—Transitions for Dinosaurs

Figure 13.6 Transitions for History

To write a well-ordered or cohesive paragraph, you often have to use transitions. These are words that tie together or unite ideas. In the following activity there is a list of transitional words, followed by nine sentences. Put the appropriate transitional words in front of each sentence. Compare your answers with a partner. Read your paragraph aloud to your partner and discuss how the transitional words help this story on American history hang together.

Transitional Words	
at last	furthermore
at the time	however
but	in addition
consequently	nevertheless
despite	repeatedly
eventually	therefore
finally	thus
frequently	

_____ the Revolutionary War broke out at Lexington and Concord on April 18, 1775, very few colonists wanted independence _____ their differences with England. Most colonists merely wanted the right of self-government from the British Empire _____ Parliament and King George refused to allow the colonists to levy their own taxes. _____ King George removed the colonies from his protection and blockaded their ports _____. The colonists hoped that King George would come to his senses and listen to their arguments. _____ the British enlisted the help of hired Hessian troops and incited the Indians to fight the colonists. _____ The colonists had no choice but to rebel, _____ the embittered colonists declared their independence on July 4, 1776.

Now write your own paragraph using some of the transitional words listed earlier.

Figure 13.7 Transitions for Greek Gods

Following is a set of notes on four of the gods from Greek mythology. By using transitions words, you can write a paragraph for each of these gods using the information from the notes. Here are the transition words, followed by an example of a paragraph about Hades, the god of the underworld.

Transition Words or Phrases You Can Use

although, as a result of, even though, however, in fact, nevertheless

Sample Paragraph:

Hades, a brother of Zeus, ruled the underworld and controlled its wealth. **Although** he lived in this unwelcome part of the Earth, he was not evil. **In fact**, his job was to protect the dead. **However,** he was not a pleasant character. **As a result of** living without sunshine and flowers, he had a dark and gloomy character. **Even though** he left the underworld from time to time to visit his brother Zeus or other siblings, he was rarely cheerful or pleasant. **Nevertheless,** Hades could be sympathetic and understanding, as when he permitted his wife Persephone to return to Earth for several months each year so that she could see her mother Demeter and enjoy the brightness and beauty of the Earth.

Notes for Your Paragraphs

Name of God	Role or Function	Positive or Strong Characteristics	Negative or Weak Characteristics
Zeus	supreme ruler of the Greek gods	fair and just; helped his brothers; despised war	deceived his wife Hera; was easily deceived by others
Hera	wife of Zeus; protector of marriage and married women	helped women in childbirth; inspired heroic deeds	fiercely jealous; inflicted cruel punishments
Athena	daughter of Zeus; goddess of wisdom and the city	sponsored arts and crafts; inspired wisdom, reason, and purity	fierce and ruthless when attacked; unforgiving
Apollo	god of light and truth	never uttered false words; kind and generous to humans	could be unpitying to humans when angered

Figure 13.8 Transitions for Comparing and Contrasting

Here is a set of notes about Earth and Venus separated by a Venn diagram. Following the notes is a Frame to guide you in writing a paragraph about these two planets. The opening sentence states how these two planets are similar. Complete the rest of the paragraph or paragraphs by using the notes on Earth and Venus. When you have finished, underline the transition words that organize what you have written. Then use these transition words to write your own paragraph or paragraphs on a topic you are studying in class.

Figure 13.8 (Continued)

Frame to Complete Paragraph(s)

Earth and Venus are considered to be twin planets because they have a similar diameter, density, mass, and gravity, as well as similar internal structures. Venus, however, differs from Earth in several significant ways. First, _____. It also _____. In addition _____.
Unlike Venus, Earth _____. It also _____. There are other major differences between the two planets. Venus _____, while Earth _____. Furthermore, _____.
So while Earth and Venus are "twins," they _____.

Figure 13.9 Transitions for Dinosaurs

Following is a set of notes about three different dinosaurs.

1. Using the notes, write three separate paragraphs, one for each dinosaur. Indent for each paragraph.

2. Begin with this starting sentence:

   Three dinosaurs have always interested me. (Name the three dinosaurs from the notes.)

3. Start your second and third paragraphs with transition words such as

   "Unlike Allosaurus" or *"Another dinosaur"* or *"Different from . . ."* or *"Similar to . . ."* or *"In contrast to . . ."*

4. End with the following sentence:

   I plan to continue studying about dinosaurs so that . . . . (Put in your own words so that you have a conclusion.)

Notes on Three Dinosaurs

Allosaurus	Ankylosaurus	Diplodocus
meat eater	plant eater	plant eater
more than 30 feet long	about 10 feet long	about 88 feet long
moved on two large hind legs	body covered with bony plates	long whip-like tail
used powerful tail for support in walking or standing	row of spikes on each side of body	brain about the size of a fist
	clublike tail with mass of bone on end	

Combining for Paragraphs and Powerful Paragraph Starters (Figures 13.10 and 13.11)

Figure 13.10   American Folk Heroes

Here is a set of notes on heroes from American folk literature, with five categories or organizers:

- Literary Character
- Occupation
- Locale
- Childhood Influences
- Characteristics

Write a paragraph about each of these literary characters using the information provided. You can add your own words and ideas to the paragraph. Here is an example:

Joe Magarac was a **steel worker** from **Pittsburgh**. According to the legend, Joe Magarac was born in an iron ore pit where he was found by explorers searching for metal to make steel. He grew up to be a **gigantic man, made of steel muscles and bones. He would eat enormous amounts** of food to satisfy his great hunger and was known to **work like a mule** and be able to **stir molten iron with his arms**.

Literary Character: Davy Crockett

Occupation: explorer of the frontier

Locale: Tennessee

Childhood Influences: excellent hunter and marksman at an early age

Characteristics: could talk with animals; friendly to everyone; powerful of build

Literary Character: Pecos Bill

Occupation: cowboy

Locale: Texas, the Southwest

Childhood Influences: brought up on mountain lion's milk; lost by his parents; raised by coyotes

Characteristics: great strength and daring; could hug a bear to death; could ride a cyclone like a bronco; invented the lasso, six-shooter, spurs, and the branding iron

Literary Character: Johnny Appleseed

Occupation: planter of apple trees

Locale: Pennsylvania, Ohio, Indiana

Childhood Influences: always carried apple seeds; could make plants grow

Characteristics: selfless, gentle, a healer; loved apple trees and animals

Literary Character: John Henry

Occupation: railroad man; hammer man

Locale: the American south

Childhood Influences: first thing he reached for as a baby was a hammer; loved trains

Characteristics: great strength and endurance; hardworking; natural ability for steel-driving; devoted husband and father

Figure 13.11 Numerous Combinations

Here is information related to the numbers two through nine. Combine the information for each of these numbers into one sentence. Then write three or four more sentences that explain or "elaborate" on the information in your combined sentence. Here is an example for the number one.

Number One

I once had a **unicycle.**

It was **unique.**

I rode it **each day.**

I rode it to get to the **monorail.**

Combined: I once had a **unique unicycle** which I rode **each day** to get to the **monorail.**

Number Two

The **twins** ride to school.

They ride **biweekly.**

They ride on their **bicycle.**

The **bicycle** is built for **two.**

Combined: _____ .

Number Three

There was a **trio** of **triplets.**

They sang every **third** day.

They sang **three** songs.

They played the **triangles** in the school band.

Combined: _____ .

Number Four

There was a **quartet** of **quadruplets.**

They walked over to the **quadrangle.**

They wanted to see four **quadrupeds.**

The quadrupeds were dancing a **quadrille.**

Combined: _____ .

Number Five

We went to the **Pentagon** building.

We went to hear a family of **quintuplets.**

The quintuplets were playing a **quintet** written by Mozart.

Their playing was the **quintessence*** of musical brilliance.

Combined: _____ .

* In case you want to know, the five "essences" according to Aristotle were four known "elements"—water, earth fire, air—and ether, said to permeate all things. Their extraction was one of the chief goals of alchemy.

Number Six

We heard a **sextet** sung by **sextuplets**.

They sang a **half a dozen** songs.

Each song was composed of six **sextains.**

The sextet sang on a **hexagonal** stage.

Combined: _____.

Number Seven

We gave my grandmother a pin in the shape of a **heptagon.**

We gave her the pin when she was **seventy** years old.

We gave her a birthday card that said, "To our favorite **septuagenarian."**

Her seven grandchildren were thrilled to celebrate her **septennial** year.

Combined: _____.

Number Eight

My uncle is having his **eightieth** birthday.

He will be come the eighth **octogenarian** in our town.

He will join an **octet** of singers.

The singers are called the **Octaves**.

Combined: _____.

Number Nine

My great grandfather celebrated his **ninetieth** birthday.

He celebrated for **nine** days.

He became the first **nonagenarian** in our family.

The family gave him a watch in the shape of a **nonagon**.

Combined: _____.

Writing With the Polyglot of English

By now you have realized that the English vocabulary is composed of words from many different languages. Figures 13.12–13.15 provide an opportunity to include some of the words in your writing. Here are the names of the activities:

- Figure 13.12—Roman Zoo
- Figure 13.13—"Geo-"—Greek for Land
- Figure 13.14—Foreign Exchange
- Figure 13.15—African American Proverbs

Figure 13.12   Roman Zoo

In ancient Rome, the people spoke a language called Latin. By the time of the period called the Renaissance, many Latin words had become part of the English language. These Latin words almost doubled the vocabulary of English, giving speakers two word choices for the same idea or concept. For example, we have the word *dog*, which comes from the early English called Anglo-Saxon, and we also have the word *canine*, which comes from the Latin word for dog (and related animals). In addition, we often have words of Latin origin for our common English words. For example, the Anglo-Saxon word *hug* can be replaced with the Latin-based word *embrace*.

In the activity that follows are English sayings or proverbs that use our Anglo-Saxon words for common animals. Replace the underlined Anglo-Saxon words with words of Latin origin, which you would find in an "Ancient Roman Dictionary." Here is an example of the substitution of Latin words for Anglo-Saxon words:

Keep the wolf away from your door.
Keep the lupine away from your portal.

Saying or Proverb	Latin Words for the Animals	Other Latin Words
1. Let sleeping dogs lie.	canine(s)	remain dormant, somnolent
2. A bird in the hand is worth two in the bush.	avine	a duo
3. Don't put the cart before the horse.	equine	carriage, chariot
4. Keep away from a bear that hugs.	ursine	embrace
5. Don't kill the goose that lays the golden egg.	anserine	ovum
6. When the cat is away, the mice will play.	feline, muridine	cavort
7. Don't behave like a bull in a china shop.	taurine	comport yourself
8. Beware of a wolf in sheep's clothing.	lupine	garments, vestments

Figure 13.13   "Geo-"—Greek for Earth or Land

Without words from the Greek language, speakers of English would have a hard time today explaining science, medicine, history, geography, and the Bible. We depend on Greek words for these and many other topics. Following is a group of words that all have the prefix geo-, which in Greek means Earth or land. Work with a partner and check the meanings of the words that you don't recognize. Write their definitions in your notebook. Then write a story using as many of these words as you can. Compare your story with your partner's.

Geo- Occupations	Geo- Subjects	Geo- Adjectives
geographer	geography	geographical
geologist	geology	geological
geometer, geometrician	geometry	geometrical
geophysicist	geophysics	geophysical
geobotanist	geobotany	geobotanical
geochronologist	geochronoloy	geochronological
geochemist	geochemistry	geochemical
		geodesic
		geothermal

Figure 13.14 Foreign Exchange

In the following template are English words that have entered the language through French, Spanish, and Italian. (Spellings may have changed.) Write a humorous or fantasy story using as many of these words as possible. You can add other words from these languages. Here are some suggestions to get you started.

You can include

- several characters who were born in France, French Canada, Spain, Mexico, South and Central America, the Caribbean Islands, or Italy
- a description of the setting (place and time)
- what is happening to these characters
- what problems the characters have or face
- how the problems are resolved

Words From French	Words From Spanish	Words From Italian
ballet	alligator	broccoli
banquet	bonanza	carnival
chandelier	barbecue	cameo
chauffeur	bronco	carousel
chef	fiesta	confetti
dialogue	hammock	cartoon
elegant	machete	finale
intrigue	mosquito	lagoon
parachute	mustang	opera
pigeon	patio	piano
rendezvous	rodeo	pizza
sabotage	sombrero	pistachio
unique	vigilante	spaghetti
voyage	vanilla	umbrella

Figure 13.15 African American Proverbs*

When the African slaves were brought to the American colonies, they brought with them the wisdom of their family heritage. Much of this wisdom was carried in their words, the only thing they could bring from Africa that belonged uniquely to them. Here is a selection of proverbs from different places where slaves came from or were brought to. Proverbs are a form of wise sayings that express wise thoughts.

Read each proverb and, with a partner, discuss what you think it means. Then use each proverb to explain what this wise saying means to you. There is an example for you to follow.

Proverb from the country of Kenya

A person who does not know one thing, knows another.

My explanation

Even if you don't know much about the sky, you can still know about the land.

Proverb from African Americans

Tell me whom you love, and I'll tell you who you are.

My explanation

_____

Proverb from the country of Tanzania

That which is good is never finished.

My explanation

_____

Proverb from Jamaica

Do more, talk less.

My explanation

_____

Proverb from Central Africa

No one is without knowledge except the one who asks no questions.

My explanation

_____

*These proverbs come from http://geocities.com/warmautumnsrealm/africanproverbs.html (retrieved on July 13, 2007).

HAVING FUN WITH GRAMMAR AND WORDS

Figures 13.16 and 13.17 have activities that can make you (or your audience) laugh. We hope so.

Figure 13.16 Double Meanings

Here are four headlines that you may never see, but would make good stories. Choose one of the headlines, and write a funny story that explains what happened. Share your story with a partner. If you like this activity, write another story with a different headline.

Headlines:

Cops Nab Two for Shooting Basketballs

Detectives Find Criminal Killing Time

A Group of Thieves Caught Stealing Bases

Whipping Cream Declared a Crime

Figure 13.17   Acrostic Varieties

You can have varied and interesting sentence starters by using acrostics, a style of writing in which you use the letters of a word to create a story or poem. By using acrostics you learn to avoid starting your sentences with the same words. Here is an example using the word *pizza*.

"**P**epperoni!" shouted Tony.

Immediately I knew I would have a good lunch.

"**Z**esty and delicious," I told my friend.

Zealously, I bit into the hot, tasty pizza.

"**A**nother pepperoni," I said to Tony, "and heavy on the cheese."

Here is a selection of topics for writing your own acrostic stories. Write at least four of them, and share them with your family and friends. You can also add your own topics.

Friends	Singer
Baseball	Secrets
Money	Horses
School	Dancing

References

Print References

Allen, R. L (1972). *English grammar and English grammars.* New York: Scribner.

Andersen, H. C. (1914). *The ugly duckling.* New York: P.F. Collier & Son. (Original work published 1855)

Armbruster, B. B., & Osborne, J. (2001). *Putting reading first.* Washington, DC: Center for the Improvement of Early Reading Achievement, United States Department of Education.

Barber, C. (2000). *The English Language: A historical introduction.* Cambridge, UK: Cambridge University Press.

Berg, C. (2003). The role of grounded theory and collaborative research. *Reading Research Quarterly, 38*(1), 105–111.

Bryson, B. (1990). *The mother tongue.* New York: William Morrow and Company.

Campbell, J. (1988). *The power of myth.* New York: Anchor Books.

Carle, E. (1984). *The very busy spider.* New York: Penguin Young Readers Group.

Carroll, L. (1995a). *Alice's adventures in wonderland.* New York: Random House. (Original work published in 1861)

Carroll, L. (1995b). *Through the looking glass and what Alice found there.* New York: Random House. (Original work published in 1872)

Chomsky, N. (1957). *Syntactic structures.* New York: Humanities Press.

Chomsky, N. (1965). *Aspects of the theory of syntax.* Cambridge, MA: MIT Press.

Claiborne, R.. (1989). *The roots of English.* New York: Times Books.

Crystal, D. (1995). *The Cambridge encyclopedia of the English language.* New York: Cambridge University Press.

Crystal, D. (2003). *The Cambridge encyclopedia of the English language* (2nd ed.). New York: Cambridge University Press.

Crystal, D. (2006a). *The fight for English.* New York: Oxford University Press.

Crystal, D. (2006b). *Words, words, words.* New York: Oxford University Press.

Cullen, R., & Kuo, I-Chun. (2007). Spoken grammar and ELT course materials: A missing link? *TESOL Quarterly, 41*(2), 361–386.

Delpit, L. (1995). *Other people's children.* New York: The New Press.

Delpit, L. (1998). The silenced dialogue: Power and pedagogy in educating other people's children. *The Harvard Educational Review, 58,* 61.

Delpit, L. (2001). *The skin that we speak.* New York: The New Press.

Delpit, L., & Dowdy, J. K. (Eds.). (2001). *Thoughts and language culture in the classroom.* New York: The New Press.

Diamond, J. (1992). *The third chimpanzee.* New York: Harper Perennial.

Dillard, J. L. (1972). *Black English.* New York: Random House.

Douglass, F. (2003). *Narrative of the life of Frederick Douglass, an American slave.* New York: Barnes & Noble. (Original work published 1845)

Dr. Seuss. (1996). *The foot book.* New York: Random House.

Frith, M. (1973). *I'll teach my dog a lot of words.* New York: Random House.

Frost, R. (1916). *The poetry of Robert Frost.* New York: Holt, Rinehart & Winston.

Gardner, D., & Davies, M. (2007). Pointing out frequent phrasal verbs: A corpus-based analysis. *TESOL Quarterly, 41*(2), 339–359.

Gardner, H. (1993). *Multiple intelligences: The theory in practice.* New York: Basic Books.

Garmonsway, G. N. (Ed.). (1939). *Aelfric's colloquy.* London: Methuen.

Gomez, K., & Madda, C. (2005). Vocabulary instruction for ELL Latino students in the middle school classroom. *Voices From the Middle, 13*(1), 42–47.

Hamilton, E. (1969). *Mythology.* New York: Warner Books.

Howard, P. (1985). *The state of the language.* New York: Oxford University Press.

Jackson, Y. (2005). Unlocking the potential of African American students: Keys to reversing underachievement. *Theory Into Practice, 44*(3), 203–210.

Jensen, E. (1998). *Teaching with the brain in mind.* Alexandria, VA: Association for Curriculum and Development.

Joos, M. (Ed.). (1957). *Readings in linguistics: The development of linguistics in America since 1925.* Washington, DC: American Council of Learned Societies.

Juster, N. (1989). *The phantom tollbooth.* New York: Random House.

Labov, W. (2003). When ordinary children fail to read. *Reading Research Quarterly, 38*(1), 128–131.

Lakoff, G., & Johnson, M. (1980). *Metaphors we live by.* Chicago: University of Chicago Press.

Lederer, R. (1991). *The miracle of language.* New York: Simon & Schuster.

Lederer, R. (1994). *Adventures of a verbivore.* New York: Simon & Schuster.

Lederer, R. (1998). *Crazy English.* New York: Simon & Schuster.

Lowth, J. (1762). *A short introduction to English grammar with critical notes.* London: J. Lodsley.

Macrone, M. (1991). *It's Greek to me.* New York: HarperCollins.

Macrone, M. (2005). *Mad libs.* New York: Penguin Books.

Mallory, J. P. (1989). *In search of the Indo-Europeans.* New York: Thames & Hudson.

McArthur, T. (Ed.). (1992). *The Oxford companion to the English language.* New York: Oxford University Press.

McArthur, T. (2002) *Oxford guide to world English.* New York: Oxford University Press.

McCrum, R., Cran, W., & NacNeil, R. (1986). *The story of English.* New York: Viking.

McWhorter, J. (1998). *Word on the street.* Cambridge, MA: Perseus Publishing.

Milne, A. A. (1957). *The world of Pooh.* New York: Dutton Children's Books.

Morrison, T. (1987). *Beloved.* New York: Alfred Knopf.

National Council of Teachers of English. (NCTE, n.d.). *Some questions and answers about grammar.* Retrieved July 3, 2008, from http://www.ateg.org/grammar/qna.php

National Council of Teachers of English/International Reading Association. (NCTE/IRA, 1998). *Standards for the English language arts.* Retrieved July 3, 2008, from http://www.ncte.org/about/over/standards/110846.htm

Nessel, D. D., & Graham, J. M. (2007). *Thinking strategies for student achievement* (2nd ed.). Thousand Oaks, CA: Corwin Press.

Nurnberg, G. (2001). *The way we talk now.* New York: Houghton Mifflin.

Oxford English dictionary. (2008). New York: Oxford University Press.

Paterson, K. (1977). *Bridge to Terabithia.* New York: HarperCollins.

Peregoy, S., & Boyle, O. (2004). *Reading, writing, and learning in ESL* (5th ed.). New York: Allyn & Bacon.

Perkins, D. (1992). *Smart schools.* New York: Free Press.

Perry, T., & Delpit, L. (Eds.). (1998). *The real Ebonics debate.* Boston: Beacon Press.

Piaget, J. (1954). *The construction of reality in the child.* New York: Basic Books.

Piaget, J. (1972). Intellectual evolution from adolescence to adulthood. *Human Development, 15,* 1–12.

Pinker, S. (1994). *The language instinct.* New York: HarperCollins.

Pinker, S. (1999). *Words and rules.* New York: HarperCollins.

Pinker, S. (2007). *The stuff of thought.* New York: Viking.

Random House Webster's unabridged dictionary. (2000). Seattle, WA: Random House.

Rosten, L. (1982). *Hooray for Yiddish.* New York: Simon & Schuster.

Rothstein, A., Rothstein, E., & Lauber, G. (2007a). *Writing as learning.* Thousand Oaks, CA: Corwin Press.

Rothstein, A., Rothstein, E., & Lauber, G. (2007b). *Write for mathematics* (2nd. ed.). Thousand Oaks, CA: Corwin Press.

Rothstein, E. (2005). *My great grandma Clara.* New York: Marble House Editions.

Rothstein, E. (2006). *My great grandpa Dave.* New York: Marble House Editions.

Rothstein, E. (2008a). *Dave the boxer.* New York. Marble House Editions.

Rothstein, E. (2008b). *Clara becomes a citizen.* New York: Marble House Editions.

Rothstein, E., Berliner, L., & Berliner, S. (1986). *Staying at the top.* Nyack, NY: ERA/CCR Corp.

Rothstein, E., & Gess, D. (1992). *Teaching writing.* Suffern, NY: The Write Track.

Ruhlen, M. (1994). *The origin of language.* New York: John Wiley & Sons.

Sachar, L. (1998). *Holes.* New York: Dell Yearling.

Simmons, J., & Baines, L. (Eds.). (1998). *Language study in middle school, high school, and beyond.* Newark, DE: International Reading Association, Inc.

Tennyson, A. (1854). *The charge of the light brigade.* London: The Examiner.

Trudgill, P. (1974). *Sociolinguistics.* New York: Penguin Books.

Truss, L. (2003). *Eats, shoots & leaves.* New York: Gotham Books.

Twain, M. (1876). *The adventures of Tom Sawyer.* Boston: Harvard College Library.

Twain. M. (1885). *The adventures of Huckleberry Finn.* New York: Harper Brothers Publishers.

United States history. (4th ed.). (2004). Parsippany, NJ: Globe Fearon.

VanTassel-Baska, J., Johnson, D. T., & Boyce, L. N. (1996). *Developing verbal talent.* Boston: Allyn & Bacon.

Vygotsky, L. S. (1936). *Thought and language.* Cambridge, MA: The MIT Press. (Original work published 1934)

Wolfram, W. (1998). Linguistic and sociolinguistic requisites for teaching language. In J. Simmons & L. Baines (Eds.), *Language study in middle school, high school, and beyond* (pp. 79–109). Newark, DE: International Reading Association, Inc.

Internet References

Beyond root words: morphology and the connection to reading skills. (1997). Retrieved April 10, 2007, from Scientific Learning Corporation Web site: http://www.brainconnection.com/content/6_1

Blue, T. (2000). *When is a comma splice not an error?* Retrieved July 28, 2007, from http://www/grammartips.homestead.com/spliceok.html

Greek and Latin roots for GRE preparation. (n.d.). Retrieved April 10, 2007, from http://www.msu.edu~defores1/gre/roots/gre_rts_afx1.htm

Text messaging abbreviations. (n.d.). Retrieved July 28, 2007, from http://www/webopedia.com/quick_ref/textmessagingabbreviations.asp

The verb of "to be." (n.d.). Retrieved July 28, 2007, from http://grammar.ccc.commnet.edu/grammar/to_be.htm

What is phonology? (n.d.). Retrieved July 28, 2007, from http:www.sil.org/linguistics/glossaryoflinguisticterms/whatisphonology.htm

Index

"A," 135
ABC books, 177–178, 179 (figure)
Accent, 21
Acrostics, 96, 211 (figure)
Address, forms of, 14–15
Adjectives, 57–58, 59–62 (figure), 171 (figure), 199 (figure)
  adverbs and, 63–64 (figure)
  Latin roots for, 92–93 (figure)
Adventures of a Verbivore, 155
Adventures of Huckleberry Finn, The, 191
Adventures of Tom Sawyer, The, 191, 192 (figure)
Adverbs, 63–65
Advertising sentences, 73, 74 (figure)
Aelfric's Colloquy, 7
Affixes, 43, 58, 59 (figure), 60–61 (figure), 161–162 (figure)
African American/African words and expressions, 121–122 (figure), 210 (figure)
Agreement
  tense, 147–148, 149–150 (figure)
  verb, 150, 151 (figure)
"Ain't," 50–51
Alice's Adventures in Wonderland, 154, 173
Allen, Robert L., 1, 66, 100, 148
  on determiners, 134
  on elliptical sentences, 71
  on morphology, 30
  on parts of speech, 50
  on semantics, 33
  on sentences, 141
  on two-part verbs, 128
Alliterative writing, 107 (figure)
American folk heroes, 205 (figure)
American Indian languages, 121–124
"An," 135
Andersen, H. C., 83 (figure)
Anglo-Indian English, 124, 125 (figure)
Anglo-Saxon languages, 17, 35, 84, 108–109
  parts of speech, 47, 52, 53, 58
  See also Germanic languages

Animal similes, 156 (figure)
Anthony, Susan B., 193 (figure)
Apostrophes, 189–191, 192 (figure)
Application to learning, morphology, 23–27, 28 (figure)
Apposition, people in, 199–200 (figure)
"-arch" words, 97, 98–99 (figure)
Armbruster, B. B., 21
Articulation, 21
Assembly for the Teaching of English Grammar, 5
Assessment, punctuation, 183–184 (figure)
Awareness, phonemic, 21

Beloved, 193–194 (figure)
Berg, C., 14
BE verb, 47–51
Beyond Root Words, 28
Bible, Greek words from the, 102–103 (figure)
Black language, 4
Blending, phoneme, 22
Blue, T., 75, 185
Body language
  idioms, 157
  verbs of, 54, 55 (figure), 81 (figure)
Boundaries in written sentences, 144
Boyce, L. N., 166, ix
Boyle, O., 20
Bridge to Terabithia, 148
Britain. *See* England
Bryson, Bill, 22, 29, viii
Building sentence power, 198, 199–201 (figure)
"By" verb, 131 (figure)

Cambridge Encyclopedia of the English Language, The, 142
Campbell, Joseph, 100
"Can," 57
"Can/could," 138–140
Carle, Eric, ix
Carroll, Lewis, 37, 154, 173, 174–176 (figure), xiii

Categorization
    noun, 47 (figure), 171 (figure)
    phoneme, 22
    verb, 54–57, 80, 81 (figure)
Characters, comedic, 163–164 (figure)
Chaucer, Geoffrey, 40
Children's literature, 169–173
Chinese language, 125, 126 (figure)
Chomsky, Noam, 3, 33, 38, 82
    on children and grammar instruction, 167–168
    on sentence deconstruction, 144–145
Churchill, Winston, 127
"Ch" words, 104 (figure)
Clarification, commas for, 185 (figure)
Clarifying and sorting, 88–89
Clauses, 142, 143 (figure)
Clipped words, 191, 192 (figure)
Codes of power, 15
Colons, 192–193
Color, adjectives of, 171 (figure)
Colorful expressions, 160
Columbus, Christopher, 116
Combining reading with grammar, 166–178,
    179 (figure)
Comedic characters, 163–164 (figure)
Commas, 185–186
Comparison
    adjectives of, 171 (figure)
    transitions for, 203–204 (figure)
Complete sentences, 2
Composing with keywords, 82
Conjugation forms, 51–54
Conjunctions, 132–133, 137
Consonant changing, 23
Contractions
    apostrophes in, 189–190 (figure)
    and the BE verb, 50–51
Contrasting, transitions for, 203–204 (figure)
Coordinating conjunctions, 133
Correct usage, 2
"-crat" words, 97, 98–99 (figure)
Crazy English, 155
Creole, 12–13
Crystal, David, 19, 39, 148, ix
    on parts of speech, 127, 134
    on punctuation, 181, 182
    on sentences, 141, 142
Culture of power, 15

"Dare," 138–140
Dashes, 192–193
Davies, M., 168
Deconstructing sentences, 144–146, 147 (figure)
Deep structure of sentences, 144–146,
    147 (figure)
Delpit, L., 4, 11, 14, 15, 70
Department store, noun, 41–43
Determiners, 134–135
Developing Verbal Talent, 166

Dialect, 8–11
Dictionaries, unabridged, 44–45
Dinosaurs, transitions for, 204 (figure)
Dominant group members, 15
Double meanings, 211 (figure)
Douglass, Frederick, 177, xiii
Dowdy, J. K., 14, 15
"Down" verb, 131 (figure)
Dr. Seuss, ix

East Indian languages, 124, 125 (figure)
Eats, Shoots & Leaves, 181, 182
Elliptical sentences, 71–73
England
    and the Indian subcontinent, 124
    Norman invasion of, 17, 111
English Grammar and English Grammars, 66
English language. *See* Language, English
Eponyms, 158–159
Etymology, 22, 24 (figure), 34–36, 95 (figure),
    99 (figure), 101 (figure)
    spelling and, 104
Expanders, verb, 50
Expressions, colorful, 160

Fairy tales, 167–168
Fight for English, The, 39
Foot Book, The, ix
Formal to friendly voice, 152, 153 (figure)
Forms of address, 14–15
Fragments, sentence, 75, 76 (figure),
    142, 143 (figure)
French language, 86, 108–109, 111–112,
    113–115 (figure), 209 (figure)
Friendly to formal voice, 152, 153 (figure)
Frith, M., 83 (figure), 169–170
Frost, Robert, 167
Fun with grammar and words, 211 (figure)
Future tenses, 57

Gardner, D., 168
Gardner, H., 19, 20
Garmonsway, G. N., 7
Germanic languages, 17, 36, 47, 109,
    110–111 (figure)
    See also Anglo-Saxon languages
Gesture, verbs of, 54, 55 (figure), 81 (figure)
"Gh" words, 194–195 (figure)
"Global lingua franca," 84
Gomez, K., 14
Graham, J. M., 82
Grammar, English
    ABC books for building, 177–178, 179 (figure)
    Black Language, 4
    children's literature and, 169–173
    combining reading with, 166–178, 179 (figure)
    as correct usage, 2
    current standards related to teaching, 5–6
    defined, 1–3, 10 (figure)

fairy tales and, 167–168
as glue holding language together, 3
Greek grammar and, 18
having fun with words and, 211 (figure)
high literary purposes of, 4
history of teaching, 3–4
inflections, 39
as it is, viii
language, dialect, and, 8–11
Latin grammar and, 3–4, 18, viii–ix
Lewis Carroll and the teaching of,
    173, 174–176 (figure)
spelling and, 104, 194, 195 (figure)
text messaging, 196, 197 (figure)
traditional rules, 1–2, 127–128, vii–viii
what should be taught in, ix–x
for word play, 154–155
See also Language, English
Grammar, Latin, 3–4, viii
Grammatical voice, 152, 153 (figure)
Great Britain. *See* England
Greek language
    in the Bible, 102–103 (figure)
    grammar, 18
    Greek pantheon and, 100, 101 (figure)
    influence on English spelling, 104
    Latin linked to, 104, 105–106 (figure)
    in mathematics, 96
    in myths and literature, 99, 100 (figure)
    Olympian Gods and, 100, 101 (figure),
        203 (figure)
    in the sciences, 95
    in the social sciences and related subjects,
        97, 98–99 (figure)
    taxonomy, 95–97, 100–106 (figure)
    words in English, 85–86, 93–104, 94 (figure),
        105–106 (figure), 208–209 (figure)

Haitian Creole, 12–13
Hamilton, Edith, 100, 101 (figure)
Hardy, Thomas, 141
Harris, Joel Chandler, 191
Harte, Bret, 191
High literary purposes of grammar work, 4
High literate performance, 21
History
    of the English language, 16–18, 34–36
    of teaching grammar in the U. S., 3–4
    transitions for, 202 (figure)
Holes, 148, 187 (figure)
Holmes, Oliver Wendell, Jr., 108
Homophones, 195, 196 (figure)
Howard, P., 7

Identity, phoneme, 22
Idioms, 157, 176 (figure)
I'll Teach My Dog a Lot of Words, 83 (figure),
    169–170
Imitation writing, 82, 83 (figure)

Incomplete sentences, 142, 143 (figure)
Indian subcontinent languages, 124, 125 (figure)
Indo-European languages, 124
Infinitives, split, 148, 149–150 (figure)
Inflections, 39
International Reading Association (IRA), 5
Isolation, phoneme, 22
Italian language, 118, 119 (figure), 209 (figure)

"Jabberwocky," 173, 174–176 (figure)
Japanese language, 125, 126 (figure)
Jensen, E., 20
Jews and Yiddish, 119
Johnson, D. T., 166, ix
Johnson, M., 155
Johnson, Samuel, 18
Jones, William, 124
Joos, M., 13, 14
Juster, Norton, 154, 176–177

Keywords, composing with, 82

Labov, W., 14
Lakoff, George, 155
Language, English, 7–8
    brief history of, 16–18, 34–36
    creole and pidgin, 12–13
    defined, 8–9
    dialect, grammar, and, 8–11
    etymology, 22, 24 (figure)
    five major aspects of, 19–20
    morphology, 22–30, 31–32 (figure)
    phonology, 20–22, 24 (figure),
        28–30, 31–32 (figure)
    registers, 13–16
    semantics, 33, 34 (figure)
    slang, 11–12
    sounds of, 21
    spelling, 104
    structure of, 38–39
    syntax, 2, 33
    taxonomy and, 8
    whole, 22
    See also Grammar, English; Parts of speech;
        Polyglot composition of English;
        Punctuation; Word play; Words
Latin language
    grammar, 3–4, 18, viii–ix
    Greek linked to, 104, 105–106 (figure)
    words in English, 84–85, 85 (figure), 86–87,
        91 (figure), 92–93 (figure), 208 (figure)
Lauber, G., 8, 21
Lederer, R., 19, 84, 166, 173
Linguistic power, 15
Linking words, 136 (figure)
Literature
    ABC books, 177–178, 179 (figure)
    apostrophe for word clippings in,
        191, 192 (figure)

children's, 169–173
combined with grammar, 166–178, 179 (figure)
Greek words in, 99, 101 (figure)
of Lewis Carroll, 37, 154, 173,
    174–176 (figure), xiii
of Norton Juster, 154, 176–177, xiii
Locomotion, verbs of, 54, 55 (figure), 78 (figure),
    80, 200 (figure)
Lowth, Robert, 18

Macrone, M., 155
Madda, C., 14
Mad Libs, 155
Major sentences, 142
Manifest Destiny, 116
Mathematics, Greek words from, 96
"May," 57
"May/might/must," 138–140
McArthur, T., 138
    on American Indian words, 122
    on determiners, 134
    on the English language,
        4, 8, 11, 12, 38, 63, 108
    on "global lingua franca," 84
    on Greek, 93
    on Latin, 87
    on morphology, 33
    on phonology, 21
    on punctuation, 182, 189, 192
    on sentences, 66, 68
McWhorter, J., 67, 141
Meanings
    deep structure and, 144–146, 147 (figure)
    double, 211 (figure)
    surface structure and, 147 (figure)
Memory, rote, 27
Messaging, text, 196, 197 (figure)
Metacognition, 76–79
Metalanguage
    defined, 8
    language, dialect and grammar in, 8–11
    register and, 16
Metaphors, 155
Middle English period, 17
Milne, A. A., ix
Mind, verbs of the, 54, 55 (figure), 81 (figure)
Minor sentences, 142
Modal words, 138–140
Morphology, 2
    as an extension of phonology,
        28–30, 31–32 (figure)
    application to learning, 23–27, 28 (figure)
    of the BE verb, 48, 49 (figure)
    Latin roots, 91 (figure)
    nouns and, 41–45
    parts of speech, 39, 40 (figure)
    pronouns and, 40–45
    templates, 29–30
    verb, 32 (figure), 173–174 (figure)

Morrison, Toni, 193–194 (figure)
Mother Goose, 167, 188 (figure)
Mother Tongue, The, viii
Murphy, Jill, 181
Murray, Lindley, 3
Mythology, 100 (figure)
Myths, Greek, 99, 101 (figure)

Names
    comedic characters and, 163–164 (figure)
    eponyms, 158–159
*Narrative of the Life of Frederick Douglass, an
    American Slave*, 177, xiii
National Council of Teachers of
    English (NCTE), 5
Native American words, 121–124
"Need," 138–140
Negative meanings, verbs that denote,
    54, 56 (figure)
Nessel, D. D., 82
Nonadvertising sentences, 73, 74 (figure)
Non-morphological words, 30, 39, 64–65
    taxonomy of, 40, 41 (figure)
Norman invasion of England, 17, 111
Norse language, 17
"Not," 190 (figure)
Nouns
    agreement with verbs, 150, 151 (figure)
    apostrophes for singular and plural, 191
    by categories, 47 (figure), 171 (figure)
    defined, 45 (figure)
    Latin roots for, 92–93 (figure)
    and morphology, 41–45
    proper, 47
Null change verbs, 53
Numerous combinations, 206–207 (figure)
Nurnberg, G., 16

Olympian Gods, 100, 101 (figure), 203 (figure)
Origins of English, 17
Osborne, J., 21
"Out" verb, 131 (figure)
*Oxford Companion to the English Language,
    The*, 2, 4, 11, 15, 63, 138, 182
Oxymora, 157, 158 (figure)

Pantheon, Greek, 100, 101 (figure)
Paragraphs
    starters, 205–207 (figure)
    transitions and, 202, 203–210 (figure)
Parentheses, 193–194 (figure)
Parenthetical phrases, 186
Parts of speech, 29, 38, 87–88
    adjectives, 57–58, 59–62 (figure), 63–64
        (figure), 92–93 (figure), 171 (figure),
        199 (figure)
    adverbs, 63–65
    conjunctions, 132–133, 137
    determiners, 134–135

expanding definitions of, 46–51
modal words, 138–140
morphology, 39–45
nouns, 41–45, 92–93 (figure), 150, 151 (figure)
"other," 65
prepositions, 129, 132 (figure)
pronouns, 40–41, 75 (figure)
teaching English through the structure of the
    English language and, 38–39
transition, 133–134
verbs, 31 (figure), 32 (figure), 47–57,
    75 (figure), 92–93 (figure), 128, 129,
    130–131 (figure), 150, 151 (figure), 177
"wh-" words, 136–137
See also Words
Paterson, Katherine, 148
Patterns in written words, 27, 28 (figure)
People in apposition, 199–200 (figure)
Peregoy, S., 20
Perry, T., 11
Phantom Tollbooth, The, 154, 176–177, xiii
Phonemes, 21–22, 194
Phonemic awareness, 21
Phonetics, 21
Phonics, 21
Phonology, 20–22, 24 (figure)
    morphology as an extension of,
        28–30, 31–32 (figure)
Phrases, 142, 143 (figure)
    parenthetical, 186
Piaget, J., 14
Pidgin, 12–13
Pinker, S., 3, 141, 148
    on determiners, 134
    on morphology, 30, 33
    on parts of speech, 37, 38
    on sentences, 67, 142, 145
Plural determiners, 135 (figure)
Plural nouns and apostrophes, 191
"-polis" words, 97, 98–99 (figure)
Polite speech, 14
Polyglot composition of English
    African American/African words in,
        121–122 (figure), 210 (figure)
    American Indian words in, 121–124
    Chinese and Japanese words in,
        125, 126 (figure)
    East Indian words in, 124, 125 (figure)
    French words in, 86, 108–109, 111–112,
        113–115 (figure), 209 (figure)
    Germanic words in, 17, 36, 47, 109,
        110–111 (figure)
    Greek words in, 85–86, 93–104,
        105–106 (figure), 208–209 (figure)
    Italian words in, 118, 119 (figure), 209 (figure)
    Latin words in, 85 (figure), 85–87, 91 (figure),
        92–93 (figure), 208 (figure)
    Spanish words in, 116, 117 (figure),
        209 (figure)

writing with, 207, 208–210 (figure)
Yiddish words in, 119, 120 (figure)
Positive meanings, verbs that denote,
    54, 56 (figure)
Power
    building sentence, 198, 199–201 (figure)
    paragraph starters, 205–207 (figure)
    register as, 15–16
Pragmatics, 69
Predicates, sentence, 68, 75, 146–147
Prepositions, 129, 132 (figure)
Prior statements, 76 (figure)
Pronouns, 40–45, 75 (figure)
Pronunciation, 21
Proper nouns, 46
Prosody, 69
Punctuation
    apostrophes, 189–191, 192 (figure)
    colons, semicolons, and dashes, 192–193
    commas, 185–186
    importance of, 181–182
    learning about, 183, 184 (figure)
    parentheses, 193–194 (figure)
    personal assessment, 183–184 (figure)
    quotation marks, 187, 188 (figure)
    text messaging and, 196, 197 (figure)
    types of, 182–183
Putting Reading First, 21–22

Quotation marks, 187, 188 (figure)

Random House Webster's Unabridged Dictionary,
    2, 11, 50, 51 (figure), 57, 66, 128, 138, 140
Reading combined with grammar,
    166–178, 179 (figure)
Reclassifying adverbs, 64–65
Registers
    defined, 13–15
    as power, 15–16
    as solidarity, 16
Religion, Greek words and, 100–101 (figure),
    100–101 (figure)
Restatements, story, 168
Roots, word, 89–90 (figure), 94 (figure)
Rote memory, 27
Rothstein, A., 8, 21
Rothstein, E., 8, 21, 34, 76, 79, 82
Rule-Based camp, 18
Rules, grammar, 1–2, 127–128, vii–viii
Run-ons, 75

Sachar, Louis, 148, 187 (figure)
SAT (Scholastic Aptitude Test), 5
Scandinavian languages, 36
Sciences, Greek words from the, 95
Segmentation, phoneme, 22
Semantics, 33, 34 (figure), 68
    taxonomy of, 69
    transition words, 134 (figure)

Semicolons, 192–193
Sense, sentence, 70–75, 76–79, 76 (figure), 82
Sentences
    advertising, 73, 74 (figure)
    boundaries in written, 144
    complete, 2
    construction, 2
    converting from spoken to written,
        142, 143 (figure)
    deconstructing, 144–146, 147 (figure)
    defined, 66–68
    elliptical, 71–73
    expansion activity, 76–80 (figure)
    fragments, 75, 76 (figure), 142, 143 (figure)
    improving, 76–79
    major and minor, 142
    metacognition and, 76–79
    numbers in, 206–207 (figure)
    people in apposition, 199–200 (figure)
    power, building, 198, 199–201 (figure)
    run-on, 75
    semantics and, 70–82, 83 (figure)
    sense, 70–75, 76–79, 76 (figure), 82
    spoken, 142, 143 (figure)
    stretchers, 79, 80 (figure), 81 (figure)
    structure standards, 5
    subjects and predicates, 68, 75, 146–147
    syntax, 2, 33
    tenses, 57, 147–148, 149–150 (figure),
        201 (figure)
    units, 142, 143 (figure)
    written, 70, 142, 143 (figure), 144
"Shall/should," 57, 138–140
Sight words, 21–22, 23, 25–27 (figure), 27
Similes, 156
Singular determiners, 135 (figure)
Singular nouns and apostrophes, 191
Slang, 11–12
Snow White, 167
Social sciences, Greek words from,
    97, 98–99 (figure)
Solidarity, register as, 16
Sorting and clarifying, 88–89
Sounds of language, 21
Spanish language, 116, 117 (figure),
    209 (figure)
Speech, parts of. *See* Parts of speech
Spelling, 194, 195 (figure)
    influence of Greek on English, 104
Split infinitives, 148, 149–150 (figure)
Spoken sentences, 142, 143 (figure)
Standards related to teaching grammar, 5–6
Starters, paragraph, 205–207 (figure)
Stretchers, sentence, 79, 80 (figure), 81 (figure)
Structure of English language, 38–39, 87–88
Subjects, sentence, 68, 75, 146–147
Subordinating conjunctions, 133
Suffixes, 58

Surface structure of sentences, 147 (figure)
Syntax, 2, 33, 67, 68, 70

Taxonomy, 8, 79
    adjectives, 199 (figure)
    affixes, 161–162 (figure)
    African American words, 121–122 (figure)
    American Indian words, 122, 123 (figure)
    Anglo-Indian words, 124, 125 (figure)
    children's literature and, 169–170
    Chinese and Japanese words, 126 (figure)
    colorful expressions, 160
    comedic characters, 163–164 (figure)
    eponyms, 159 (figure)
    etymology, 35–36
    French words, 113–115 (figure)
    Germanic words, 109–111 (figure)
    Greek words, 94 (figure), 95–97,
        100–106 (figure)
    Italian words, 119 (figure)
    metaphors, 155
    non-morphological words, 40, 41 (figure)
    oxymora, 158 (figure)
    phonology, 21
    semantic terms, 69
    Spanish words, 116–117 (figure)
    "up" verb, 129 (figure)
    words of time or when, 64 (figure)
    Yiddish words, 120 (figure)
Templates, morphology, 29–30
Tenses, 57, 147–148, 149–150 (figure), 201 (figure)
Text messaging, 196, 197 (figure)
Text versions of stories, 168
"That," 137
"The," 135
Through the Looking Glass,
    37, 173, 174–176 (figure)
"To be" verb, 47–51
Tomlin, Lily, 127–128
Tone, 11–12
"To" + verb, 201 (figure)
Traditional rules for English grammar,
    1–2, 127–128, vii–viii
Transformational meaning, 145
Transition words, 133–134
    for comparing and contrasting,
        203–204 (figure)
    for dinosaurs, 204 (figure)
    for Greek gods, 203 (figure)
    for history, 202 (figure)
    paragraphs and, 202, 203–210 (figure)
Trudgill, P., 14, 15
Truss, Lyne, 182
Twain, Mark, 191, 192 (figure)
Two-part verbs, 128, 129, 130–131 (figure)

Ugly Duckling. In Tales., 83 (figure)
Unabridged dictionaries, 44–45

Unclassified words, 172 (figure)
United States History, 145
Units, sentence, 142, 143 (figure)
"Up" verb, 129 (figure), 130 (figure)
Usage, correct, 2
Using Commas, 185

VanTassel-Baska, J., 166, ix
Verbs, 75 (figure), 177
    agreement with nouns, 150, 151 (figure)
    BE, 47–51
    categories, 54–57, 80, 81 (figure)
    conjugation forms, 51–54
    contractions, 50–51
    defining, 47, 48 (figure)
    expanders, 50
    forms, 31 (figure)
    of gesture, 54, 55 (figure), 81 (figure)
    Latin roots for, 92–93 (figure)
    of locomotion, 54, 55 (figure), 78 (figure),
        80, 200 (figure)
    of the mind, 54, 55 (figure), 81 (figure)
    morphologies, 32 (figure), 173–174 (figure)
    OUT, BY, and DOWN, 131 (figure)
    tenses, 57
    that denote positive and negative meanings,
        54, 56 (figure)
    "to" +, 201 (figure)
    two-part, 128, 129, 130–131 (figure)
    UP, 129 (figure), 130 (figure)
    of vocalization, 81 (figure)
Very Busy Spider, The, ix
Vocalization, verb of, 81 (figure)
Voice, grammatical, 152, 153 (figure)
Vowel changing, 23
    verb, 52–54

Webster, Noah, 3
"What," 136–137
When Is a Comma Splice NOT an Error, 185
"Which," 136–137
"Who," 136–137
Whole language, 22
"Wh-" words, 136–137
"Will," 57
William the Conqueror, 17, 111, 112 (figure)
"Will/would," 138–140
Word play
    affixes and, 161–162 (figure)
    colorful expressions, 160
    comedic characters, 163–164 (figure)
    eponyms, 158–159
    grammar for, 154–155
    idioms, 157, 176 (figure)
    metaphors, 155
    oxymora, 157, 158 (figure)
    similes, 156

Words
    African American/African,
        121–122 (figure), 210 (figure)
    American Indian, 121–124
    from the Bible, 102, 103 (figure)
    Chinese and Japanese, 125, 126 (figure)
    clippings, apostrophes for, 191, 192 (figure)
    East Indian, 124, 125 (figure)
    etymology, 22, 24 (figure),
        34–36, 95 (figure)
    French, 86, 108–109, 111–112,
        113–115 (figure), 209 (figure)
    German, 17, 36, 47, 109, 110–111 (figure)
    Greek, 85–86, 93–104, 105–106 (figure),
        208–209 (figure)
    having fun with grammar and, 211 (figure)
    homophone, 195, 196 (figure)
    Italian, 118, 119 (figure), 209 (figure)
    Latin, 85, 85 (figure), 86–87, 91 (figure),
        92–93 (figure), 208 (figure)
    mathematics, 96
    modal, 138–140
    morphology, 2, 22–30, 31–32 (figure)
    in myths and literature, 99, 100 (figure)
    non-morphological, 30, 39, 40, 41 (figure),
        64–65
    patterns in written, 27, 28 (figure)
    phonology, 20–22, 24 (figure)
    roots, 89–90 (figure), 94 (figure)
    science, 95
    semantic inferences from specific,
        33, 34 (figure)
    sight, 21–22, 23, 25–27 (figure), 27
    social science, 97, 98–99 (figure)
    sorting and clarifying, 88–89
    Spanish, 116, 117 (figure), 209 (figure)
    terms for understanding structures of, 87–88
    of time or when, 64 (figure)
    unclassified, 172 (figure)
    word play, 154–164
    Yiddish, 119, 120 (figure)
    See also Parts of speech
Words and Rules, 142
World of Pooh, The, ix
Write for Mathematics, 8, xi
Writing
    alliterative, 107 (figure)
    imitation, 82, 83 (figure)
    with the polyglot of English,
        207, 208–210 (figure)
Writing as Learning, 8, 9, 76, 82, xi
Written sentences, 70, 142, 143 (figure), 144
Written words, patterns in, 27, 28 (figure)

"Y" and "ly" ending adjectives, 62 (figure)
Yiddish language, 119
Yinglish language, 119